To Barbara,
Thanks for helping so many
live the DREAM!

Love

"Brian is a dear friend and professional colleague. In between the words of this book, which can change your life and your children's future, is a love for serving and for people, which comes through him every day in everything he does. This book is so much more than just a template for healthy natural living; it is a lifeline to our children to save them from another generation of misinformation, unhealthy behaviors handed down from a perpetually sick culture, and an attack on them by Big Pharma and the profiteers of ill-health. This is a positive approach to living a life of physical, social and emotional fulfillment. As the Dalai Lama told me one day, 'Live your life with integrity and you'll get to enjoy it twice; first while you're living it and again when you look back on it at the end.' What a beautiful opportunity we have to offer this 'gift of life' to our children. Brian, kudos to you."

—Dr. Guy Riekeman, Chancellor Emeritus Life University

"This is the ultimate easy to read, easy to implement reference book for any parent looking to raise a healthy child. Jammed packed with practical and powerful ways to ensure your happy and healthy child's future. A must read!"

—Bob Hoffman, D.C., Co-author of
Discover Wellness and Your Flourishing Brain

"Reading *D.R.E.A.M Wellness* is like reading a fun and insightful instruction manual on self-care, for the entire family."

—Shira Miller, M.D., Top Doctor in Concierge Medicine

"I found this book to be a great resource for families wanting to be proactive in their overall well-being. Dr. Brian has put together a very thoughtful and complete guide toward that goal. A healthy family (physical, mental, social) is not just a matter of luck. You have to work at it. This is the road map you need."

—Armand Rossi, D.C., F.I.C.P.A., ICPA instructor and Dean of Clinical Sciences at Sherman College of Chiropractic

"Dr. Brian Stenzler has distilled decades of clinical experience into a readable book providing practical advice. When facing the challenges of today, people are seeking workable strategies for expressing their potential as human beings. This book helps take the reader from the mitigation of illness to the creation of health."

—Christopher Kent, D.C., J.D.

"As an occupational therapist who helps families end mealtime battles and grow food choices, I LOVE how this book incorporates factors that go well beyond just food and diet. Dr. Brian eloquently explains the 5 Keys of wellness, providing a framework that families can follow. He includes actionable steps to improve your life and your child's future so you can create a D.R.E.A.M. family. This is a must have book for families who desire to have a united, healthy life!"

—Becky Miksic, OTR/L

"As a family therapist and mother of four sons, I can attest that Dr. Stenzler hits the mark in *D.R.E.A.M. Wellness*. Creating a family culture that encourages harmonious communication, self-awareness and healthy habits is critical for the mental well-being of the entire family. Dr. Stenzler's guidance is fun and easy to implement for all families."

—Amber Trueblood, LMFT, MBA
(Author, speaker, podcaster, mother of four)

"Dr. Brian's brilliant book is a perfect example of the saying: 'If they knew what you knew, they'd do what you do.' He's amassed a wealth of knowledge and shared it in a simple yet profound format. His book will help you take action and create DREAM wellness for you and your family so you can live your Epic Life!"

—David Jackson, D.C., Best-selling author, and
CEO of Epic Practice, Del Mar, CA

"Brian's message is vital for families who want to raise healthier kids who grow into healthy adults. At a time when there is so much confusing information, Dr. Stenzler gets straight to the facts and makes them easy to follow. More importantly, he has been living these principles for decades. This book is a must read!"

—Eric Plasker, D.C., Author of *The 100 Year Lifestyle*

"There has never been a better time to read and equip your family with the RIGHT tools to make better health choices. If your family life is full of stress and unhealthy habits, and you're about to fold like a deck chair, read this book. Brian is the real deal, and his true calling is helping families live their D.R.E.A.M."

—Matt Hubbard, D.C., True Chiropractic and Awaken Church, Executive Pastor, San Diego, CA

"Dr. Brian's book should be the foundation upon which you build a healthy lifestyle. His direction will guide you to a lifestyle that prevents the need of going through the jungle of dangerous and unnecessary medication and interventions. This book will teach you everything you need to know to maximize your innate health potential both for you and your family."

—Billy DeMoss, D.C., California Jam Founder, DeMoss Chiropractic, Newport Beach, CA

"If you're ready to take your family's physical, mental and emotional health to new heights, put this book on your required reading list. Brian shows you how to live like a champion and make daily choices that will impact your family and legacy forever."

—Phil McConkey

D.R.E.A.M. WELLNESS

D.R.E.A.M. WELLNESS

THE 5 KEYS TO RAISING KIDS FOR A LIFETIME OF PHYSICAL AND MENTAL HEALTH

Dr. Brian A. Stenzler
M.Sc., D.C.

JONES MEDIA
PUBLISHING

CONTENTS

FOREWORD

If you're a parent, just like me, you want to know that you're doing everything you can to help your kids thrive—physically, emotionally, and mentally. But with so much information out there, often conflicting, you want to know what's real, what's hype, and what you really need to do—without spending day and night doing the research.

Long before the COVID-19 pandemic, children were already facing an epidemic of chronic childhood disease. The pandemic has shined a glaring light on the need to reverse chronic disease in children and adults with diet and lifestyle modifications.

With more than 50% of our nation's children currently being diagnosed with at least one chronic condition and that number projected to increase to greater than 80% by 2025, we need to know how to help our children now so they don't just become another statistic.

As an internationally recognized holistic pediatrician, pediatric functional medicine expert, and mom to two thriving kids, I have helped thousands of kids get to the root cause of their health concerns and helped their parents understand how to help their children thrive—body, mind and spirit. These health concerns have ranged from frequent colds, ear infections, asthma, and eczema; to autism, ADHD, PANS/PANDAS, anxiety, depression, and autoimmune illnesses.

My extensive training has given me the opportunity to help so many families in need, but most of them would not have needed my help if they had previously applied the information and principles found in this book. We do not just need to know how to keep our kids from getting ill, we need to know how to help them thrive. I am a physician who has dedicated my life to caring for our youth, and I know firsthand how important the family's lifestyle is to prevent and reverse chronic disease in our children.

That's why I'm so grateful to have Dr. Brian Stenzler's book as a go-to resource for the busy parent who wants to cut to the chase and trust that the information they're given is evidence-based, doable, and sustainable. Dr. Brian breaks down the 5 Keys to raising healthy kids in easy-to-understand and practical ways, so that you can help your family thrive.

Our kids need help now, but parents are struggling with what to do and how to help them. This book is so needed now more than ever. It gives parents the tools they need to take action today and raise their kids for a lifetime of physical and mental health.

Dr. Brian Stenzler is not only a dedicated and caring pediatric and family wellness chiropractic doctor, but more importantly, he is a father who knows firsthand that his approach works! I have gotten to know Dr. Stenzler through an amazing community of health and wellness professionals who are working to change health across the globe. With his approach, Dr. Brian is paving the way for a future of thriving kids for generations to come.

And now—you can learn Dr. Brian's approach in this book!

I am honored to share with you what I know will become one of your go-to resources to help your kids thrive—body, mind and spirit.

Elisa Song, MD
Holistic Pediatrician and Pediatric Functional Medicine Expert
Founder, Healthy Kids Happy Kids

PREFACE

I could not hold back my excitement . . . I was finally a Doctor of Chiropractic, and I now had the opportunity to serve dozens of children, babies and their parents . . . without a clinic doctor looking over my shoulder!

It was Friday, March 13, 1998, when I officially graduated from Life University in Marietta, Georgia. A local, very successful family chiropractor about 50 miles outside of Atlanta hired me to cover her practice the following Monday. That Friday evening prior to the doctor leaving for her trip, she handed me the key to the office and left my cell number on the voicemail in case there was a weekend emergency. Little did I know that I would learn an important lesson in caregiving, respect and the power of natural healing the very next day.

On Saturday morning, a woman called my cell phone and begged me to see her "little one" following a fall down the stairs two days prior at their house. This woman did not actually have any children that she had birthed; her children were her dogs. When she explained to me what had happened and that the dog had not gotten better after two days, I agreed to meet her in the office that afternoon to see if I would be able to help. I let her know that I had some but little experience adjusting dogs at this point, but I would do my best. I warned her that I would potentially need to refer her to a chiropractor that specializes in canines or possibly even a veterinarian. I never thought in my wildest dreams that my first official paying patient would be a dog . . . but here is where the story gets even wilder.

The woman did not tell me on the phone what kind of dog she had, nor did I ask. I did not think it would matter as the anatomy would be the same for any type of dog. She pulled up in a large van and parked in front of the office. The door opened and out came a little brown Cocker Spaniel. I thought to myself, I cannot wait to help this little guy and get his body working again. As I went to pat the little fella, his mom said, "That's not the dog with the problem." Seconds later, a huge Great Dane with a shiny black coat limped out of the van. I do not think I had ever seen a dog that large before, let alone laid my hands on one.

With my heart pounding out of fear and excitement, we proceeded into the office reception area. The woman told me about the fall, and I began to feel the dog's spine. Rocco was not able to stand on his own for more than 30 seconds, and he could not turn his body without falling. He would just drop to his knees. I felt misalignments in the hip and spine, but just by feel I could not rule out fractures or small dislocations. I asked the woman why they had not taken him to an emergency clinic for an evaluation and x-rays first. She told me that she wanted to try chiropractic as that has always been her first course of action for herself and her dogs. I explained to her that I did not have x-ray vision and I would do a very gentle adjustment, just in case there was a fracture or something unstable, as I did not want to cause any harm to Rocco. I also told her that regardless of the outcome of the adjustment, she should still consider taking him for x-rays.

I told the woman how I planned to adjust Rocco so she knew what to expect. I said that it is very common for a dog to make a yelp sound, jump up and run in circles when this particular area of the spine/hips is adjusted. I used my hands for some manual adjustments and then an Activator instrument for the part with the greatest subluxation and most tender spot. Vertebral subluxations are dysfunctions within the spine, typically caused by misaligned vertebrae, that place stress and tension on the nervous system (*see Ch. 8–5*). At the moment of the instrument's click, Rocco yelped as expected, jumped up and ran in circles. This time, he did not fall. The woman was elated by the quick turnaround (no pun intended).

After Rocco stood on his own and showed off his ability to walk, stand and turn without falling, he took a squatting position. Rocco then proceeded to drop the largest poop of his life in the middle of the reception area. What the woman did not tell me was, Rocco had not defecated for the past two days, since the incident.

The woman and I were mortified and ecstatic at the same time. While I knew I had intended on having a family practice with lots of babies, I never would have imagined that my very first official patient would be a dog that pooped all over the office!

The early stages of my career were filled with numerous opportunities to witness and participate in amazing natural healings. First, as a student clinician in chiropractic college with a ten-month-old toddler who had terrible eczema that cleared up following chiropractic care (*see Ch. 8-6*). This was after invasive medical procedures failed her. Then my first experience as a licensed doctor helping Rocco. And it was not just Rocco's hip issue that was helped but also his constipation likely caused by the interference to the nerves controlling his digestive organs following the fall. These experiences and so many more helped build a foundation of certainty that fuels my passion every day.

This book is not about chiropractic, though it does address a lifestyle that so many chiropractic doctors and other naturally based healthcare providers choose to live. If you want an 'insider's look' into how *we* live *our* lives and raise *our* kids, then buckle up and keep reading. Over the decades of serving families, I have met numerous *holistically* minded parents. They prefer to avoid using medications for their children, but they often do not take all the necessary measures to set themselves up for success. The world needs to know what we know so they can also live healthfully, happily and purposefully.

I began writing this book more than ten years prior to completion, but I had not been successful at creating enough time to finish it. Truthfully, finishing this book was important to me, but it did not become urgent until the year 2020. The coronavirus global pandemic shifted the necessity of this information to receive widespread attention. While the survival rate of the virus is over 99%, there have still been hundreds of thousands of needless deaths in the United States alone.

The vast majority of those who succumbed to the virus were either those of elderly populations or individuals who suffered from a chronic disease, many of which may have been preventable through lifestyle. In fact, while age was the most prevalent factor affecting risk of hospitalization and death, obesity was a close second.

The unfortunate truth is, if those with lifestyle created illnesses had made changes back in March 2020 when the pandemic became a known concern, then I believe the death rate would have decreased even more significantly and more quickly. Fewer incidences of obesity, high blood pressure and diabetes alone would most certainly have increased the odds of those who contracted the virus to survive.

In fact, on March 5, 2021, CNN and several other news outlets reported on the findings from the World Obesity Federation. The report revealed that countries where at least half of the adults are overweight, COVID-19 death rates were 10 times higher. According to Johns Hopkins University and the World Health Organization, 2.5 million deaths had been reported by the end of February 2021. Eighty-eight percent (2.2 million) of those deaths occurred in countries where more than half the population is overweight. Sixty-eight percent of the United States population happens to be overweight.

While there have been tremendous advances in therapeutics and preventative measures, few things would be more advantageous to an infected individual than not having these risk factors in the first place.

Dr. Tim Lobstein, the author of the report said, "Governments have been negligent, and ignored the economic value of a healthy population at their peril. For the last decade they have failed to tackle obesity, despite setting themselves targets at United Nations meetings."

This is not about shaming or blaming those who are overweight and/ or suffering with health problems. This is about bringing attention to a huge crisis that is not being handled properly. The government has been failing us for many decades (to be covered in more detail in Chapter 1.1). If governments had placed a larger emphasis on preventing obesity and other chronic illnesses, perhaps hundreds of thousands of COVID-19 related deaths would have been avoided. Instead of encouraging more exercise, eating healthy food, and utilizing health promoting professional services, they shut down the gyms, stopped sports activities for children and adults, shut down most "mom and pop" restaurants (only leaving open fast-food chains) and closed the practices of all "non-essential" health and wellness services. While some of those decisions were done with good intentions to prevent the spread of the virus, they inadvertently created a situation of making the vulnerable more vulnerable.

> *A book cannot change your life; only you can do that. I am providing you with the tools and resources necessary to set your entire family on a course of conscious living that consists of constructive choices for you to make now that will impact your legacy as a parent and for generations to come.*

When combined with appropriate action, your family's future can be significantly transformed. The goal of this book is to inspire, educate and empower you and those you care for to realize that "good enough" does not have to be good enough anymore, and ultimately realize that you were created perfectly and you have the opportunity to express that perfection.

Individuals, parents, lawmakers, regulators, employers, preachers and teachers alike will benefit from the contents of this book, as the 5 Keys will unlock the "mystery" of health creation (salutogenesis) that has eluded so many for too long. You will likely find many of the suggestions within this book to be obvious, while others will likely surprise you.

You may currently be suffering from health issues, financial woes and/or relationship problems; all of which prevent you from living your best life possible. Perhaps your kids are often missing school because of constant runny noses, "unproductive" coughs or other health ailments, which ultimately causes you to miss work or interfere with your daily routine. This book can be a launching pad to a new life if you so choose.

If you are reading this book and have no known issues and your kids appear to be very healthy, this book will hopefully inspire you to make choices and take action to create even greater health throughout your lifetime and that of your progeny.

I expect you to find takeaways and easy wins from every chapter, whether you are reading it straight through from front to back or poking around when using it as a reference. This book will provide a lot of information, and I do not want it to overwhelm you. Read it through and take notes as you go and follow the workbook found in the bonus/resource section. In the conclusion, I provide you with three easy steps to start integrating what you learned into practice. All my anecdotes have a lesson built in. My intent is not to disparage in any way but rather to share my experiences that I learned along the way so that you can either avoid those lessons or see how to get out of current situations that are not serving you or your family.

Regardless of your race, religion, ethnicity, socioeconomic status, current health status or any other demographic or psychographic group that you may relate to, your life can change for the better when you implement this information. I am aware and acknowledge that not all people have the same access and the resources to healthcare and information. I am also aware that some populations have higher predispositions toward certain health issues for a variety of reasons, many of which may not be in their control.

We all must start somewhere, and the smallest of changes can be the catalyst to some of the biggest breakthroughs in your family's health and quality of life. Parents may claim that they cannot afford to make significant changes in their home, but the reality is, they can't afford not to. More than 50% of bankruptcies in the U.S. are related to healthcare debt and more than 70% of healthcare dollars are spent treating diseases caused by their lifestyle. While not everyone has the financial resources to afford all of my recommendations (such as organic food, top of the line cookware and many proactive healthcare services), making as many changes as possible is much better than making zero changes.

This is exactly why I have chosen to put all this information into a book and combine it with an easily accessible lifestyle survey: the DREAM Score. Throughout my decades of consulting with clients, I recognized that I was giving most people similar information (with nuances based on their individual lifestyles) and realized that I needed to bottle up this information so everyone could access it. No longer does this information need to be accessible only to people who can afford to pay for private consulting sessions.

There are hundreds of suggestions in this book that can be implemented into your life that cost nothing and will improve your family's health and quality of life dramatically. You are now being armed with information which should make it more difficult for you to make excuses about your lifestyle patterns and habits. The *choice* is yours.

My insights come from decades of clinical practice, formal education and living a wellness lifestyle every day. And I must say, my wife and I have been putting everything that I am recommending to you into action as we raise our son. We too have been reaping the benefits as we watch him grow into a healthy, happy and mindful young man. Do we do everything perfectly? No, of course not. But we do live consciously and purposefully, and those are the first and most important steps toward living your dream life by living your DREAM, every day (*see Ch. 4-1*).

I am excited to introduce you to the 5 Keys or Facets of the wellness lifestyle, DREAM, representing Diet, Relaxation, Exercise, being in Adjustment and Mental wellness.

At times I make suggestions that may seem to be out of the ordinary, but to live an extra-ordinary life, you must do extraordinary things. I teach people that when you are living purposefully, you will choose excessive *goodness,* and maybe a little bit of *bad* stuff. Rather than use the judgmental terms, *good* and *bad* moving forward, I prefer to use the terms *constructive* and *destructive*. Something that is constructive serves a useful purpose, and in the context of this book, will enhance your overall health and quality of life. Anything that is destructive, however, can be considered something that will cause harm or damage in the short- or long-term.

I would have preferred to write this book in a completely positive manner, one that is only inspiring by informing you of what you *should* consume and do to live a wellness lifestyle and raise healthy children. However, if you are not also made aware of what to *avoid*, then all the constructive suggestions will become marginalized at best.

People too often say, "Everything in moderation." Well, that is certainly a great way to live an average life. My friend and mentor Dr. Bob Hoffman who is referenced quite a bit in this book often says, "Once you lick the lollipop of mediocrity, you'll suck forever." (I believe that quote was initially that of *The Beach Boys'* Brian Wilson.)

I do not suggest anything that I would not do myself. I meet people all the time, whether they connect with me on the road or come into one of my centers and tell me they *want* what I *have*. Well, if you truly *want* what I *have*, you must *do* what I do. In all actuality, while what you *do* is very important, who you choose to *be* matters more.

Be-Do-Have principles have been around in personal development for quite some time. All too often, one person looks at another and wants what the other has. They ask, "What did you *do* to get X?" The problem is, too many people focus on the *do* so they can *have* what they want, but they do not consider who they need to *be*, or whether or not they really want X and if so, why? What purpose would it serve?

The *be* is about who (and what) you are. What are your beliefs? How do you show up in this world innately? What drives and motivates you? Dr. Hoffman taught me early on in my career, "Who you are determines how well what you do works." This explains why one course of action works for one person but not necessarily everyone. Two people can perform the exact same activities and tactics, yet they yield completely different results.

This book will cover all of the necessary tools to help you understand who you "*be*" and what *you* need to *do* in order to *have* a *dream* life.

I am not going to fill your time reading about natural cures for diseases, specific exercise routines or reasons to avoid drugs and surgery. There are several books already out there that do a great job at that. Instead, I want to inspire you to live the life you were created to live and lead by example for your kids. If you follow the steps in this book, hopefully you will avoid needing any cures as most health issues will be avoided. By reading this book you are already on the road to living your DREAM, everyday!

Oh, one other thing . . . I unapologetically reference God quite a bit in this book. Feel free to mentally change the word/name to whatever is more comfortable to you, such as Universe, Soul, Spirit, Intelligence, Source, Energy, Innate or Nature. For the purposes of this book, it will work just fine.

To set the tone of the book, I would like to share with you a passage from Marianne Williamson's bestselling book, *A Return to Love: Reflections on the Principles of a Course in Miracles*:

15

Our deepest fear is not that we are inadequate. Our deepest fear is that we are powerful beyond measure. It is our light, not our darkness that most frightens us. We ask ourselves, "Who am I to be brilliant, gorgeous, talented, fabulous?" Actually, who are you not to be? You are a child of God. Your playing small does not serve the world. There is nothing enlightened about shrinking so that other people won't feel insecure around you. We are all meant to shine, as children do. We were born to make manifest the glory of God that is within us. It's not just in some of us; it's in everyone. And as we let our own light shine, we unconsciously give other people permission to do the same. As we are liberated from our own fear, our presence automatically liberates others.

THE FORMAT

Because this book is full of reference points, I expect you to jump back and forth while reading so you have the necessary background information related to certain topics. I cover many topics that relate to previous and ensuing sections and give you cues to easily jump back and forth. The book can be read cover-to-cover or used as a reference on specific topics.

Throughout this book I will recommend my favorite products and services that will help you live your DREAM. I do not want to waste valuable book real estate on shopping lists, specific products or tools you can use, especially since they are always changing. You will also receive tons of bonus material that will enhance the health of your family.

All of those resources and bonuses can be found at https:// DREAMWellnessbook.com/bonuses. After I cover a particular subject, you will know if there is a resource or bonus by seeing **BONUSES & RESOURCES** followed by a brief description of what you will find on the page. (Note: Some bonuses and resources may change from time to time and may not reflect what is printed in the book at the end of each section.)

BONUS: Your very first bonus and most important download is the "Living Your DREAM Workbook." This workbook will follow along the entire book and serve as your *wellness journal, family manual* and accountability partner as you read the book and beyond!

If you were referred to this book by another healthcare provider (or under the care of a trusted healthcare provider), please ask your providers if they have other recommendations prior to exploring mine. There may be good reason to go with their suggestions.

This book also serves as a report for the DREAM Score lifestyle assessment. Some of you have already taken the extensive questionnaire and purchased this book to go along with the report. The report demonstrates where your opportunities exist and references the pages that you should focus on so you can make improvements to your lifestyle and score higher the next time you answer the questions. While some of you may only look at the specific pages to increase your score (and ultimately your health), I encourage you to read the book in its entirety for context and additional gems. There are also online courses (found on the reference webpages) that you can take if you would like to delve much deeper into any of the concepts in this book.

For those who are reading this book first (and maybe didn't even know about the DREAM Score), you are in for a treat! At the end of Chapter 4-2, you will be prompted and encouraged to take the questionnaire and see how well you're currently living your DREAM. You too will receive a complete report with a score and references within the book to improve your wellness lifestyle.

PART I

INTRODUCTION TO WELLNESS

1-1

AMERICA'S REAL HEALTHCARE CRISIS

"I want my kid to grow up obese and riddled with lots of health issues including diabetes, high blood pressure and depression," said no parent ever.

All parents want their children to become happy and healthy adults themselves. The guilt, shame and pain that parents experience when their child's quality of life is poor is very real. Fortunately, that is often avoidable.

Your lifestyle as a parent creates not just your future but also your children's. If you want healthy kids, you must get healthy yourself first, or at least start the journey. Your lifestyle impacts theirs. Healthy, happy kids start at home.

While much of this may sound like common sense, it is even backed up by research. The *British Medical Journal* performed a study in 2018 titled, "Association between maternal adherence to healthy lifestyle practices and risk of obesity in offspring: results from two prospective cohort studies of mother-child pairs in the United States." The results of the study revealed, "When all healthy lifestyle factors were considered simultaneously, offspring of women who adhered to all five low risk lifestyle factors had a 75% lower risk of obesity than offspring of mothers who did not adhere to any low risk factor." This led to their conclusion of the study, which read, "Our study shows that mothers' overall healthy lifestyle during the period of their offspring's childhood and adolescence is associated with a substantially lower risk of obesity in their children. Importantly, adherence to a healthy lifestyle in both mothers and their children could result in an even further reduction in the risk of offspring obesity. Our findings highlight the potentially critical role of maternal lifestyle choices in the etiology of childhood obesity and lend support to family or parent-based intervention strategies for reducing childhood obesity risk."[1]

There are dozens of research studies confirming the role you have as a parent in determining the outcome of your child's health, which carries into their adulthood. This book will make you aware of many of your habits that may be detrimental to the outcome you desire. You will have a choice to make necessary changes and to create the future you want. If you will not do it for yourself, at least do it for your kids. They are counting on you! Our country is counting on you. Heck, the world is counting on you.

> *"You can't medicate yourself out of something you behaved your way into."* —Dane Donahue, DC

The United States of America makes up approximately 4% of the entire world's population. Interestingly, the U.S. spends more than 50% of the world's healthcare dollars on that 4%. I guess that should make us the healthiest nation, right?

U.S. Population Compared to the World

Spend of Healthcare Dollars

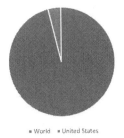

■ World ■ United States

■ Rest of the World ■ United States

If that were the case, we would see hospitals closing their doors, physicians going out of business and a more energetic, vibrant, productive and vital society. Instead, we see hospitals expanding because they are filled to capacity; long wait times for scheduled doctor appointments, and a shortage of healthcare workers to handle the 'needs' of the U.S. population.

Interestingly, I finished writing this book in the midst of the COVID-19 global pandemic, which arguably can be referred to as a *syndemic*. A syndemic is a term coined by medical anthropologist Merrill Singer in the mid-1990s. It is essentially the confluence of two or more disease processes, or epidemics, that complicate the effects of one particular disease itself. Tens of millions of people are living with obesity, diabetes, cardiovascular disease, high blood pressure and other health conditions at epidemic proportions. Throw all of those *pre-existing* conditions, or epidemics, into the mix with a highly infectious potent pathogen, and the result is millions of deaths.

While the virus has sadly taken the lives of hundreds of thousands of people in America alone, our problem is not that of an infectious disease; it is that of a chronic disease problem. More so, it is a lifestyle problem!

While there are many (seemingly) healthy individuals losing their lives or struggling to survive the effects of the coronavirus, they are the vast minority.

In the middle of the year 2020, the governor of New York summarized a survey of 1,200 COVID-19 hospitalizations in New York that revealed that 96% had at least one underlying, pre-existing serious health issue. *The San Diego Union-Tribune* reported that of the 194 deaths in San Diego (at that point), only 6 of the victims were purely related to COVID-19 according to County Supervisor Jim Desmond. The majority of pre-existing health issues that are hospitalizing and taking the lives of these people include obesity, hypertension, cardiovascular disease and adult-onset diabetes, all of which are often avoidable through lifestyle modifications.

Center for Disease Control and Prevention (CDC) former Director Dr. Robert Redfield testified before Congress on June 23, 2020. He reported that the CDC looked at 1.3 million patients confirmed with COVID-19, of which 15% were hospitalized. The majority of those with serious issues were over the age of 80 and/or had pre-existing health conditions such as heart disease (32%), type 2 diabetes (30%), chronic lung disease (18%) and obesity. The study found that patients with underlying health conditions were six times more likely to be hospitalized and twelve times more likely to die from COVID-19, than otherwise healthy patients (https://www.cdc.gov/mmwr/volumes/69/wr/pdfs/mm6915e3-H.pdf).

Our country is dealing with a higher incidence of obesity, heart disease, diabetes, auto-immune disorders and other lifestyle related diseases in our population. In 2020, 60% of Americans reportedly suffer from at least one chronic disease (https://www.cdc.gov/chronicdisease/resources/infographic/chronic-diseases.htm).

Our schools are filled with children who are on medications for ADHD, asthma, depression and anxiety, just to name a few.

Businesses have employees who are unproductive, underproducing and costing their employers millions of dollars each year with high health insurance rates, absenteeism or worse yet, *presenteeism* (being at work physically, but not producing at 100%; usually related to health issues). For a country that spends more than any other country on healthcare, you would think the trend would be quite different (https://hbr.org/2004/10/presenteeism-at-work-but-out-of-it).

In the year 2000, the World Health Organization (WHO) did its first ever (and only, I believe) analysis of its 191 member countries to examine and compare aspects of healthcare systems around the world. The United States ranked 38 out of the 191 nations when it came to overall level and distribution of health in the populations and the responsiveness and financing of healthcare distribution. In comparison, Saudi Arabia and United Arab Emirates ranked significantly higher on the chart, ranking 26 and 27 respectively. Also interesting to note, while the United States' expenditure on healthcare per capita was number 1, Saudi Arabia was 63 in its expenditure on healthcare per capita. The country Oman which ranked way above the U.S. at 8 on the list ranked 62 in its spending on healthcare per capita (http://www.who.int/whr/2000/media_centre/press_release/en/).

We can clearly draw a conclusion that just by spending more money on healthcare does not make for a healthier nation. In fact, I would venture to say that the amount the U.S. spends on healthcare, which is really "sick," "disease" and "crisis" care, is a big part of why we rank so poorly. While there are many people with the belief that having more access to medical care through a socialized medical system would make for a healthier nation, I would tend to believe that will not solve our country's health issues. It doesn't matter who is in control of our healthcare system; the government, the hospitals, the pharmacies, the people, the Democrats, the Republicans (or any other political party). If the number one priority is not about education toward prevention of disease and the promotion of health through a wellness lifestyle, then all models will fail.

Okay, let's tackle another controversial topic for the moment and explore the majority of charities raising money for "disease cures" around our nation. How much closer to a cure for cancer, ALS, diabetes, multiple sclerosis or Alzheimer's are we now? Who is really getting the most benefits from these charities and events? While many of the organizations have good intentions and do good work and research, how much of your hard-earned dollars that you contribute are going to finding a cause and solution, versus treatments (albeit important), marketing and administration expenses?

According to a 2011 study by Charity Navigator analyzing 3,929 charities, 11 non-profits paid their CEOs more than $1 million for annual salaries, not including bonuses. In fact, 78 CEOs of the charities looked at were paid between $500,000 and $1 million.

My intent is not to discourage you from contributing to research. In fact, it is vitally important and must continue. However, that should not be the end all, be all, and I encourage you to do you own research on the organizations you may choose to contribute to.

Is the "Race for the Cure" the absolute best we can do? What if we took the attitude of "Run to Prevent XXX Disease" or even better yet, "Run to promote health and wellness"? Sure, once someone has a particular issue or disease, we want to have the best care possible available, whether it be allopathic (traditional medicine), holistic or a combination of both. We also know that no matter how healthy of a lifestyle we live, there are no guarantees that we can prevent these issues. However, if the majority of money raised goes into researching and developing treatments for these problems, then what is the end game? A sick nation that pops a pill or cuts something out when something goes wrong?

Ben Franklin said, "An ounce of prevention is worth a pound of cure." I wholeheartedly agree with that statement, but I would take it one step further and say, "An ounce of DREAM living is worth infinite pounds of cure." While preventing disease and promoting health may sound the same, the outcome is extremely different. Some people say that they want to "maintain" their health, but I see that as problematic as well. Because your body is dynamic and constantly changing, I do not believe that you are ever maintaining health. Your quantity of health is constantly increasing or decreasing, every single moment of your life.

While not all chronic illnesses are created by lifestyle choices, the vast majority are preventable in one way or another. This is not about shaming those with issues, it is about inspiring those to take action to prevent and/or heal them (naturally) when possible and to proactively create health.

As mentioned in the Preface of this book, there are certain populations that are more predisposed to certain illnesses than other demographics. That does not mean they should sit around and wait to be inflicted. Some have opportunities to take massive action and try to prevent them. However, not all people have the same access due to geographic or financial constraints to some of the proactive wellness lifestyle services I cover in this book. Whatever the government can do to support higher risk populations through social services that may include free care and education, I support 100%. It cannot be just free care though. It must include education and empowerment.

It is vitally important for you to understand, for the future of your family's legacy and that of our entire nation, what you do with the information you read in this book can impact the lives of generations to come. Change for the country and the world starts at home.

Children love to play *follow the leader*. They watch you. They hear you. They know what you are doing. I implore you to be very conscious with every word you say and action you take as your children will likely follow in your footsteps. Be the leader you want your kids to follow. Families get healthy and stay healthy together.

1-2

SICK CARE VS. HEALTHCARE

THE PARABLE OF THREE RUNNERS

Joe, John and Jane are triplets, all members of their high school's varsity cross country team. They decided to participate in their first marathon together during their summer break.

Joe read a couple of books about how to train for this marathon but did not prepare his body for the punishment he would endure. A couple of weeks before the race, he noticed a dull ache at the bottom of his foot. Just to make sure he was okay, he went to the doctor to get it checked out. Turns out Joe had a stress fracture in his foot. By checking it out early, Joe prevented further damage that could have come if he ran the race. This is an example of *prevention*.

Joe's brother John was a little more proactive than Joe. John started training months before Joe. He stretched and he did other exercises to strengthen his body. By *maintaining* his body the way he did, he ensured himself an opportunity to not only compete but possibly even finish the race without injury.

And then there's Jane—Joe and John's sister. In addition to stretching properly and exercising, Jane also made sure that she fueled her body efficiently and maintained ideal form and spinal alignment. This decision ensured optimal nerve flow throughout her body and made sure that her muscles, organs and glands were functioning optimally before the race. Jane's preparation gave her the best chance to finish the race without injury and the best chance to *win the race*!

PREVENTION: EARLY DETECTION

In our current "healthcare" system, most of what is referred to as prevention is really early detection. Certain tests are important to have done routinely to catch disease, (or what I refer to as "dis-ease") processes before they get out of control. However, once an issue is identified, even if it is early, it is already a problem in many cases. Early detection is a very important aspect of caring for an individual, but if there is already a problem, is it really prevention, aside from preventing it from getting worse?

PREVENTATIVE INTERVENTIONS

There are also medical interventions that fall under the category of prevention with the goal to avoid contracting an infectious disease and controlling an existing illness. These prophylactic measures may include vaccinations, cholesterol medications, bypass heart surgery and antibiotics. However, most of these are not without some form of risk, and they certainly will not make a person healthier. At best, they may prevent the disease they want to avoid, but these interventions are not salutogenic (*see Ch. 10-1*). *Salutogenesis* is a term coined by Dr. Aaron Antonovsky, a professor of medical sociology. The term comes from the Latin root "salus" which means health and the

Greek word "genesis" which means origin or creation. Salutogenesis ultimately focuses on the factors that lead to the creation of health. This is contrary to pathogenesis.

There are numerous resources that layout the potential risks and benefits of various medical interventions that should be explored if you desire additional information. Your decisions regarding any medical procedure for you or your child should begin with background research followed by an open conversation between you and your trusted healthcare provider(s) to determine what is best. True informed consent should be the cornerstone of any relationship between an individual and any healthcare intervention.

PREVENTION: MAINTENANCE

A lot of people talk about their goal to maintain their health, like John in the example you just read about. The individual who desires this is ultimately seeking the same or similar goal as prevention. Essentially, they want to remain free from health issues. As noble as that may be, they are just maintaining the status quo.

HEALTH PROMOTION

Then there is an entirely different thought process that I refer to as health promotion, or salutogenesis. Health promotion is about taking purposeful steps within a wellness lifestyle to encourage optimal health as the result. This entails conscious choices and actions throughout the lifetime to not only avoid bad things from happening, but by making your body and mind as strong and fit as possible to encourage great things to happen!

A wellness lifestyle is for the people who want to win the race of life!

REFLECTION OPPORTUNITY

What do you currently do in your life for disease prevention for yourself and your children?

What do you currently do in your life for injury prevention for yourself and your children?

What do you currently do to promote health and wellness in your household?

1-3

PARADIGMS: SHIFT HAPPENS

> *"Small shifts in your thinking, and small changes in your energy, can lead to massive alterations of your end result."* —Kevin Michel, author

A paradigm is a group of ideas about how something should be done, made or thought about. It is basically a way of thinking and for many, a way of life. Every paradigm has its own values, its own beliefs and its own way of doing things.

I am going to compare two lifestyle paradigms. The purpose of this exercise is not to comment on which is right or wrong or better or worse. Instead, I want you to think about where you spend the majority of your thoughts, actions and money when it comes to lifestyle and healthcare for yourself and your household. Perhaps by the time you finish reading this chapter, you too will be ready to make a paradigm shift.

The *outside-in* approach is basically the model of our current healthcare system in the United States. This tends to be more of an allopathic model, which is basically the practice of medicine; but of course, there are exceptions. When something is not working correctly, medical doctors typically look to the outside and see what they can bring in (to the body or mind, for example) to make it "better." The *inside-out* approach, however, tends to be more holistic, understanding that the human body is created with all it needs to return to a state of normalcy without the need to bring something artificial into the body. It is the thoughts, words and actions of the individual that determines the person's health destiny. We will refer to this as a wellness model.

ARTIFICIAL VS. NATURAL

The outside-in allopathic approach tends to be an artificial process. Drugs are typically manufactured synthetically in a laboratory and often contain ingredients that do not exist in nature. While they may often save or sustain life, they are not necessarily the best answer toward increasing the health of an individual.

We all know that many medications often prove to have value in helping get through and sometimes overcome a litany of health problems, and they do save lives. All I can say is, thank goodness for the brilliant minds that have created some of the most important life-saving treatments. However, medicinal use, especially long-term, can create problems that are as bad if not worse than the original problem.

All drugs make the body behave in a way that it would not ordinarily function; that is how they work. They change your chemistry to bring about a particular result. All too often, however, people rely on taking certain medications for conditions that could potentially resolve through more natural means and/or lifestyle changes.

Medications have many effects on the body, some desired and some not. We often refer to the undesired effects as side-effects, but they are not really side-effects. They are actually effects of the drug working properly, just not always desired.

Ask yourself, "Why is it a bad idea for healthy people to take medications when they do not need them?" Your answer is probably something to the effect of, "Because medicine will make a healthy person sick." Exactly. So, if medications would likely make a healthy person sick, then how does one think that medications can make a sick person healthy?

They won't. They can get you from point A to point B when needed, and even make certain symptoms disappear. But if you need a drug to keep a symptom or disease process away, does that mean you are really healthy?

The inside-out wellness approach typically considers the body's very own *pharmacopeia*, or internal pharmacy. It is known that a healthy body is constantly creating all of the chemicals and hormones needed to regulate the body and keep it functioning optimally. When an imbalance occurs, the natural approach would be to help that person overcome the stress by looking at the person's inborn natural healing ability and doing what may be necessary to help it heal without the introduction of artificial substances. This is done through lifestyle modifications.

BATTLING DISEASE VS. BUILDING HEALTH (SALUTOGENESIS)

The outside-in approach is mostly about battling disease when something is apparently wrong. The mission more often than not is to treat the symptoms and, in some cases, get to the root of the problem.

While medical doctors tend to treat diseases with medicine that often have side-effects, there are other healthcare professions that provide options that are more natural and do not typically stress the body as much, if at all. These may include naturopathic doctors, acupuncturists, functional medicine and functional nutrition providers, herbalists, homeopaths, physical therapists and some chiropractic doctors (depending on their philosophy of practice). Even though many of these options are natural, they are still a form of "sick care" as they are *treating* a pathology. While it may be *natural*, it is not *wellness*.

With the inside-out approach, however, the value is placed on healthy habits and positive lifestyle actions. This is essentially the purpose for living the DREAM, which is covered in great detail throughout this book. Importantly, many of the above-mentioned natural providers will *treat* the pathology while simultaneously providing lifestyle advice to encourage better health throughout the lifetime.

INTERVENTION VS. (RE)-CONNECTION

This was a big one for me because as I began to understand this concept, my entire thought process shifted. The outside-in approach looks to intervene and make the body do what "textbooks" say it should do. The inside-out approach, however, is quite different.

The inside-out approach understands the concept of innate intelligence and that ultimately the power that made the body heals the body. In a later chapter, you will see a reference to the

Michelangelo painting that is found on the ceiling of the Sistine Chapel in Rome, Italy. When I was in chiropractic college at Life University, many of my fellow classmates wore shirts with an image of the painting on it. Not knowing much about art or spirituality at that point in my life, I asked my friends why they had it on their shirt. The response was almost always the same, "Because it's spiritual." I would always respond back and say, "Yes, I can understand that, but what is the significance of that particular picture and chiropractic?" The next answer again was, "I don't know, it's spiritual." We would go around and around and never get me my answer.

Then, finally during a trip to Italy and a tour of the Sistine Chapel, my 96-year-old tour guide explained that the painting I had seen over and over again in chiropractic circles was that of God giving Adam the spark of life. That's it! I immediately went back in my mind to my first month of chiropractic college in Dr. BJ Harmon's philosophy and chiropractic history class. D.D. Palmer, the founder of chiropractic (*see Ch. 8-6*), said that the purpose of chiropractic was to re-unite "man the spiritual with man the physical." At the time, that really made no sense to me; I thought chiropractors just realigned the spine to help a person feel and function better. But now it was all starting to make sense to me. Now the purpose of my life started to become clearer in understanding that I would help ensure the quality of one's life by helping humanity express true connection with Source. The reality is, we are never actually disconnected from God or Life Source, otherwise we would not be alive. That said, we often do not demonstrate that connection at times. The true expression of divine connection is a perfect example of atonement (*see Ch. 4-1*).

The inside-out approach understands and honors the importance of that connection and does everything possible to help the individual harness his/her natural healing abilities, as opposed to trying to play God with manmade interventions. Young children are living examples of innate intelligence. With very little educated intelligence at that point in life, they are essentially living on instinct.

PHYSICAL VS. MENTAL, EMOTIONAL, PHYSICAL AND SPIRITUAL

The outside-in approach often looks at the body solely as a physical being made of flesh and bones. Many healthcare treatments only consider the way it would affect that body part. Also, many of the causes are looked at as purely physical.

The inside-out approach, however, considers the thoughts, the traumas, the toxins and the energy of the individual and how those have an effect on the cause and/or resolution of issues. Looking at and working with one's mental and emotional state as well as spiritual connection often helps people overcome and avoid many physical ailments.

MECHANISTIC VS. VITALISTIC

The outside-in approach views the body as an incredible piece of machinery. Think about Frankenstein for a moment. (Many people think of Frankenstein as the monster in the movies, but those that really know the story are aware that Frankenstein was the doctor who created the monster.) Dr. Frankenstein believed that if he could take all the parts of a dead human and zap it with enough electricity, he could make that body come back to life. That is a *very* simplistic view of mechanism, but hopefully you get my point.

While wellness providers also see the body as an incredible piece of machinery, they also see it as a perfect and complete being. The word vitalism comes from the Latin root of *vital* meaning that it pertains to life. A vitalistic approach considers that something we cannot see on the surface exists to keep us alive and separate from a piece of meat. This is very much tied into the concept of innate intelligence (*see Ch. 3-1*).

Let's do a thought experiment. Imagine if you cut a steak. In one week, go back and look at the steak. What will the steak look like? That's right, still cut and rotted out. Now imagine your son cuts his hand. What would his hand look like after a week? That's right, it's healed or in the process of healing. What is the difference between that steak and his hand? You got it, *life*. Whether we are referring to a bovine or human, a living being has the ability to heal.

REPLACES VS. RESTORES

The outside-in approach is quick to take out body parts that are not working correctly as if we are created with too many organs. I can say with certainty that *we were not created with too many organs or too few drugs* in our bodies. Now I am not saying that removing body parts at times does not save lives. I am again oversimplifying a concept. Though I will say that if you think your children were created with organs that they do not need, like tonsils and the appendix, that is just ludicrous. Those organs have been shown to be part of the immune system, as well as a first line of defense to helping fight disease and infection. But even if we did not have knowledge as to what certain organs do, where do we come off thinking that they are extra?

The inside-out approach looks to help the organs, muscles and glands that may be stressed and naturally restore their ability to function as intended.

TREATING SYMPTOMS VS. CORRECTING CAUSES

The outside-in approach often helps people feel and function better. However, it often falls short of actually fixing the problem that caused the symptoms in the first place, making someone a customer for life. A perfect example of this would be type II diabetics whose doctors only prescribe insulin (or other medications), as opposed to helping guide them with a change in lifestyle habits, such as diet and exercise.

The inside-out approach in a wellness model desires to get to the root of the problem and do the best possible job at restoring the person to optimal function, again, through lifestyle modifications. The outside in approach mostly uses drugs to resist death whereas the inside-out approach helps people take action to promote life!

CHEMICAL VS. CHEMICAL AND ELECTRICAL

The *chemistry of life* is a term I learned from a mentor Reggie Gold, DC. Your chemistry keeps you alive as your body is run on chemicals every second of every day.

The outside-in approach often looks to modify chemistry. If your blood pressure is too high, you would be given a chemical, whether it be a drug or supplement, to lower it. If your heart is beating too fast, you would be given a chemical to slow it down. If your pancreas is not producing insulin as in the case of diabetes, you will be given a chemical to breakdown sugar. The chemistry of life is an ebb and flow of chemicals and hormones regulating every single body process. Chemistry must be balanced for the body to function and regulate.

You may have learned at some point in your education that your body produces all the chemicals and hormones needed for your body to function. Your organs and glands have an inborn intelligence that knows exactly how much of each chemical to produce and when to produce it.

The brain is in constant communication with your organs and glands, informing them of how much to produce of each hormone. The brain sends electrical messages down the spinal cord and out to the spinal nerves that feed vital information to every organ, every muscle, every gland and every cell of the body, every moment of your life. If optimal communication between your brain and organs were to become compromised, that could potentially impact the performance and function of that organ.

In an outside-in approach, it would not be typical protocol to check the electrical flow of energy in your body prior to putting you on a medication or natural therapeutic. That is why it is extremely important to look at both the chemistry and the electricity in an inside-out model. I can't tell you how many times I have someone visit my centers with a problem that they were medicated for, but when I was able to remove the interference to the nervous system with a specific chiropractic adjustment, the problem resolved itself from the inside. The true wellness part of this scenario is in determining the stressor that caused the interference in the first place.

* * *

A true wellness provider who really gets the inside-out approach would not ever claim to heal or treat any condition. While many issues resolve through natural approaches, the provider would rather honor the power that made the body and work within that realm to bring back balance to you so that you can express your true perfection.

Many in the chiropractic profession use the term, ADIO (Above-Down, Inside-Out). They are referencing that the optimal expression of health, life and vitality is dependent on nerve signals arising from *above* (referring to the brain), travel *down* the spinal cord which is located centrally *inside* the body from the spinal cord and then travels *out* the various nerves. The nerves feed vital information to every organ, gland, tissue and cell of the body. (Some chiropractors with a more spiritual perspective refer to the *above* aspect as being God, more so than to the brain.) A true wellness lifestyle helps ensure that the nervous system continues to function optimally, all of the time.

REFLECTION OPPORTUNITY

What are your current beliefs within the 8 paradigms listed above?

Which of the paradigms explained do you see shifting to the most for yourself and your family?

What actions do you take each day to reduce your risk of ill health?

What more could you do to take an inside-out approach in your daily life?

1-4

THE AUTHOR'S JOURNEY

My passion for a career in wellness was sparked by tragedy. When I was a student in my sophomore year attending the State University of New York at Oneonta, back home on Long Island my mom started dating a retired NYPD officer named Nat Lindner. The first time I met Nat he asked me about college and my interests.

I told him that I had recently decided to change my career path 180 degrees from the desire to be a movie producer to becoming a physical therapist. I did not know much about physical therapy, but with my passion for health and fitness and having been a personal trainer, varsity wrestler and avid martial artist, it seemed like it would be a good fit. He asked if I ever considered being a chiropractor and suggested that I talk to his son Steve who was studying at Life Chiropractic College (now Life University) in Marietta, Georgia. Nat thought that Steve and I would get along and chiropractic may be a good career choice for me.

When Steve introduced me to the philosophy of chiropractic, I felt like I was *home*. It made so much sense to me. He explained how health is the natural state of our being, and how chiropractic helps the body heal itself without drugs or surgery. This made perfect sense to me. I loved to exercise to keep my body healthy: I lived on salads before salads were even an entrée on restaurant menus, and I did not take drugs, "pushed or prescribed." I always wanted to treat my body like a temple. This chiropractic thing sounded like it was perfectly aligned with my values.

Steve and I spoke many times on the telephone that year and planned to meet in person at our parents' wedding. Steve promised to spend much of winter break introducing me to chiropractors in our hometown and surrounding areas. We had no idea that 36 hours before the wedding, everything would change.

As my mom and Nat were leaving the house to visit friends, Nat said he didn't feel well. On the way to the hospital his condition worsened. By the time he was on a gurney outside the emergency room, Nat was gone. He was 44 years young when he suffered his first and only symptom of heart disease, a deadly aneurysm.

If you asked Nat when he woke up that morning about his health, he would have told you he was perfectly healthy.

I met Steve for the first time at his dad's funeral. Even in his grief, Steve was committed to start our tour of chiropractic offices the next Monday. He was on a mission to save the world through chiropractic and was not going to allow the state of a man's physical existence change that, even if that man was his dad. I owe much of my passion and commitment as a healthcare provider to both Nat and Steve.

Steve and I spent days together watching the masters of the chiropractic profession— most notably, Dr. Pasquale Cerasoli who later became one of the most influential mentors in my life. Though we were a day shy of becoming stepbrothers, Steve and I continue to enjoy a friendship that is stronger than most brothers share.

From the time after Nat's passing even through today, Steve and I often talk about his dad and whether he would still be around had he made different lifestyle choices. We will never know the answer to that question, but Nat's story and millions of others' untimely deaths and unnecessary suffering inspires and drives us every day to help people take control of their health and vitality.

REFLECTION OPPORTUNITY

What pivotal moments in your life were derived from a tragedy and how did it turn out?

Where does your inspiration come from?

Nat did not have an opportunity to meet his amazing grandchildren who were born decades after his premature departure from this plane of existence. As a parent and reader of this book, I can only assume that you desire to watch your children grow up and possibly start a family of their own. I would like you to take a moment, close your eyes and visualize what grandparenthood would look like for you. Make a declaration, right now, that you will make substantive changes to your lifestyle, no matter how good it may currently be, to put the odds in your favor for your vision to come to fruition. Your kids need you to be around for a long time, and children deserve to know their grandparents. Take a few moments and write out what being a grandparent could look like for you.

2-1

HITTING THE MARK!

THE PARABLE OF THE GOOD ARCHER

There once lived a world-class archer, back in the 1800s. This archer would easily beat his competitors, day after day after day. Then one afternoon after winning a big competition, he stumbled upon a barn in a small village with targets painted all around it. Surprisingly, each and every target had an arrow shot through the dead center. The archer was shocked and needed to meet that other archer, for he could not call himself the best if he had not beaten all the greats.

He knocked on the barn door to introduce himself to the talented villager, but no one was around. He walked into the town and asked several locals, "Who is the world class archer with the barn?" Each time he asked that question, he would first get a funny look and then a snicker from the other person but still failed to get the answer. It was not until several hours of investigating that an elder in the town told him who it was.

She said, "You see, good sir, the man you refer to as this world class archer, we refer to him as the village idiot." "Village idiot?" he replied, "How could such a talented individual be mocked like so?" The lady proceeded to tell him, "Well, I can see why you would say that, but the truth is, he shoots the arrows into blank barn walls, and then he paints the targets around them!"

* * *

When I first heard that story, everyone of course laughed and that was the end of the story. However, I found it to be quite profound . . . much more than a simple joke, this was a parable in the making!

Personally, I think that we could all take a page out of the book of the village idiot every now and then.

The villagers may have perceived this gentleman to be the village idiot, but I see him as the village genius. He was so clear on what he wanted his outcome to be, he created the environment around him to make it happen, rather than blame any shortcomings in his life on "bad luck, bad germs or bad genes," as a mentor, Dr. James Chestnut says. The archer chose to do what was necessary to bring his vision to fruition.

You may not be aware, but much of what you have in your life right now is a result of your past thoughts, words and actions. Dr. Pasquale Cerasoli always said, "Thoughts are things and things are thoughts." It is very likely that you have heard the phrase, "What we speak about, we bring about."

Many have heard these sayings from personal development books and movies, like the 2006 documentary *The Secret*. In fact, I put *The*

Secret to the test about someone who was in the movie, and magic happened.

I was at a restaurant in San Diego shortly following my move from New York to San Diego not long after the release of the movie. The friend I was dining with mentioned to me that two or three of the stars of the movie lived in San Diego. I was particularly interested in meeting John Assaraf, so I said to David, "Okay, then let's use the law of attraction and 'conjure' him up." Minutes later, John walked into the restaurant. I'm not going to lie, I was a bit in disbelief, even though I did believe in the power of thought and intention.

As much as I enjoyed that movie and viewed it dozens of times, it was not new information (though it was new to me at the time); and it is certainly not a secret. You can go back more than 5,000 years and read in the Bible: *"Death and life is in the power of the tongue: and they that love it shall eat the fruit thereof."* (Prov. 18:21, 21st Century King James Version)

Lao Tzu said:

Watch your thoughts, they become words;
Watch your words, they become actions;
Watch your actions, they become habits;
Watch your habits, they become character;
Watch your character, for it becomes your destiny.

Of course we were not going to miss an incredible opportunity to meet someone who greatly impacted our lives, so we introduced ourselves to John and told him about our little experiment. I even invited him to speak to a group of chiropractors in San Diego, and he graciously accepted. Many people in the personal development world are quite different when the cameras are off. I will say that John is the epitome of caring and authenticity. I have gotten to know John over the years, and I have seen him in his roles as a father, a husband and a brother. John has had a tremendous influence in my life since that moment, both personally and professionally, and I have the privilege to continue to see him in his role as a friend. Never underestimate the power of your thoughts, words and actions!

When your thoughts and actions are not in *alignment*, you will miss opportunities in life and potentially cause needless suffering. Many refer to *sin* as an offense against a religious or moral law. However, the word's origin is quite different. The Hebrew word for sin is חטאה (hhatah) and literally means to go astray or to *miss the mark*. A sin can be deliberate or done mistakenly. Interestingly, the word sin was initially (and still today) used in archery. When an archer does not hit the bullseye, he or she has sinned.

What you and your family currently have in terms of health, wealth and happiness is very much a result of your past, your previous thoughts, words and actions. That means that your health, wealth and happiness (and that of your kids), in the future will be a result of what is done today . . . and tomorrow . . . and the next day.

Let us use food as an example. If your daughter is hungry and wants a snack and has before her a cookie and a carrot, which one would she grab?

Cookies and carrots both taste pretty good, yet the net result will be quite different. Is she hitting the mark if she chooses the cookie?

If she chooses to eat the carrot, her body will acquire more nutrients. After eating the carrot, will her eyesight immediately improve? Of course not. And she will not gain weight by eating one cookie if she chooses that route. However, if she chooses to eat a carrot every day for a snack versus a cookie, she will certainly benefit from the nutritional content of that vegetable versus the empty calories and carbohydrates. You and your kids share the fact that destiny in health, wealth and happiness is ultimately determined by the compound effects of words, actions and habits.

When you sin in archery, the consequences can range from damaging your arrows to losing the match. When you sin in life, the consequences can ultimately be summed up as not living to your perfection. Fortunately, life is filled with numerous opportunities for do-overs and reconciliation.

REFLECTION OPPORTUNITY

Are you conscious of the words you choose?

Think of a time in your life when something great resulted that was unexpected. Perhaps you were running late or made a last-minute decision and ended up being in a place at a time that was not planned. What can you do to create more *serendipitous* moments in your life?

How can you use this information to teach your children something about their language?

2-2

BRAINWASHED: A RUDE AWAKENING

THE BLUE PILL OR THE RED PILL?

Neo, the main character in the 1999 movie *The Matrix*, had to make a big decision. He had the opportunity to take the blue pill, which would keep him ignorant of reality and follow the status quo. Had he made that choice, he would have continued to live the life he was accustomed to and nothing in his life would change. The other option he had was to take the red pill which would turn his entire life upside down because he would finally learn the truth about reality and how he could make constructive changes for the entire world.

Given the opportunity, which pill would you take?

No one wants to be brainwashed but let us look at it differently. We go through our lives, day after day, hearing lies, false truths, "alternative facts" and negative information. Whether it is mainstream media, social media, politicians or private companies with their advertisements, this constant bombardment of mostly inaccurate and misleading information affects our beliefs about ourselves, our society and everything around us.

You have been getting brainwashed for years and your kids are being "programmed" like never before. In the past, it was television ads, radio ads and newspapers as the biggest culprits. These days, however, there is a plethora of technology that has created more and more opportunities to seep information into the minds of young ones. As a parent, you must be more vigilant than ever. Not only is it time to decide to limit these exposures, but it is also time to wipe the slate clean for you and your kids.

There is great irony in the analogy above, as pills are one of the biggest deceptions in existence. I am not saying drugs do not work. In fact, they often do exactly what they are supposed to do. What I am calling deceptive is the belief that we need these pills to be healthy.

> *If health came in a pill bottle, the world would have a plastic shortage.*

When I was a child, I was taught that when I had a problem, medicine would heal me. Pharmaceutical companies spend tens of billions of dollars each year convincing us to believe that health comes in a little orange bottle. They also spend billions of dollars finding creative ways to subsidize and fund medical schools, doctors' offices and lawmakers' elections. It is time to stop committing the sin (*see Ch. 2-1*) of bowing down to the idols of medicine and to start taking responsibility for your health.

I never thought that I would be on this side of the aisle when it came to healthcare. It was so much easier not knowing the truth, as it would have been for Neo (spoiler alert) had he not chosen the *red pill*. Instead, he chose to save the world.

This is not about putting "pharma" on trial. I just want to clear the misinformation stuck in your brain that has been there from your childhood and prevent as many future *sins* as possible. This is your opportunity, for the benefit of your entire family, to start from scratch and use critical thinking moving forward.

While reading this book, try to not think about what you currently believe and just try and receive it with an open mind. When you are done with the book, if you genuinely feel that your old beliefs were serving you better than this new information will, then by all means, go back to where you were.

REFLECTION OPPORTUNITY

Think of at least three beliefs you currently hold that may or may not be based on sound evidence. These can be about yourself, other people, health, the world, politics or anything else important to you. Then consider whether those beliefs serve you well or potentially hold you back and prevent you from learning or experiencing more. If so, think about what you can do to learn more about those things and either verify your beliefs or modify if needed.

Bonus Opportunity: There is a great quote: "Being taught to avoid talking about politics and religion has led to a lack of understanding of politics and religion. What we should have been taught was how to have a civil conversation about a difficult topic." Talk about these with someone you care about and trust and have an intellectually honest conversation about these issues. You may learn something new!

3-1

INNATE INTELLIGENCE

LIFE WITHOUT FEAR

Within the minutes that followed the most exciting and surreal moment of my life, I learned that it could have been the most tragic.

One thing that my wife, Brooke, and I knew for sure was we wanted our son to be born at home. As a chiropractor, I had learned of the numerous health benefits of homebirth and pledged that I would only start a family with someone holding similar values. Fortunately for me, my wife, Brooke, was born at home, as were her two brothers.

We weighed both the risks and benefits of a homebirth versus a hospital birth, and for us, it was a no brainer.

We interviewed many midwives until we chose the perfect one for us, Michelle F. We also hired an amazing doula who was also our amazing Bradley Method birth class instructor.

After 12 weeks of intense Bradley classes (taught by our doula, Julie) chock full of birth education, some of which was a refresher for me from chiropractic school, we were ready for anything. We were confident that if there were a reason to be transferred to the hospital, we would do what needed to be done to ensure a safe, healthy birth process. We also knew that throughout this pregnancy, there were other decisions that we were going to make down the road.

One of the more controversial decisions we had made early in the pregnancy was to not perform any ultrasound tests.

There are several reasons why we chose to not use ultrasound, but the most meaningful reason of all was, it did not fit into our philosophical and spiritual paradigm. We know that there are many benefits that ultrasound provides throughout pregnancy, but there are also potential risks. Understanding that we were created by God in His perfection (with no mistakes), there is no way the one process required by humankind to persist would require this particular medical intervention. People have been birthing babies before ultrasound ever existed. We explained our decision to Michelle and she just made us agree that if she found a cause for concern that we would agree to having one done. We took no issue with that deal.

Forty weeks went by blissfully for Brooke. Not a single complication or cause for concern. Brooke loved being pregnant, every moment of it.

January 24, 2016, was the day. For those sports fans, yes, it was the day that the Denver Broncos beat the New England Patriots to clinch the AFC Championship and learned they would face the Carolina Panthers in Superbowl 50; but that is not what I'm referring to. I should mention, however, the reason I remember that so well is because Brooke is from Denver and a huge Broncos fan. She was literally in the middle of heavy breathing through contractions when we got a text from her friend telling her the good news. Her friend did not know at the time that Brooke was in labor pushing out baby Zion while the Broncos defense was pushing Tom Brady to the ground. But I digress . . .

At 4:44 p.m., Zion Gabriel Stenzler made his entrance into this world. As I caught him, the midwife and I saw that the cord was wrapped around his neck a bit. We untangled him, and I carefully adjusted his delicate little spine as I handed him to Brooke with the cord and placenta still intact.

At 4:55 p.m. while Brooke and I were coddling our beautiful miracle, we noticed the midwife and doula whispering and taking pictures. Only they were not shooting photos of us, it was the placenta they were photographing. We thought that was a bit strange, but maybe it was a common procedure. I asked Michelle what was going on and she told us that the placenta presented with a velamentous cord insertion.

This is a rare condition in which the umbilical cord is inserted in the fetal membranes rather than the middle of the placental mass and is completely encased by the amniotic sac. (Don't worry, you do not need to know what that means). Normally the blood vessels would be protected by Wharton's jelly which prevents rupture during pregnancy and labor. Without Wharton's jelly protecting the vessels, the exposed vessels are susceptible to compression and rupture with too much movement in utero. While the incidence of rupture is relatively low, if it were to happen, it could be catastrophic for mom or baby, or both.

Velamentous cord insertion occurs in approximately 1% of pregnancies and do not come with many (if any) symptoms, and it is typically only diagnosed with an ultrasound. Once diagnosed, the doctor would require frequent monitoring and multiple ultrasounds throughout the remainder of the pregnancy. Based on other potential complicating factors, these pregnancies commonly end with a pre-term C-section.

Fortunately for us and Zion, everything turned out perfectly. But what if it hadn't? Perhaps we set ourselves up for a potential tragedy which easily could have been avoided had we done an ultrasound.

Many of you have probably heard the term innate intelligence, but a good definition has eluded most. Some refer to it as life force, chi, spirit, soul or even God within. I define innate intelligence as the divinely infinite, inborn wisdom that animates our internal living world. This *gift from God* is your inner voice that tells you and your body all kinds of stuff . . . whether it is on the conscious level or not.

Brooke and I have such strong convictions in prayer, healthy lifestyle and innate intelligence that we know that we did everything the way we were supposed to. We prayed for Zion prior to his conception and throughout the pregnancy. I adjusted Brooke throughout the pregnancy and performed a special technique called Webster, which helps ensure proper fetal positioning by relieving constraint in the uterus. (Interestingly, from the first moment that Zion's head was detectable by the midwife, she told us that he barely moved from that perfect head-down position, which was in just the right spot. Most fetuses are much more active doing their "fetal gymnastics." It is almost as if he innately knew not to move too much.) In addition, Brooke ate the right foods and exercised appropriately, and she kept her thoughts pure on the perfection of Zion as he was developing. With all that intentional focus on the perfect pregnancy, we counted on the belief that we would be protected from anything that could potentially go wrong.

Had we strayed from our belief system out of fear and performed the recommended ultrasounds, what could have been the result?

Well for one, we would have missed an opportunity to experience a true, natural pregnancy and birth from beginning to end, and the expression of faith in God and innate intelligence. Then there is the issue of the multiple ultrasounds. What if the potential negative effects of ultrasound that concerned us became a reality and Zion had complications as a result? What if we were required to do an early term C-section? Aside from the plethora of benefits of vaginal births, Zion was born on the day he was supposed to, not just because it was the Broncos special victory. Zion was only 6 pounds at 40 weeks. How much smaller would he have been if delivered early? How long would he have lain in the incubator in the NICU? How would that have potentially affected his survivability or health as an infant and beyond? Maybe that is the tragedy that we avoided.

These are questions that we will never have answers to, thank goodness! But what Brooke and I both agree is, had we done it the way we did and had a negative consequence, it would be tough for us to live with. However, had we compromised our beliefs and values and had a negative consequence, that is something we could not live with.

While many readers may feel that the choice Brooke and I made was completely irresponsible and we are lucky it did not turn bad, I am reminded of an impactful book I read decades ago as a student in chiropractic college, *Life Without Fear*, which was by a mentor and teacher, Dr. Fred Barge. Barge taught about the necessity to understand that innate intelligence always knows what is best for an individual's survival, and we will thrive if we just let the body do what it needs to do. Innate needs no help; just no interference. Fear is often created for malevolent reasons, whether it is for profit or control. Fear also comes from lack of faith, understanding and trust.

There is a very fine line between living with faith and being irresponsible.

A CLOUDY PARABLE

In the middle of an afternoon on a cloudy or rainy day, it would appear that the sun is not shining. However, if you were to get into an airplane and travel above the clouds, you would see that the sun is shining just as brightly as it does each and every day when the clouds are not blocking the rays. On the ground level, the expression of the sun is inhibited by the clouds making it appear that the sun is not shining. The sun never ceases to shine at 100% within the solar system, but the expression of the sunshine may appear less than 100% based on your location on the planet or existing weather patterns. Same goes for innate intelligence. Your innate is always shining at 100%, but the expression may often appear less than perfect.

* * *

What your innate knows does not have to be thought about, studied, researched or understood. In fact, your innate intelligence controls body functions and processes that even one percent of your conscious mind could never begin to handle. It knows your heart should beat 60–72 times per minute to pump blood throughout your body; it knows your lungs should expand and contract every 10–12 seconds to breathe; it knows your spleen should replace red blood cells every 4–6 months, and so on. Imagine if you had to think about every single body function every moment of the day. I don't know about you, but the second I were to answer my telephone, I would drop dead!

Your intuition, thoughts and gut feelings are also encompassed within your innate intelligence (as opposed to *educated intelligence*: that which we have learned). Innate intelligence is knowing right from wrong; your thought whether to go right or left when driving and lost; the angel sitting on your right shoulder arguing with the devil on your left shoulder prior to sneaking that chocolate bar just before bed; and so on. The question is whether or not we listen to innate enough.

Without getting too spiritual here, I would like to mention that I believe that innate lives in the mind, not to be confused with the brain which is an organ. The mind can be defined as the element of people that enables them to be aware of the world and their experiences, to think and to feel, the faculty of consciousness and thought. The mind is not made of physical matter and ultimately encompasses our entire being.

Every person on this planet has the exact same amount of innate intelligence. It does not matter if it is a newborn baby, disabled individual, person with infirmities or a seemingly healthy Nobel Prize recipient. Innate intelligence is 100% in every living person, 100% of the time. However, the expression of that innate may be less than 100%.

As discussed earlier (*see Ch. 1-3*), the fresco painting by Michelangelo called *The Creation of Adam* can be found on the ceiling of the Sistine Chapel. It illustrates the Biblical creation narrative from the Book of Genesis in which God breathes life into Adam, the first man.

The very popular version of that painting shows two fingers close together but not quite touching. That is the gap between man (Adam) and God just before God gives Adam the spark of life.

The true goal of life should be for us to all live to our 100% innate potential and perfect expression of self. Since we are created in the likeness of God, it is our responsibility to treat our bodies as a temple or a house for the spirit; and express our divine perfection. Many people will say that we were not born perfect. This sometimes comes from a practical perspective and other times from a religious or spiritual frame of reference. If you cannot accept that we are all created perfect, then at least consider accepting that we are all created *imperfectly perfect*.

Hopefully by now you are getting inspired and educated on how to live purposefully and consciously during this journey we call life, and how to pass it on to your progeny. It is extremely important to focus our actions and thoughts daily and to work with mentors, spiritual leaders and wellness providers who work within that gap to help you express that 100% connection with source.

Zion's birth story was an exhibition of innate intelligence in its most perfect expression.

REFLECTION OPPORTUNITY

What is an example in your life where you made a decision that was contrary to normal standards based on your faith and/or philosophy and how did it turn out?

Think of a time that you listened to your *innate* on something very important. How did it turn out?

What are some examples of *brilliance* that you saw in your kids that demonstrated their connection with innate?

3-2

HEALTH VS. SICKNESS VS. EXPRESSING HEALTH

I will never forget this one particular consultation I was doing on a patient when I was relatively new in practice. She was 38 years old and seemed to have it all together. She had a wonderful family, which included a husband she adored and three children all under the age of 12. She was referred to my office with the hope of naturally resolving her headaches, just as her best-friend's migraines resolved shortly after receiving care at our office months earlier.

As I was going over Beth's health history, she did not think she had much to tell me. When she said she was healthy and had an "uneventful history," I poked and prodded because most people, especially with headaches, have at least one thing to share. She mentioned a car accident she had when she was in college but no known injuries from that "fender-bender." She also informed me that in high school when she was the flyer on her cheerleading team, she fell from the top of the pyramid. Her neck and her mid-back hurt for a few weeks, but it was "no big deal." That was all she thought was important to tell me about her prior health.

When I asked about any previous surgeries, she told me that she had her tonsils removed when she was seven years old. I asked if there were any other surgeries. She thought and said, "Oh yeah, six years ago I had a double mastectomy as part of my treatment for breast cancer."

I did everything I could to not look shocked, but I could not understand why that was not top of mind for her and why she did not tell me about the breast cancer when I was asking about any prior health issues. When I asked why she did not mention anything about the cancer, she said, "Because prior to the cancer, I was completely healthy."

I needed to take a second to compose my thoughts and choose my next words wisely. I wanted to let her know that "healthy" people do not suddenly *get* cancer, but I chose to tread lightly as I did not want her to misunderstand my intention. Like most of you, I too have painfully lost people close to me due to cancer and other horrible diseases, and the last thing I wanted was to come across insensitive. Instead of saying anything, I just listened to her with compassion and knew I would have opportunities throughout her care to educate her on the real meaning of health.

Most disease processes, including cancer, diabetes and high blood pressure, do not form overnight. They are gradual and often do not reveal themselves with symptoms until they have progressed considerably. While these issues are developing, the individual is no longer completely healthy, whether symptoms are present or not.

Most people determine their health status based on how they feel. We all know that many people visit healthcare practitioners when they do not feel well. So, if you are not experiencing pain, symptoms or other obvious problems, does that mean you are healthy?

That may seem like a silly belief now that you are seeing it in print, but just think about how you live your life and raise your kids. Remember my mom's fiancé Nat (*see Ch. 1-4*), who was not experiencing any symptoms the morning he awakened for the last time. When was the last time you visited a healthcare practitioner when you felt great? Aside from a routine physical examination, most people do not seek care or advice from healthcare providers unless they do not feel well. But then the question again is, are you healthy even if you do not have symptoms?

The World Health Organization defines health as *the state of complete physical, social and mental well-being, not merely the absence of disease or infirmity.*

I personally think that is a pretty good definition and I wish it were more publicized and understood. It is unfortunate, however, that in our society so many people believe that they are healthy if they do not have any known illness. It is not obvious to most people when they are physically, socially and mentally unwell, especially if they *feel* "fine."

So much of what we have in our lives, including our relationships, finances, successes, failures, perceptions and our physiques are a huge reflection of our physical, mental and social well-being. But what kind of *doctor* would you see if you do not like your friends, or they don't like you? Or you do not like the way you look? Or you do not have enough money? Or you do not have your dream job? Or you lack energy? Or cannot sleep at night? Or you don't have time for your kids? Or your kids can't stand being around you?

Maybe the job of healthcare should *not* be left in the hands of your medical doctor. In fact, most doctors treat sicknesses, diseases and injuries. So why is it even called healthcare when what they really do is sick care? I am certainly not knocking medicine, but let's be honest for a moment. If you went to your doctor's office and told the doctor you were feeling great and you weren't there for a routine physical examination, that doctor would likely look at you as if you had three heads wondering what you were doing there.

Historically, medicine has not been known for its *proactive* approach toward creating health. In the 1970s, the medical community was outspoken about the potential dangers of exercise and how it can cause heart attacks. At the turn of the millennium (and even still today), many doctors discourage taking vitamins and supplements, "because they're not regulated like medications." Give me a break! Let's not even start the conversation about the medical doctors who actually did commercials promoting cigarette smoking and tobacco usage in the 1950s.

In Paul Zane Pilzer's book *The Wellness Revolution: How to Make a Fortune in the Next Trillion Dollar Industry*, Pilzer wrote, "Approximately one-seventh of the U.S. economy, about $1.5 trillion, is devoted to what is erroneously called the 'healthcare' business. It is really a sickness business that is reactive. People become patients only when they are stricken. . . . The wellness business is proactive because people voluntarily utilize these services . . . to feel healthier, to reduce the effects of aging and avoid becoming patients of the sickness business."

I believe that the United States has the best sick care system in the world. If my health is in crisis and I find myself in a life-threatening situation, there is no place I would rather be than in a hospital surrounded by the best medical doctors. However, I think that they should leave healthcare to those who focus on the creation of health through a wellness lifestyle.

WHAT IS SICKNESS?

When I was in college, I remember hearing about a tragic story that took place at another local university. Two lacrosse players went out binge drinking one evening to celebrate their victory. The two students went *shot for shot*, drinking the exact same tequila and the exact same quantity. By night's end, they were both inebriated. One of the students woke up the next morning with the worst hangover of his life. He was vomiting nonstop, had a terrible headache and could not keep his eyes open. The other young, talented lacrosse player did not wake up. He died of alcohol poisoning.

Which student was sick; the one whose body recognized the toxin and got it out of his system, or the one who died from alcohol toxicity? Obviously, they were both dealing with challenges. However, the student whose body was not able to recognize and rid the body of the invader, alcohol in this case, was the sick individual. The other student's body was doing exactly what it should be doing.

What do you think of when you think of *sickness*? When you say you are *sick*, what do you mean by that?

If your son has a fever, is he *sick*? How about coughing up phlegm? Sneezing? How about even vomiting?

Sure, when you or your kids have any or all the above symptoms, you are typically very uncomfortable; but are you *sick*? Well, again that comes down to how you define sickness.

Just because your son may have symptoms, that does not necessarily mean he is sick. In fact, in many cases, the symptoms, which are his body doing what it needs to do, are an expression of health. Symptoms are typically annoying and uncomfortable, but we should be grateful that we have them. Symptoms are often not the problem; in fact, they are frequently the solution or at least part of the solution. Symptoms are there to inform you that something is going on and/or to bring your son's body back to balance. I can assure you that he was not created with a faulty mechanism that would cause him to overheat every now and then, giving him a fever.

Fevers, up to a certain temperature, are a gift that help immobilize, retard multiplication and eventually kill the unwelcomed invaders in our bodies. Yet parents are constantly giving their children medications to lower fevers, which may not always be the best course of action.

Artificially lowering these fevers can leave a breeding ground in your kid's body for more invaders. Remember, kids (especially young ones) are constantly touching objects that are infested with bacteria and viruses, and they are around other kids that have done the same. Then they put either the object or their fingers in their mouths causing a *natural* immune response.

The mucus (snot) carries dead pathogens (virus, bacteria, parasites and tumor cells) out of his body once they are killed by interferon, which is a substance his body produces constantly. If he has a dead virus in his body, do you really want to suppress its expulsion?

Let's examine the common care for a sprained joint like the ankle. What is the typical first call to action? That's right, ice the injury. In fact, the acronym RICE is currently used to remind people that an injury should first be rested, then iced, then compressed and kept elevated. Additionally, doctors often recommend anti-inflammatory medications to keep down the swelling, and inflammation and often pain medication is used. This all seems pretty sound . . . or does it?

Personally speaking, I had sprained my ankle multiple times while playing soccer and other sports; probably for the first time when I was around 8 years old. Two of those sprains resulted in torn ligaments. I received the typical treatment that included RICE and a few casts on the ankle. Fortunately, I never required surgery. The problem is my ankles never fully healed and that is why they were considered *weak ankles*. Instead of the doctors wondering why my ankles were weak and changing their approach, they just treated them the same way each time, which led them to get weaker and weaker.

Why does an injury get inflamed? That too is not a faulty mechanism of the body.

Inflammation occurs right after an injury so that the healing can begin. In the case of the ankle, the joint begins to fill with fluid, healing tissue and blood flow which causes it to get warm. The swelling also creates its own cast to ensure you keep it immobilized so you do not cause further injury. Those cells and healing tissues that bombard the area are there to fix the injured area. However, the swelling and heat is scary and painful, so we often choose to "play God" and get rid of it before the body does what it needs to do.

Ice is wonderful at reducing pain and inflammation. By making the area colder, it causes the blood vessels to constrict, the warm areas to become colder and the swelling to diminish. However, just because you feel better, that does not necessarily mean that you are better off. All the necessary healing has not yet taken place. Speeding up the process may come at a cost to your long-term strength and health of the body part. Therefore, I believe my ankles were always weak because they were never given the proper amount of time to heal.

The last time I sprained my ankle, which was while playing tennis in 1997, I treated it completely differently, and it healed stronger than ever before. I stretched and strengthened the surrounding area that was injured, and I had the ankle adjusted when needed. I did not put ice on the injury and I certainly did not cast it. (Disclaimer: I am not recommending a particular treatment protocol, especially since all injuries are unique and have differing severities. I am suggesting that there are other ways to handle certain injuries and it is important to make wise decisions. You should discuss all options with your healthcare provider.)

Injuries and symptoms should be watched closely to prevent them from getting out of control or spreading to others when they are contagious. You do not want over swelling, fevers, vomiting or other major symptoms to get out of hand, and you certainly do not want to circulate viruses and bacteria to others. The problem is, most people are usually too quick to take medication and use outside influences to rid themselves of their symptoms that they do not even give the body a chance to heal naturally.

In non-life-threatening situations, solely ridding your body of symptoms before healing runs its course can be a major cause of chronic problems in our society. There are many exceptions to this thought process, particularly in situations when the symptoms themselves can be a cause of greater concern or even deadly. It is wise to always rule out a serious health issue with a trusted healthcare provider. The bottom line is, as a society we tend to over medicate in situations where there is no serious underlying condition.

I define *sickness* simply as the body not doing what it is supposed to do. If you have an invader in your body and you did not have a symptom or a mechanism to neutralize it, then you may actually be sick.

Hopefully this gets you thinking about what medications you take or may give to your child that may be unnecessary or even hazardous. Again, I am not recommending that you never take medications, I am suggesting that you consider allowing some symptoms run to their natural course before interrupting your body's innate healing ability. While symptoms may be annoying, they are not typically the enemy.

If we are in fact created in God's image and therefore perfect, then how could we believe that we were built with faulty software and cannot heal naturally? This discussion needs to take place between yourself and a trusted healthcare provider. I encourage you to do a considerable amount of research before and after receiving advice. Regardless of what your doctor advises, *you* are ultimately responsible for *your* health and need to live with your body for the remainder of *your* life. Whether it is you or your child, remember, doctors advise . . . you decide!

Now that you know what sickness really is, what are you going to say when you do not feel well and have symptoms? First off, let us consider the power that words carry.

EXPRESSING HEALTH

As you learned in Chapter 2-1, words have power. If you say that you are sick, what do you think you may be attracting? That's right, more sickness. Instead, I propose that we have an attitude of gratitude (*see Ch. 9-11*) when you don't feel well and be grateful that you were created with your own amazing pharmacy that constantly wants to bring you back to balance. Instead of saying you are sick, I suggest you say that you are *expressing health* or *cleansing*. After all, if you are having symptoms that are designed to heal you, you are truly expressing health, just like the case of the lacrosse player who consumed too much alcohol.

Have you ever noticed that people who get symptoms and complain about it constantly typically stay in bed "sick" for many days or even weeks?

How about those people who will not give their symptoms any power by complaining, but instead choose to remain positive? You may ask them if they are sick, but they will just swear their sneeze, stuffy head and runny nose is just an allergy. As long as they take care of their body appropriately and rule out any serious health ailment or infectious disease, they usually re-balance quickly and get back on their feet and return to normal life within a few days.

Of course it is wise to keep your children out of school or daycare when they are experiencing symptoms. They need to rest, and if the issue is contagious, the last thing you want to do is spread it to others whose immune system may be weakened.

It is important to note that just because a person is exposed to a pathogen or toxin, it does not mean that the person is doomed. We have all heard of households where a member of the family gets a stomach virus, common cold or flu, and it runs its course through the house. However, there is often at least one member of the household who does not get the symptoms at all, or just a milder case. Why does that happen?

There are a lot of unanswered questions regarding the *germ theory* and why some pathogens affect some people more than others. What we do know, however, is the stronger the immune system, the better chance someone has of not experiencing the same severity of the infection, if any at all.

Additionally, if your daughter has chronic illnesses, such as ear infections and common colds, and you treat them with antibiotics and other medications, you should begin to wonder why they are reoccurring so often. Is there something going on in her body that is making her so susceptible to these infections?

An analogy I like to use is a dumpster. If you lift a dumpster's lid that is full of garbage, there is a good chance that flies and other pests will be found swarming the trash. If you spray bug repellent into the dumpster, you will effectively kill most if not all the pests. If you return to that same dumpster the next day, what do you think you will find? That's right, more flies.

The problem was not a lack of Raid in the dumpster. The problem was the garbage inside the dumpster. Until you remove the trash, the flies will continue to return. Until you remove the cause(s) of the reoccurring infections, they will continue to return.

If your daughter appears to have a weakened immune system where she always seems to have a cold, ear infection or other chronic health concern, it is very important to look at her entire lifestyle as you will read in the next chapter and to ensure that her nervous system is functioning the way it should.

REFLECTION OPPORTUNITY

Take a moment and think about your current overall health status . . . yes the physical, social *and* mental well-being.

- Do you believe you are healthy? If so, what do you base that on? What about your kids?
- Is there room for improvement? If so, where?
- Are there potential issues you are ignoring?
- Are there things you can do better that would bring you and your family better health?
- Are there things you are ignoring that are detracting from your health or that of your family?

Has this chapter changed your mindset about *sickness* and how you think about it?

What do you do when your children are showing symptoms of a common cold or even chronic ear infections? Is it possible that there may be a better course of action?

Does it make sense to you that symptoms occur for a reason and that they are not typically the *problem*, and in fact, they are often part of the *solution*?

How do you feel about the concept of words having power?

Can you see yourself changing your language from saying you're sick (or even someone else such as a child or spouse) and instead using the phrase *expressing health*?

3-3

WELLNESS LIFESTYLE FOR THE FAMILY INTRODUCED

WHAT IS WELLNESS?

Now that you hopefully have a better understanding about *sickness* and *health*, you can finally begin to understand the word that this book is about!

Wellness is a word that is frequently misused, and all too often people use health and wellness interchangeably. Worse yet, they speak of wellness in the treatment of disease, such as medical offices called *wellness centers*. While health and wellness are very much intertwined, they are quite different.

The amount of health you have at any given time is directly proportional to your wellness lifestyle.

So what is wellness?

Wellness is a proactive approach toward creating physical, mental, social and spiritual harmony.

It is a lifestyle, encompassing the complete integration of mind, body and spirit, affecting not only your visible body part, but also the trillions of cells that make up your entire body.

Wellness is much more than just how you feel; it determines how you function.

Wellness is a choice, a lifestyle and a process. You cannot reach a destination of wellness because it is ever changing. At every moment of your life, you are either getting healthier or "sicker" based on your lifestyle choices and actions.

The more complete your wellness lifestyle is, the more health you will experience. Every choice that you make and action that you take throughout your life either contributes to or detracts from your wellness lifestyle, therefore having a direct effect on your health and that of your family. You can say that wellness is the *process* and health is the *result*.

On the next page, you will see a diagram that demonstrates the *Illness-Wellness Continuum* as so brilliantly illustrated by John Travis, MD. Consider where you and your family members would find yourselves at any given time. Given that the wellness lifestyle is dynamic and always changing, fortunately you can always move in your desired direction based on your actions. Given that more than

60% of Americans suffer from at least one chronic disease, you can put the majority of them to the left side of the Neutral Point.

The more destructive behaviors that you and your family participate in, the more to the left you will fall on the Continuum. A little to the left is where health begins to diminish and normal function decreases causing symptoms to develop. People to the left side of the spectrum pretty much let life happen. They don't concentrate on what they eat, they have poor attitudes, and the only exercise they do on a regular basis is jumping to conclusions. Those people are in trouble, but the one thing they have going for them is that they are aware that a problem exists. Their lifestyle often leads down a path with the need for medications and surgery. Continuing down that path will ultimately lead to chronic diseases, multiple medications, significantly limited function, poor quality of life, and ultimately, an untimely death.

However, when constructive behaviors are the norm in your household, you should typically enjoy optimal health and well-being. If your family engages in more constructive behaviors and lives consciously by exercising regularly, eating well and keeping your nervous system free of subluxations (*see Ch. 8-5*), then you should experience good health

Then there are the families who choose the DREAM lifestyle every day. You know these people; they are the ones running, hiking and biking together; eating raw nuts and sprouts; and they don't spend much time in front of the television. They typically make great decisions about how to live their lives and are very conscious of their thoughts, words, choices and actions. These achievers typically enjoy optimal health with 100% function and are continually growing and developing more and more health and enjoying the compound effects of a wellness lifestyle.

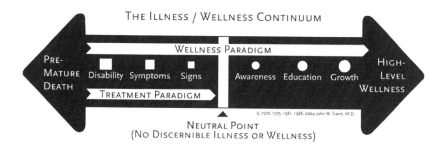

Illness-Wellness Continuum © 1972, 1981, 1988, 2004 by John W. Travis, MD. Reproduced with permission, from *Wellness Workbook: How to achieve enduring health and vitality*, 3rd edition, by John W. Travis and Regina Sara Ryan, Celestial Arts, 2004. www.wellnessworkbook.com.

Then there is the most dangerous group of people: the ones in the middle who have no known illness. Unlike the people to the left who are aware that they have problems, those in the Neutral Point are in a comfort zone and think they are healthier than they actually may be. They feel pretty good most of the time. They think they are maintaining their health because they have no symptoms. Their idea of good nutrition is a bacon cheeseburger, a diet soda and side salad. They exercise sporadically. They do not make health a high priority. They may get a check-up or physical annually but don't really do much to promote health between doctor visits.

The reason this is the most dangerous group is because the ones on the left pretty much know what is coming if they don't make a change; whereas those in the middle feel fine and their attitude is typically, "If it ain't broke, don't fix it." These are the people who go to bed feeling fine and wake up the next day with cancer, diabetes, high blood pressure, or worse yet, don't wake up. This is what you hear at the funeral, "I just don't get it, John was only 35 and was so healthy, he wasn't sick a day in his life." Or, "Before I had the cancer, I was completely healthy," like with Beth (*see Ch. 3-2*). The fact remains, "healthy people" do not drop dead of heart attacks, get cancer or get diabetes, but people without symptoms do.

Does that mean that if you live a wellness lifestyle that you will never get any disease? Of course not! There are many factors that go into the creation of disease (*see Ch. 10-1*), but surprisingly most of them are within our control, but surprisingly most of them are within our control. In fact, genetics plays a much smaller role when it comes to lifespan than we are led to believe, estimated at 25 percent.[2]

When I took a genetic saliva test, I was informed that I had a predisposition to obesity. This did not shock me based on family history. Fortunately, many genetic predispositions can be overcome through lifestyle, which my 11–12% body fat on average demonstrates. There is a complete field of study called epigenetics. In short, epigenetics explores how a person's phenotype (physical traits) can be influenced and modified without a change in the genotype (the inherited genetic makeup) by one's environment, lifestyle and overall well-being.

The good news is that we have the power to make changes in our daily lives to improve our well-being, rather than just being victims of our genetic codes. Physical, mental, emotional and even spiritual well-being is in our hands no matter what cards we were dealt when we entered this world.

REFLECTION OPPORTUNITY

Where do you think you fit on the Illness-Wellness Continuum? What about the rest of your family?

- Is your current lifestyle leading you toward the left or the right? (Hint: you should know this answer if you have taken the DREAM Score)
- If you are heading toward the left, what can you do, starting today, to shift the momentum in the other direction?
- If you are heading toward the right, what can you do today to accelerate the momentum in that direction?

4-1

THE 5 KEYS OF WELLNESS REVEALED

It was my first Passover Seder as a doctor in April 1998. I had just graduated from chiropractic college a few weeks earlier, and I had essentially been away from the family in New York for the previous 4 years getting "brainwashed." I was excited to share what I had learned after taking the *red* pill as referenced previously in the book (*see Ch. 2-2*). My family totally thought that I had lost it. While they were proud of me for becoming a doctor, based on their reactions, I'm certain that some of them wondered if I made a wrong turn on my way to school in Atlanta and became a "witch doctor."

My uncle who is a brilliant, very successful dentist in New York began to question my way of thinking. He asked with understandable skepticism, "Are you saying that with my genes, if I lived this wellness lifestyle you preach, you could guarantee me that I would not have to take medication for these conditions?" I simply responded by asking him a question in return. I said, "You tell me that I should floss my teeth every day, brush at least 2 times per day and rinse daily with mouthwash to prevent tooth decay. If I do that, do you guarantee that I won't develop any cavities?" He responded, "No, but it puts the odds in your favor." My response was the same.

So what is this Living the DREAM stuff all about anyway? Well, if I were to ask you what kinds of things would you do to live a proactive, wellness lifestyle, what would you tell me?

When I ask audiences this question, it often takes 10 minutes until I get close to the answer that I am looking for. It is rarely complete. And it should only take a few seconds. So, it is my mission in life to make the DREAM acronym understood in all households so that people will never again have to hesitate when thinking about what a wellness lifestyle entails.

DREAM® is an acronym that my former business partner Gregg Baron and I trademarked in 1997; it represents the 5 Keys or Facets of the "wellness lifestyle." The purpose of this lifestyle is to better assist your body in adapting to chemical, physical and emotional stressors, which are the ultimate causes of most health issues. Avoiding them, however, is the first step.

There are an infinite number of activities you can do in your life to satisfy each facet, and many that you do will overlap into different ones. It is, however, important to understand that these facets are categories, not services or products. Below is a description of each facet. In the next chapter, you will learn how you can live your DREAM every day.

DIET

Everyone has heard the saying "You are what you eat." The truth is, you are what your body *gets* from what you eat. Actually, the whole truth is, you are what your body gets from what you eat, drink, breathe, see, feel, taste, touch and hear. In other words, *diet* is everything that enters your body's internal environment from the external world.

In Dr. Masaru Emoto's book *The Message from Water*, Dr. Emoto details the changes thought, words and intention have on the crystal formation of water as it freezes. If thought, words and intention can change the shape of water crystals, what kind of effect do you think it can have during the cellular formation of a living human being?

There is an old computer term that dates back to the 1950s, "Garbage in, garbage out," or GIGO. GIGO refers to if the input of certain numbers, logic or information is inaccurate or flawed, then the output will be nonsense or garbage. That same premise can be used to the stimulus of our everyday lives. If you put garbage into your mind through your eyes and ears, you're going to get garbage out as a result. If you allow this type of garbage into your body through your diet, it will not serve you well on a mental and emotional level.

While it is important to breathe fresh air and consume foods and beverages that are rich in nutrients, it is also vital to ensure that what you see, feel, hear and touch is also *nutritious*. The nutritional value of your overall diet will ultimately be determined by your body's ability to process and adapt to its external environment.

RELAXATION

Relaxation is more than just sleeping well. In physics, relaxation is defined as the exponential return of a system to equilibrium (balance) following a disturbance. It can also be defined as a state of refreshing tranquility. We see relaxation as a combination of both. It is a physical, emotional and spiritual mind-body connection in which each and every cell gets a chance to call "timeout" for repair and regeneration. When you are in a relaxed state, your body is more likely to adapt to chemical, physical and emotional stressors that you most certainly encounter on a daily basis. How well your body adapts to stressors will have a huge impact on your state of health. Obtaining the tools necessary to bring your body to a constant relaxed state is acquired only through living a wellness lifestyle.

EXERCISE

Exercise can be defined as any activity that requires physical or mental exertion. This "stress" helps regulate metabolism while promoting biochemical balance to the many systems of the body that are responsible for running the human body. All parameters of human performance and function are directly improved through the process of exercise.

An individual's *health potential* will depend on his/her body's ability to convert the physical, chemical and emotional stressors of exercise into constructive energy.

ADJUSTMENT, ATONEMENT & ALIGNMENT

To be in adjustment means to be in balance mentally, physically, spiritually and emotionally, as well as experience optimal brain-body communication through the nervous system. When you are in *adjustment*, your brain, body and spirit are expressing connection, communication and balance. Because we live our lives through our nervous system, it is essential to be in *adjustment* for optimal health to exist, and to truly live a wellness lifestyle.

The word *adjustment* says it all. The word *just* is Latin for "balance." Think of *justice* or *justify*. The prefix *ad* is "to bring toward" or "be in"; and *ment* is a "state of." So, to be in adjustment is *to be in* or *bring toward* a state of balance; or what my longtime friend, colleague and co-founder of DREAM Wellness, Dr. Gregg Baron, would refer to as a "moving or dynamic balance." Imagine the *scales of justice* see-sawing back and forth.

Many people confuse this facet with the chiropractic adjustment. While the chiropractic adjustment is one of the most well-known and effective ways to restore a person back into *adjustment*, it is not necessarily the only way to restore balance, and there are many things a person needs to do to stay in *adjustment*. However, if you truly want to know if you are in fact in or out of *adjustment*, you would need to have a chiropractor on your healthcare team. We will certainly address this in greater detail when we talk about chiropractic care (*see Ch. 8-5*).

Being *in adjustment* also encompasses being in atonement and alignment.

Atonement is explained on Wikipedia as "the concept of a person taking action to correct previous wrongdoing on their part, either through direct action to undo the consequences of that act, equivalent action to do good for others, or some other expression of feelings of remorse."

Many religions interpret the meaning similarly but with important distinctions. In Judaism, atonement is mostly about forgiveness to sanctify a relationship with God. For Christians, atonement is essentially used as the result of salvation and redemption. Mary Baker Eddy, founder of Christian Science, refers to atonement in her book *Science and Health with Key to the Scriptures* as "the exemplification of man's unity with God, whereby man reflects divine Truth, Life, and Love."

For the purposes of this book, atonement has elements of all of that above, and the expression of a person being in a state of *at-one-ment* with all. This means they are at-one with God and with all people, creatures and the universe. There is no separation between us and Spirit.

While being in alignment physically (particularly related to body parts such as spinal bones) is vital for physical health, being in alignment in every aspect of your life is necessary to express your perfection. Your thoughts, your values and your actions must be in alignment for true sanctification. For example, if you value your health, yet you eat a lousy diet, drink tons of alcohol and consume recreational drugs, then your values and actions are contradictory and not in alignment, which will prevent optimal health. If you value a happy marriage but you choose to belittle your spouse, then your actions and values are not in alignment with one another, preventing a happy marriage. If you want to earn a promotion at work but you're not affirming that you deserve that role because of your greatness, rather partaking in negative self-talk (*see Ch. 9-6*), then your thoughts are not aligned with your beliefs and will likely result in no promotion (and maybe even worse). If you are a goal setter and your goals are not in alignment with your purpose in life (*see Ch. 9-7*), don't expect to achieve those goals . . . or at least don't expect to be happy if they are achieved. Contradictions breed discord, which in turn prevents our desires from coming to fruition. When you limit the contradictions in your life, you will reap the rewards of a person who chooses to live in alignment.

MENTAL WELLNESS

Mental wellness can be defined as the process of connecting your inner purpose and passion to your outer goals and tasks in all phases of life. It is the process that creates the *you* that you and other people get to know. Mental wellness is about being right with your self-esteem, self-worth and self-values. It's the process which enables a person to go from, "Oh God, it's morning" (with a low tone, low energy and bummed out feeling) to shouting with a joyous tone, "Oh God, it's morning!"

4-2

THE D.R.E.A.M. SCORE

If you have not done so already, this would be an excellent time to self-assess your lifestyle and determine how well you are living your DREAM. The evaluation is for you as a parent to take, but more importantly, it will serve as a predictor of your child's future health. It is incumbent upon you to be at the top of your game as an individual and healthy parent to best care for your children. You will not need a "crystal ball" to see your child's destiny, as you have the power to create it.

Go to https://DREAMWellness.com/DREAMScore to take the assessment now. It is approximately 100 questions and should not take more than 20 minutes.

Once you complete the assessment, you will receive a comprehensive report by email specifically designed to address your answers. You will receive a numerical value on how you scored. Additionally, it will inform you as to what stressors may be holding you and your family back from living the DREAM, every day.

The report will also provide reference points throughout this book to refer you to learn about what changes you can make and the reasons behind those necessary changes. By using this report, you will be able to create small wins here and there, which will eventually lead to the biggest win of all . . . creating a DREAM family!

PART II

WELLNESS WIKIS: YOUR MANUAL FOR STRESS MASTERY BY LIVING THE D.R.E.A.M. LIFESTYLE

While some of the 5 Keys or Facets may seem obvious, it is the integration of them that will dramatically benefit your family's health and quality of life. Additionally, expect to be surprised when you learn how many of your daily habits, which are considered by most to be healthy habits, are in fact often misunderstood and may be destructive to you and your family's health.

As a parent, you must always keep in mind that your words, habits and actions are constantly being observed by your children. Know that your lifestyle will be creating an imprint on them. This is why so many children end up having many of the same challenges that their parents had. This is the time to learn and make changes if necessary, not just for yourself but also for your progeny.

Inconsistencies with *diet, relaxation, exercise* and *mental wellness* will ultimately lead to the inability to avoid and adapt to chemical, physical and emotional stressors, thus causing you to be "out of *adjustment*" and stressed.

The term stress itself is a misunderstood term. In fact, there are a lot of people who actually believe that they do not have any stress in their lives. That is partly because most people think of stress similarly the same as the *Merriam-Webster* definitions: "a state of mental tension and worry caused by problems in your life, work, etc," and "something that causes strong feelings of worry or anxiety."

That is far from a complete definition, and it leaves many people who do not have anxiety or worries to believe that they are not stressed, or at least impacted by stress.

The National Institute of Health's (NIH) National Cancer Institute defines stress in medicine as "the body's response to physical, mental, or emotional pressure."

The fact is, stress is a part of everyone's life, and it is not always bad. The saying "That which does not kill us, makes us stronger" rings true in this case. Like using weights to strengthen muscles, stress puts you under tension to create a change, and in many cases, growth is the result. Stress itself is not harmful. Its impact on your life will always come down to your resilience to the *tension*.

Stress shows itself in different forms, and anxiety is only one. Stress manifests in some people as neck or back pain. In others, it shows up as belly aches. Other people display stress as being verbally abusive or having a "short fuse" and quick temper. I cannot stress enough the fact that just because you do not feel anxiety or emotional tension that you are free of stress or the impacts of it.

According to the Mayo Clinic, "Stress is your body's reaction to the demands of the world. Stressors are events or conditions in your surroundings that may trigger stress."

While we all endure stress on a regular basis, we encounter stressors almost every moment of our existence. Stressors come in three forms: physical (traumas), chemical (toxins) and emotional/mental (thoughts). Stress is the result you get when you are unable to adapt to the stressors of life.

Think of stress as the "tension" or "force" that is being placed on a person or object to create a change in response to stressors. Just like in exercise as mentioned before, when the body can overcome tension, the result is increased strength. However, if the weight is too heavy, injury occurs. When the "weight" of your stressors is too much for your body to handle, your health will be compromised, whether you feel it or not. In exercise, the weight of the dumbbell is the *stressor* and the tension in the muscle is the *stress*. *The stressor* is the cause, *stress* is the effect.

To be able to avoid stressors in the first place requires one to recognize the most common stressors we face daily. As parents, it is important to know what these stressors are for your child. Once you understand the common stressors, you will surely enjoy reading on and learning how to avoid/neutralize these stressors.

PHYSICAL STRESSORS

MOST COMMON PHYSICAL STRESSORS FOR PARENTS	MOST COMMON PHYSICAL STRESSORS FOR CHILDREN
• Sitting for long periods of time	• Being born (big body exiting a small birth canal with lots of twisting and turning)
• Sports injuries	
• Car accidents	• Being carried in inappropriate baby carrying devices
• Being overweight	
• Sleeping on the wrong mattress and/or pillow for your body	• Frequent falling when learning to walk
	• Bumping head and head banging
• Footwear that does not properly support your alignment or natural stride	• Sitting in car seat, swings or chairs for long periods of time
• Lifting improperly	• Asymmetric crawling/scooting
• Exercising improperly and Yoga moves gone wrong (and other exercises done incorrectly, with too much weight or unbalanced)	• Sports injuries, including gymnastics, trampoline, frequent falling and "rough housing"
	• Heavy & improper backpack usage
• Exercising with an improperly aligned spine and/or joints	• Car accidents and bicycle falls
• Standing on one leg frequently	• Childhood obesity
• Sitting cross-legged	• Sleeping on the wrong mattress and/or pillow for their bodies
• Text (tech) neck	• Footwear that does not support proper alignment
• Computer strain and poor ergonomic workstation	• Lifting improperly
• Poor posture & spinal misalignments	• Sitting cross-legged
• Carrying, lifting and holding small children	• Text (tech) neck
	• Computer strain and poor ergonomic setup for schoolwork
• Lifting children out of car seats	• Poor posture & spinal misalignments
• Nursing with poor posture and baby wearing with poor devices	• Being swung around by adults
• Rollercoasters and amusement park rides	• Rollercoasters and amusement park rides
• Pregnancy	• Circumcision

As you are reading this book, what is your posture like? Are you in a well-aligned position with the center of your ear directly over the center of your shoulder . . . or is your head forward? Think about how you (and those you love) spend time on your phone and computer . . . with your head so far forward that if it wasn't attached, it would roll right off your shoulders! How about when you're in the car? Did you know that having your head even a little bit forward (Forward Head Posture), can adversely affect your health? Take a look in your children's bedroom and look at their backpacks. Is it large, heavy and clunky?

CHEMICAL STRESSORS

MOST COMMON CHEMICAL STRESSORS FOR PARENTS	MOST COMMON CHEMICAL STRESSORS FOR CHILDREN
• Food colorings, additives and dyes	• Colorings, additives, and dyes in foods and toys
• Caffeine	
• Nicotine	• Sugar, artificial sweeteners and food items with caffeine
• Sugar & artificial sweeteners	
• Cigarette smoke	• Toys & objects that babies and toddlers put into their mouths that they pick up off the ground
• Recreational drug and alcohol use	• Second-hand cigarette smoke
	• Air and water pollution & environmental toxins
• Air and water pollution & environmental toxins	
• Medications and biologics	• Medications and biologics
	• Recreational drug and alcohol use
• Poor nutrition (including non-organic & GMOs) and processed food	• Poor nutrition (including non-organic & GMOs) and processed food
• Food items that may cause sensitivities or allergic reactions	• Food items that may cause sensitivities or allergic reactions such as dairy, formula & gluten
• Electromagnetic frequencies/ broadband cellular networks	
	• Electromagnetic frequencies/ broadband cellular networks
• Dehydration	
• Heavy metal and chemical toxicity from many household cleaning supplies, plastic containers, aluminum cans, detergents, cosmetics, beauty supplies, body cleansers, soaps, shampoos, lotions, toothpaste, bubble bath, sunscreen, tampons, nail polish, nail polish remover, cookware, dental amalgam fillings, insect repellent, etc . . .	• Dehydration
	• Heavy metal and chemical toxicity from many household cleaning supplies, plastic containers, aluminum cans, detergents, cosmetics, beauty supplies, body cleansers, soaps, shampoos, lotions, toothpaste, bubble bath, sunscreen, diapers, tampons, nail polish, nail polish remover, cookware, dental amalgam fillings, insect repellent, etc . . .

Take a look inside your refrigerator. Is it loaded with fresh fruit and veggies, or processed meats and soda? Look in your pantry. How many cans will you find? Look at the ingredients of the food in boxes and see how many words you recognize. Look at your cleaning products and see how many toxic ingredients are in them.

EMOTIONAL STRESSORS

MOST COMMON EMOTIONAL STRESSORS FOR PARENTS	MOST COMMON EMOTIONAL STRESSORS FOR CHILDREN
• Work frustrations and concerns	• Crying it out
• Conflicts in relationships & family drama	• Loneliness/separation anxiety
• Financial concerns	• Schoolwork frustrations (homework, tests, applying to college)
• Health concerns for themselves or family members	• Conflicts with classmates and friends, including bullying and cyberbullying
• Lack of physical intimacy or connection with a partner	• Rejection/fear of abandonment
• Too much to do and not enough time	• Fear of parents
• Not feeling in control	• Dysfunction at home
• Time constraints	• Too much to do and not enough time
• Peer pressure/keeping up with the Joneses	• Not feeling in control
• Disappointment	• Time constraints
• Traffic	• Peer pressure
• Social Media	• Disappointment
• Violence or sadness in media (movies, TV, books, magazines, news, etc . . .)	• Social Media
• Negative body image	• Violence or sadness in media (movies, tv, books, magazines, news, etc . . .)
• Gossip	• Puberty
• Parenting and co-parenting	• Dating
• Concerns about children	• Negative body image
• Lack of self-awareness	• Gossip
• Harboring feelings of guilt, shame or anger	• Lack of self-awareness
• Fear of failure	• Harboring feelings of guilt, shame or anger
• Death of a loved one	• Fear of failure
	• Death of a loved one or pet

Think about how much time you spend on social media and how it makes you feel. How about your kids and their social media exposure? What are your favorite television shows, movies to watch or books you read? How do you feel during and after? How are your relationships with those you surround yourself with? Do you enjoy their company? Do they enjoy yours? Do you feel good about yourself when spending time with them?

While this list is certainly not all-inclusive, it is important to understand that my intention is not to make you an expert on all of these subjects but rather to bring them to your attention. When a particular stressor is a part of your life, please do much more research on the topic so you can best learn how to appropriately handle it. Not all these stressors can and should be avoided as many are part of life, and sometimes needed in a temporary situation. I am providing you with the most basic information about them. It is up to you to take responsibility for your actions, learn how to avoid/ neutralize them and then take the appropriate actions. If you are not willing to make necessary changes for yourself, at least do it for your kids.

THE D.R.E.A.M. LIFESTYLE

This is the fun part. This is the section where you will learn how to avoid and neutralize chemical, physical and emotional stressors, and promote the good stuff!

Believe it or not, everything you do in life has an impact on all 5 Facets of wellness, though one facet is typically more obvious than the others for a particular action. For example, getting a chiropractic adjustment will certainly help get someone in *adjustment*. So logically you would think that the A in DREAM is for chiropractic. That could not be further from the truth. Chiropractic adjustments will also aid in relaxation, especially by helping keep the autonomic nervous system in balance and prevent sympathetic dominance (*see Ch. 8-4*).

Getting adjusted will also enable someone to get the most out of their exercise, not only because they will feel better with less pain and more flexibility but also because the nerves will transmit better information to the muscles you desire to grow and the organs that need to function while exercising. When someone is well adjusted, they also are happier, which positively impacts their mental wellness. And finally, because digestive organs are controlled by the nervous system, a perfectly aligned spine will help ensure that the food you consume will be digested properly and help you gain the best benefit from your diet.

Also note, just because everything you do has an impact on all 5 Facets, it does not mean that the impact is always constructive or destructive for all five. For example, eating an unhealthy, sugary dessert is certainly not good for your diet, for obvious reasons. The sugar content will most certainly prevent optimal relaxation. Too much sugar does not make it easy to exercise, especially if it causes increased weight. And of course, sugar is a chemical stressor so it can very likely cause you to go out of adjustment. All that said, enjoying a treat on a special occasion may do wonders for your mental wellness, at least temporarily.

While a chiropractic adjustment may have a constructive impact on all 5 Facets of wellness, pecan pie made with high fructose corn syrup is likely to be constructive for one (temporarily) and destructive for the other four. Therefore it is extremely important to live consciously every moment and make decisions that are consistent with your goals and values. This is where discipline (*see Ch. 9-10*) comes into play!

I have categorized, to the best of my ability, many lifestyle activities according to the primary or most obvious facet of wellness and key that it "lives" in. Remember, however, each activity will have an impact on all facets.

This next section is essentially your "wellness bible." Read through it at a pace that is comfortable to you. Be sure to notate and highlight areas that you want to refer to in the future. This part is categorized by the *five keys*. Each key contains multiple notes or "wikis" which are short compilations of information that will bring everyday items to your attention, so you can determine how they impact your "wellness walk." *Wikiwiki* is Hawaiian for "quick." For each of the following topics, I will quickly cover the most basic information you need to help make more constructive choices for you and your family, all of which can and should be expounded on with your own research if desired. Many of the topics are important enough for books and courses of their own; many of which you can or will find from yours truly. Be sure to check the bonus/resource section regularly as it will be updated often.

Do not beat yourself up over the things you may not have known, and do not allow it to overwhelm you. The wellness lifestyle is a process. Do the best that you can and take baby steps when implementing changes. If there are some suggestions that you do not agree with, skip them (at least for now). If there are recommendations that you cannot afford to implement (based on time, finances or ability), that is just fine. Remember, every action you take has a cumulative effect on the well-being of you and your family.

As a reminder, after I cover a particular subject, you will know if there is a resource or bonus by seeing **BONUSES & RESOURCES** (which are provided either completely free to you or may be purchased at significantly reduced rates off the vendors' retail price): https:// DREAMWellnessbook.com/bonuses. I have worked extremely hard to cultivate relationships with dozens of experts to provide you with every opportunity to put everything in this book into action, as simply as possible.

> *Be sure that if you have not yet downloaded the "Living Your DREAM Playbook," do it now! This workbook will be your wellness journal and accountability partner as you read the book and beyond.*

As a music lover and decent musician, I labeled many of the Wellness Wikis™, or "notes" within each key as song titles. If you know the song, sing it in your head to get a feel of what you are about to read. If you are not familiar with the song, feel free to look up the lyrics or maybe even listen to the song for your enjoyment. After all, wellness is a proactive approach toward creating physical, mental, social and spiritual *harmony*.

KEY 1
DIET

5-1

CONSCIOUS CONSUMPTION

> *Your diet is everything that enters your internal world to your external world . . . everything you eat, drink, taste, touch, smell, hear and see.*

When it comes to your family's diet, you want to make it as nutritious as possible. By nutritious, I'm not just referring to the food and beverages you consume. It also includes the media you watch and hear, literature you read, and even the people you spend time with. In fact, motivational speaker Jim Rohn (and I'm sure many others) said, "We are the average of the five people we spend the most time with." If you are around naysayers, gossipers and just all-around negative people, how do you think that will resonate with you and your kids on the cellular level?

Right now, think about the 5 people (outside of your household) that you spend most of your time with. Think about their lives. Are they happy? Are they healthy? Are they successful? Would you want a life like theirs? If not, consider what it would be like to spend your time with people who are very happy, healthy and successful. Do you think there's a possibility that being around people like that would lift you up? Motivate you? Encourage you to be the best version of you? How about the children that your kids play and interact with? Do they have good morals and values? Are they a positive influence on your child? Do their parents share common values and morals to your family?

I don't expect everyone's *diet* to be perfect . . . I only encourage you to do the best you absolutely can at being your best. Again, it is what I refer to as excessive good stuff and maybe a little bit of bad stuff. And when you really "get it," the bad stuff will not even be that bad. For example, if you are by a campfire with the kids, s'mores are a must. I am not suggesting you deprive your kids from this yummy treat that they are likely looking forward to, I am suggesting that you are conscious about what you use to make them. For example, you can purchase marshmallows that do not contain corn syrup, graham crackers that are not made from refined flour and chocolate that does not have all the nasty chemicals and refined sugars that so many conventional chocolate bars have. While these s'mores will not be considered "healthy treats," they are certainly a healthier alternative, and the kids won't even know the difference.

All items you and your children consume, whether they be through the mouth, eyes, ears, nose or skin, can be put into one of three categories. *Constructive* contributes to your health, *destructive* detracts from your health and neutral does not have a considerable impact either way.

There are "deal-breakers" for me when it comes to my *diet*. These are non-negotiables. If you get *nothing* at all from this chapter except for this one paragraph, it will be worth it!

> *At all costs, I strive to avoid high fructose corn syrup, artificial sweeteners, hydrogenated oils, artificial food coloring and gossip/drama. I recommend you consider doing the same for the sake of your entire family's health and well-being.*

Regarding the food non-negotiables, I know that I won't always have an ingredient list available. Therefore, there may be times where my ignorance may cause me to consume some of those items, but it would be extremely rare. Because I am aware of where most of those products show up in foods, which is mostly processed or store bought, I am confident where they may be. If I am not sure and I cannot ask, I typically will not eat it. Yes, I am the annoying guy at the restaurants and dessert shops that always asks for the ingredient list and holds up the line. It's okay; while I know it may annoy the people behind me in line, it just may inspire others.

If I am at someone's home (or they bring it to my home), I may ask about its ingredients, but I do tread lightly because I do not want to offend anyone or seem ungrateful. In those cases, I may take a tiny bite or just make it look like I did. Other times I may avoid the food and explain why to make it an educational moment for them, without being too annoying or coming off self-righteous. The good thing about the five people I spend most of my time with is, they also wouldn't typically consume that junk either. And if they do, they know me well enough to not bring it to my home or serve it when I am at their place, or at the very least, they won't be offended if I don't indulge.

As for gossip . . . that's easy. When I am with people that begin to talk about someone in an unfavorable way, I will either gently bring it to their attention, or I will remove myself from that situation. This would also be a great tactic to teach your children at an early age.

Cleaning up your diet is one of the easiest changes you and your family can make to begin your wellness journey together. Most adults have complete control over their *diet* with few exceptions. If you are not the person responsible for what you consume, do your best to share your desire with the person(s) in charge.

The food you consume will impact every aspect of your life. Your microbiome, which is essentially the bacteria and microorganisms in your body, outnumber your human cells by 10:1. Having a *dysfunctional* microbiome can be a causative factor to hundreds of health problems and diseases. Many functional medicine practitioners investigate the food you consume and other lifestyle choices that affect the health of your gut and in turn, your entire body.

Prior to having a child, I never understood why so many young children eat so unhealthfully. Now that I have a kid, I really don't understand it! Your young children, especially under three years old, will only eat what you feed them. If you do not give them sugar, they will not know to crave it. Same goes for chicken fingers, pizza and all the other junk food so many parents give their kids.

Why expose it to them in the first place? Of course, when they get a little older, it may become more difficult to manage everything they consume, but as a conscientious parent, you can let other parents, teachers, coaches, childcare providers and other family members know your desires.

> *On December 29, 2020, the U.S. federal government released its new "Dietary Guidelines for Americans" for the years 2020–2025. The updated guidelines state that children under two years old should avoid consuming any added sugars in their diets.*

As a parent reading this book, there is no doubt that you want the best for your children. When it comes to recreational drugs, you may even discourage them from experimenting by using the words of the late First Lady of the United States of America Nancy Regan, "Just say no!" You likely feel strongly about that because you know the harmful addictive nature of most drugs. I am convinced that if all parents truly understood the harmful and addictive qualities of sugar (especially refined sugar), they would think twice before celebrating their child's first birthday with a cake made of conventional white flour, refined sugar, frosting and corn syrup (*see Ch. 5-12*).

Part of conscious parenting is understanding that it is never too early to talk with your child about what foods will make them healthy and strong, versus the alternative. If you build value at an early age, like Brooke and I have done with our son, Zion, you will be setting your child up for success. This will empower your children, and they will be less likely to deal with the results of the poor choices that so many adults are trying to overcome later in life.

If you feel it is too late to teach your children to eat healthier foods and not be so picky, I can assure you, it is never too late! As a bonus with this book, I have a 5-Step Playbook to end your child's picky eating.

Just like children cannot eat food that you don't give them, *you* cannot eat food you don't put on your plate. In fact, if you don't buy junk food in the first place, there will be no temptation to eat it. Becoming aware of food that is salutogenic versus pathogenic (*see Ch. 10-1*) will be the first step, but after learning from this book, it will be up to you to make better choices.

We all know the saying "knowledge is power." While that is true, putting that knowledge to work is even more powerful. Experience separates knowledge from wisdom, and if you want to be wise, I recommend you start putting some of these suggestions into action. Unfortunately, you will not learn most of this information from your medical doctor. In fact, when Zion went to his pediatrician for his required "checkup" prior to starting preschool, the doctor was being playful and said, "What's that in your belly, Cheerios?" Zion looked at her and asked, "What are Cheerios?" The doctor looked at us and said, "He doesn't have Cheerios and milk for breakfast"? Zion replied, "Cow's milk?" with disgust. It was an entertaining and empowering moment; and I think a little humbling for the doctor. We proceeded to explain to her what we choose to feed him instead, and why. And by all means, Cheerios are not necessarily the worst option, but there is much better available. She could not argue with anything we said because we had more knowledge than she did on this very important topic. In fact, she thought we were very wise. Annoying . . . but wise.

It is very important to know what ingredients are in the products you purchase and to understand why some are better than others and what to avoid. As a gift, I have provided you our label reading guide as an additional bonus.

The following section of this book will provide you with practical information about your family's diet and how it can be improved, no matter how good it may be now. This information is rather basic, and I encourage you to dive more deeply into the topics that interest or concern you the most.

BONUSES & RESOURCES *End Picky Eating Bundle*
BONUSES & RESOURCES *Guide to Reading & Understanding Food Packaging Labels*

5-2

PURIFICATION/DETOXIFICATION

♫ TURNING OVER A NEW LEAF

At least once per year, my wife and I participate in a detoxification program. While most nutritional detoxification programs may not be appropriate for young children, it is a good idea to take "inventory" as a family of what you all have been consuming and determine what should be added and avoided moving forward.

As for actual detoxification programs for adults, it is always good to make sure you are keeping your digestive systems clean, regardless of how well you eat throughout the year. The programs that I recommend are based on lifestyle eating, not diets per se. Therefore, most of the food consumed and avoided during these programs are suitable for children. However, it is recommended to leave out the cleansing supplements that are part of the program, unless they are approved for children.

Detoxifications (Detox), cleanses and purification programs are designed to purge the body of unwanted chemicals and toxins, which, in some cases, are means to achieve your desired weight.

For purposes of this book, we will use these terms interchangeably, though there are subtle differences between them all.

These programs can benefit the body in a sense that they cleanse the body of toxins that can cause digestive issues, weakness, bloating, nausea, mood swings, and skin issues. Also, detoxification diets can boost energy, cleanse the liver, aid in achieving desired weight and reduce inflammation.

While some participants swear by detoxes, some say that the diets deprive the body of protein and fluids, leading to dehydration, headaches and fatigue, and may lower the metabolism. Detoxes can be quite dangerous especially for people with diabetes, as it could lower blood sugar. It is important to do one of these programs under the guidance of your trusted healthcare provider and make sure that the program you choose does not starve the body of important nutrients.

Since many detoxification programs are not appropriate for young children, be sure to ask your healthcare provider how to modify the program for your children so they can also benefit and be a part of the process. Heck, this could even be a fun family challenge when it is introduced in an entertaining way.

When choosing which purification program to do, make sure it allows for fresh organic salads, raw fruits and vegetables and perhaps high-quality lean proteins at some point and in some quantities during the cleanse. If the program allows for bread, pasta, candy, refined sugar, artificial sweeteners, caffeine, soda, alcohol or foods high in saturated fat, then I would look elsewhere, as most of those foods contain the very impurities you're trying to eliminate. Of course that is not an all-inclusive list, just some of the more popular items I find in what I consider to be bad cleanses. Also, I do not typically recommend starvation cleanses, especially for children. While there may be some value to them, I believe the benefits do not outweigh the risks; and honestly, they are not necessary in most cases.

Many of the popular "diets" and programs can change the way you eat to suppress one hormone and increase another to burn fat, but they typically do not address the toxins. Also, just cutting calories or carbohydrates is not the be-all and end-all. Your body uses the liver to store toxins in fat cells to protect vital organs. While diets and cleanses may be used in tandem, it is important to understand that going on a diet for "weight loss" without starting with a cleanse beforehand may prove to be in vain and potentially harmful.

A diet alone will not typically support long term "weight loss" because it does not cleanse the body and liver of the impurities beforehand. A successful program must balance hormones, maintain the proper macro and micronutrients, and remove harmful toxins from your body. Also, we should consider the words we use, as referenced earlier in this book. Using a term like weight loss may already be setting you up for failure. When you lose something, your subconscious mind is always looking to find it again. But if you release something, it is gone forever, so if anything, try to reframe weight loss to weight release.

BONUSES & RESOURCES My favorite purification programs

5-3

VITAMINS AND MINERALS

♫ MILKMAN

People are always asking me what supplements I take and give my son. I am not a huge supplement person, though I do understand that our soil is so depleted these days that even a well-balanced meal plan can make it difficult to consume all the appropriate nutrients. Dietary supplements in general are either intended to provide nutrients to increase the quantity of their consumption, or to provide non-nutrient chemicals which are claimed to have a biologically beneficial effect. Many multi-vitamins provide all the basic micronutrients that your body needs, but more specific supplements can provide additional nutrients where your diet may be lacking.

While taking supplements has benefits when certain vitamins and nutrients may be deficient, not all of them are regulated, and it is difficult to prove whether their use is safe or effective. With some supplements, large doses can have strong biological effects on the body and can even be dangerous in some instances. Mineral supplements such as iron or boron can be dangerous in large doses.

It is important to choose vitamins and supplements that are made as naturally as possible and are *whole food supplements* whenever possible. Look for ones that are organic, non-GMO and disclose all the ingredients. Many companies don't list all of their ingredients because of "proprietary reasons," which essentially means either they don't want to disclose their ingredients for fear of a competitor stealing their formulation or because they don't want to reveal potential destructive ingredients. Either way, if you don't know the ingredients, beware that you are playing "roulette." Some companies can be trusted more than others, so be sure that you completely trust either the company itself or the person recommending the supplement.

If you walk into any health food store, or heck, even any grocery store or pharmacy these days, you will see tons of vitamins and supplements on the shelves. Supplements are supposed to do exactly what their name states: supplement. Supplement what though?

We need to have adequate supply of micronutrients and macronutrients for the human body to function properly and ultimately express optimal health.

Micronutrients are vitamins, minerals and antioxidants that are needed to enable the body to produce enzymes, hormones and other substances essential for healthy growth and development. Think of them as the tiny chemicals that enter our bodies through every day living. We do not only receive micronutrients from our food through ingestion, but we also absorb some through our skin, such as vitamin D from exposure to sunlight.

Macronutrients are essentially what make up the calories we receive from foods, which include fats, proteins and carbohydrates.

A well-balanced, healthy diet should provide a person with enough micronutrients and macronutrients to function optimally . . . in theory. However, there are issues with that theory when it comes to reality and application.

First off, there are so many different thoughts on what a healthy diet includes. If you look at the history of advice we received from our government via the United States Department of Agriculture (USDA), you will see considerable changes over the past century. In the 1940s, the USDA had 7 food groups that we were told we needed to consume on a regular basis. In the '50s, '60s and '70s, they changed it to 4 food groups, which included milk, meat, vegetables/fruit & breads/cereals. In the 1990s they came up with the food pyramid which was not much different from before but it did include the portions along with a hierarchy of importance based on serving sizes, placing bread, cereal, rice and pasta as the foundation of the pyramid, recommending more than double the servings (6-11) of the next food group of vegetables and fruits (2-4 each). Then in 2005 they changed their illustration to something they called *MyPyramid*, where they literally turned their pyramid on its side. In 2011, the USDA introduced *MyPlate* which is essentially a simple graphic that helps personalize the pyramid.

While the items in the food groups recommended by the USDA do contain both micronutrients and macronutrients, there are many issues with their guides. For one, how is it possible that something created in a factory should be considered a food group? Have you ever seen a bagel tree? How about a Lucky Charms bush? Oh that's right, it can be found just under the rainbow next to the pot of gold!

I will now address dairy, but please don't hate me. Dairy products in general do have plenty of redeeming qualities because of their vast amount of nutrients. And I know that people love the taste as well, so that's a plus. However, just because something tastes good and has lots of important vitamins and minerals does not mean that it should be consumed in large quantities.

First off, what other animal normally drinks milk from another species of animal in the wild? Have you ever seen a goat suck on the udder of a cow? I'll answer that question for you . . . no, not likely. Nature did not intend on one animal consuming milk from another species, except perhaps in rare life and death situations.

Dr. Walter Willett, MD, PhD, from the Harvard School of Public Health refers to the USDA guidelines as, "Udderly ridiculous and out of step with what we know about sound nutrition." In fact, humans are the only species that consume milk in adulthood.

Newborns produce the enzyme lactase, which breaks down the carbohydrate found in milk called lactose. Did you know that adults lose the ability to breakdown lactose? This is why so many people, nearly 70% of the adult population, suddenly find themselves not enjoying the effects of dairy products later in life as they have become lactose intolerant.

Aside from the carbohydrate lactase that is found in milk, let us look at another macronutrient: the proteins casein and whey. Thirty-eight percent of the solid matter in cow's milk is protein, of which 80% is casein and the other 20% is whey. An issue with casein is something that so many parents have dealt with and never realized where the issue was coming from. Many people have an allergy to the casein which causes the release of histamine. The symptoms of a casein allergy often mimic lactose intolerance, but they also include other issues such as skin irritations and rashes, including eczema; hives; swelling of the mouth, lips, face, tongue or throat; congestion; sneezing and runny nose.

Interestingly, human breast milk's protein is 60–80% whey, as opposed to casein, which is one of the many reasons why a breastfed baby from a mom with a very clean diet typically has fewer skin issues.

Another interesting comparison between human breast milk and cow's milk is the growth factor. The nutrients in cow's milk essentially promotes significant growth to the body, whereas the nutrients in human breast milk is to stimulate the growth of function of the brain. A 2013 study showed that toddlers who had been exclusively breastfed for a minimum of three months had 20–30% more white matter in their brains than toddlers who had not. The white matter connects different regions of the brain and transmits signals between those areas.[3]

Yet another benefit to breastmilk is, in the body's infinite wisdom, a mom's milk will change its chemical composition moment by moment to provide the baby with the nutrients he/she needs at the time needed. For example, when a baby is fighting symptoms of a cold, the breastmilk will have more immune promoting substances than usual. The color and taste of the milk will be evident of this change if you pay close attention.

In summary, there is plenty of research that supports the notion that dairy is not needed to complete a healthy diet as long as the nutrients are made up elsewhere, like whole plant foods including vegetables, fruits, nuts, beans, seeds and whole grains. In fact, there is an abundance of support that a diet without dairy can even be heathier.

If you do choose to consume dairy, it is recommended to source it from the most natural way possible: raw (in jurisdictions where it's legal) and organic. Choose grass-fed animals whenever possible. Try goat or sheep's milk over cow's milk when you can. And go with fermented, such as kefir and yogurt, but not sweetened. Do your best to refrain from serving your children dairy products with added sugar, as milk is already loaded with approximately 13g of sugar per serving.

There are many more issues with the USDA's recommendations, including that they do not account for the difference between people and body types (*see Ch. 7-7*). An endomorph, mesomorph and ectomorph would require different proportions of macronutrients to maintain optimal body mass.

As you can see, we have been taught false information since childhood about what real nutrition is. We have been convinced to believe that a large portion of our diet should come from a lab (processed breads, pastas and cereals) and milk from another species that doesn't necessarily do our bodies good! Whether the reasoning for the bad information was poor science or greedy motives, we need to see the light and make changes. I believe that our country can do much better than this. High incidences of obesity, type II diabetes and metabolic syndrome could be avoided if we had access to better information and made better choices.

So do we need to supplement? That's a good question and debate. It depends on your goals and needs.

If your body is deficient of a nutrient because of an issue with an organ or gland (that can't be resolved naturally), then a supplement is likely in order.

If you are not able to consume the proper amount of nutrients from your diet for whatever reason, then a supplement is likely in order.

If you think that you have a well-balanced diet but you just aren't sure if you're getting all the nutrients needed, then feel free to supplement just in case. Many argue that our soil is depleted at this point and that it is not possible to get all the nutrition from a well-balanced diet, no matter how hard you try.

While every person is different with different needs and lifestyles, there are certain supplements that should be part of everyone's household to "hedge your bet." Be mindful that dosages typically vary between adults and children.

Multivitamin
Vitamin D3
Fish Oil
Powdered greens
Digestive enzymes
Probiotics

BONUSES & RESOURCES Comprehensive list of each specific vitamin and mineral and what they do in in the body as well as how deficiencies may lead to certain cravings.

BONUSES & RESOURCES Gallery of my favorite supplements and products.

5-4

ANTI-INFLAMMATORY DIET

♫ THE HEAT IS ON

As a chiropractor, some of the people that I take care of suffer from pain caused by inflammation. I find that with many of them, even once their subluxations (*see Ch. 8-5*) are corrected, their inflammation does not always completely go away. There are many causes of inflammation, but one of the easiest changes to make is to remove foods from your meals that can cause additional inflammation.

An *anti-Inflammatory* diet is low in processed foods and saturated fats and is rich in fruits, vegetables, fish, nuts, beans and olive oil. Studies show that by following an anti-inflammatory diet, these foods can help lower blood pressure, curb inflammation and benefit joints. Nuts are especially known for reducing inflammation as they are packed with inflammation-fighting monounsaturated fat. Many fruits and vegetables are high in antioxidants and polyphenols, protective compounds found in plants.

Eating these foods has been shown to reduce inflammation and combat the risks of diseases associated with inflammation, especially arthritis. Lastly, anti-inflammatory foods positively affect the body by improving overall mood and quality of life.

Foods that have been known to increase inflammation include (but are not limited to) sugar, vegetable oil, fried food, refined carbohydrates, dairy, gluten, artificial sweeteners, artificial additives, saturated and trans fats, conventional grain fed meats, processed meats, alcohol and most fast foods.

While most children do not complain of pain related to inflammation (such as arthritis), inflammation can still affect their gut and joints considerably creating long-term issues.

BONUSES & RESOURCES *Chronic Inflammation Related to Food Guide*
WORKBOOK ACTIVITY *Inflammatory foods Worksheet*

5-5

NON-TOXIC COOKWARE

♫ MAN OF STEEL

Most people do not consider the effects cookware can have on one's health, especially young children. However, it has a significant impact and can be a leading chemical stressor, causing toxic overload in your body. We know that air pollution, water pollution and many household chemicals can be hazardous to your health and that of your family, but what about the material you cook your food on?

What about your current cookware . . . is it safe?

Many people feel safe with their typical stainless-steel cookware (referred to as 18/8 or 18/10; the ratio is based on the percent of chrome and nickel added to the alloy). Stainless steel cookware is made from a metal alloy consisting of mostly iron and chromium along with differing percentages of molybdenum, nickel, titanium, copper and vanadium. Unfortunately, this ratio of stainless steel allows other metals to potentially leach into the food you are cooking. The principal elements in stainless that have negative effects on a person's health are iron, chromium and nickel.

Many people are already wise to the fact that non-stick surfaces can be detrimental to one's health, especially since they scratch, chip and flake very easily. "Exposure to Teflon® resins at temperatures above 393°F may produce a condition termed polymer fume fever characterized by flu-like symptoms such as chills, fever, body aches, nausea and occasional vomiting," according to the Federal Aviation Agency Occupational Health & Safety Bulletin. A chemical, C-8, used to make non-stick coated pans has been linked to birth defects in humans and cancer in laboratory animals. The chemical is also present in the blood for up to 4 years and can show up in breast milk.

How about cast-iron cookware? Iron is the most porous of all metals, and when the iron heats up, the pores in the metal expand. When the iron cools, the pores contract (close), leaving the grease trapped in the pores and allowing the oil to turn rancid. Some people believe that they can get (nutritional) iron from a cast iron pot. In reality, iron comes in a ferrous and a ferric form. Ferrous iron is what makes our red blood cells and comes from our foods—and is extremely important for your body to function properly. Ferric, however, is the type of iron that comes from cast-iron cookware and your body cannot properly assimilate this metal. Too much ferric can have significant negative effects on one's health. Cast-iron cookware is very durable but iron is constantly leaching into the food, changing the enzymes in it. Iron can reach toxic levels in the body with regular use and becomes a pro-oxidant which causes stress, oxidation and eventually disease.

Aluminum cookware is one of the most common types of cookware to use, but it can be very toxic as this heavy metal is absorbed into all food cooked in it. The aluminum released into food during cooking ends up in your body. Excess aluminum has been associated with estrogen-driven cancers and Alzheimer's Disease. "All Vegetables cooked in Aluminum produce hydroxide poison which neutralizes digestive juices, producing stomach and gastrointestinal trouble, such as stomach ulcers and colitis." Dr. A. McGuigan's Report on Findings for the Federal Trade Commission in Docket Case No. 540, Washington, D.C. Note: The sale of aluminum cookware is prohibited in many countries around the globe.

Glass, enamel and ceramic cookware seem pretty harmless (aside from them being notorious for poor heat distribution, cause foods to stick and burn, and chip off into food), but some may also contain lead and cadmium.

Copper cookware is popular because it conducts heat very well. However, it releases copper into the food and usually also has nickel in the coating, which is another toxic heavy metal and can be very allergenic. If you do choose to use copper cookware (though I don't recommend it), avoid cooking vegetables in copper pots. Copper can kill vitamin C, vitamin E and folic acid.

The cookware that I choose to use for my family and recommend to my clients is made of a non-porous stainless steel (316Ti, stainless steel with titanium added). Type 316 alloys are more resistant to general corrosion and pitting crevice corrosion than the conventional chromium (nickel austenitic stainless steels such as Type 304). 316 surgical stainless steel is used in various applications, such as surgical instruments, ocean oil rigs, nuclear waste materials, and of course cookware. 316Ti Titanium Stainless Steel Interior has demonstrated to provide higher resistance to chemical reaction with the acids and enzymes in food; protect quality, purity, and flavor of food; resist pitting; and resist corrosion and oxidation.

There are a few different companies that compete in this elite space of cookware, though I choose to use the product produced by Saladmaster®. Not only do I feel secure preparing my food in 316Ti, but Saladmaster® also has a unique patented Vapo-Valve™ that allows you to know when to reduce the cooking temperature to maintain many of the vitamins and minerals; and it creates a semi-vacuum that locks in the moisture. Additionally, Saladmaster® has been around since the 1940s, and its products are manufactured by a company that has been around for over 100 years, making it one of oldest and most reputable companies in the cookware space; and the products come with a limited lifetime warranty. Saladmaster® cookware is a bit pricier than other brands, but the health benefits and energy savings of rarely needing to use my oven outweighs the costs by far. Additionally, I have had my cookware since 2008 and it still looks and works like new. Just by virtue of the fact that I will never need to replace my cookware makes the extra upfront cost well worth the investment.

BONUSES & RESOURCES: Opportunity to learn about and demo SaladMaster®, and purchase at a discount.

5-6

HYDRATION

♫ BLACK WATER

Did you know that more than 2/3 of the Earth's surface is covered by water? Did you know that approximately 2/3 of a person's weight is water? Coincidence? I think not.

Most people know that water is the most important nutrient to consume on a regular basis. Without water, your body would cease to work. All body functions such as digestion, circulation, muscle contraction, kidney filtration and maintaining body temperature would fail and you would cease to exist. Even elimination (yes, going to the bathroom) and weight management are significantly impacted by your water intake. Additionally, drinking water throughout the day has been shown to increase metabolism.

Most people do not realize this, but the body doesn't always know the difference between hunger and thirst. In fact, if you're between meals and starting to feel a little grumbling in your belly, drink some water and see what happens . . . you might be surprised that after sipping from your favorite water bottle (preferably made of glass), you no longer need to grab that unhealthy snack you were about to consume. In fact, if you are looking to lose some weight, try drinking a glass of water before you begin your meal. You may be surprised to find that you will not need as much food to eat, especially the empty carbs to fill your tummy. This works especially well for kids who refuse to go to bed claiming that they are still hungry. Encourage them to drink a glass of water and see if they still need food. If they are being honest, they probably won't. If it is a behavior issue, however, then a good parenting class may be in order.

How much water to consume daily is also a consideration, one that experts differ in opinion considerably. Growing up I was told to drink eight glasses of water every day. I always found that strange because I was (and still am) more than five inches shorter and 30 pounds lighter than most of my friends. How in the world would my childhood friend John, the starting linebacker of our high school football team and I need the exact same amount of water? Not to mention, we did different activities throughout the day.

I have always believed, and this is supported by scientific studies, that body type, body size and activity level should ultimately determine your water intake requirements. The first part of the equation you should start with is your body weight. I personally agree with the formula of drinking half your body weight (body weight in pounds, amount of water in ounces). If you weigh 150 pounds, you should consume at least 75 ounces of water per day. That is your baseline. After that, you need to consider how much activity and sweating you do daily, and even the climate and elevation of where you spend your time. Then you need to consider the type of food you eat and beverages you drink throughout the day. Almost all food and beverages contain water, but some are better, cleaner sources than others. Fruits and veggies are the best sources of water from your food, but they should be in addition to your baseline ounces. And if you're thinking that the 3 cups of coffee you consume throughout the day or the 24-ounce cola that you drink at the ballgame will provide you with a good portion of your daily hydration, then this just may be the most important book you will ever read!

There is a lot of misunderstanding when it comes to water quality, mostly because terms keep changing and companies often use them interchangeably. And there is a lot of marketing and salesmanship used to spin their product's qualities to make it appear better than the rest.

Purified, or pure water is water from a source that has removed all impurities and only leaves the molecules that make up water. Water may be purified through several techniques including distillation, reverse osmosis and deionization. There are many concerns that experts claim regarding purified water, including the removal of minerals such as calcium, magnesium and iron.

Water may also be filtered by several processes including carbon filtration, ultraviolet filtration and micro-porous filtration. Commercial water filters are specifically designed to work with treated water that comes out of your tap. The filtration systems use activated carbon that prevents unwanted, microscopic contaminants from entering your drinking water. Because the majority of harmful water impurities are carbon-based, water filters can be extremely effective in keeping your drinking water safe and healthy.

Filtered water typically retains calcium, zinc, and magnesium. It also removes contaminants, such as heavy metals, pesticides, mercury, lead, and arsenic. Most filtered water also has reduced chlorine and other chemicals that are found in tap water and removes many bacteria. Aside from filtration providing many health benefits, it also makes it smell and taste better.

One ingredient that most water filtration systems do not completely remove (at this point) is fluoride. Fluoride is added to tap water to strengthen teeth (and other potential health benefits are claimed), but many contend that fluoride is more harmful than helpful. Reverse osmosis filters and the distillation process removes fluoride, but there are some potential disadvantages to those processes, including removing all minerals that many believe to be important.

The benefits to drinking pure or filtered water heavily outweigh the disadvantages. Basic tap water is associated with many cardiovascular problems. Pure and filtered water does not contain chemicals that cause the harmful effects associated with heart disease. Drinking pure or filtered water has shown to help maintain a healthy body weight, properly digests and absorbs nutrients from food, promotes healthy skin, decreases joint inflammation, betters circulation and naturally detoxifies the body.

One other type of water that I would be remiss not to mention is ionized water, also known as alkaline water. This is water that goes through a process of electrolysis to raise the pH (reduce acidity) and decrease the negative effects of oxidation, thereby making it an antioxidant. Many alkaline water drinkers swear by a plethora of health benefits which include reducing headaches, skin conditions, congestion, poor digestion, gout, acne, frequent colds and allergies;

and also claim to have other long-term health benefits. Some sources claim that there are no benefits whatsoever to alkaline water and that the claims made are false, misleading and just marketing. Still, millions of consumers, including myself, contend that they are healthier and better off consuming alkaline water. While the research may be mixed and potentially biased (on both sides), I have personally heard many success stories of health conditions improved with the consumption of alkaline water.

It is important to do the research and determine which type of water you would like to consume the most. My personal opinion is to "hedge your bet" and drink a combination of filtered water and purified waters. I personally have a carbon-based household water filtration unit at home so that all of the water in my house is filtered, including the water my family showers and bathes in. I also have an ionizer in my home so that the majority of water that I drink is alkaline. When I'm in my office, I drink purified water that has gone through the process of reverse osmosis.

Why do I have all of these options? Because the truth is, I am not sure if anyone really knows the truth as to what is best. There is too much bias in the research, and quite frankly, my feeling is that you should be drinking a ton of water that is free of contaminates.

BONUSES & RESOURCES Lists and contacts for water filtration and ionization companies I recommend.
BONUSES & RESOURCES *Foods that Help with Hydration Guide*

5-7

TOBACCO CESSATION

♫ SMOKE ON THE WATER

If you are a smoker, it has more than likely been suggested that you consider quitting, not only for your benefit but also for those you live with, especially your kids. You have most certainly heard all the reasons why you should stop smoking, from social reasons to health reasons. If you are reading this book, I can only assume it is because you want to live a healthier lifestyle and give your children the best possible health outcomes as they grow up. If so, hopefully this refresher will help nudge you a little more in the direction of quitting. For the purposes of this book, you need to be aware that cigarettes are chemical toxins and stressors that do not fit into the DREAM lifestyle.

Even if the potentially detrimental effects of smoking on your health is not reason enough for you to quit, you can at least protect the rest of your household by not smoking around them. In 1993, the Environmental Protection Agency (EPA) reported that secondhand smoke is a Group A Carcinogen, which means it is known to cause cancer in humans. Other health risks include asthma and heart attacks. It is important to note that there is no safe amount of secondhand smoke exposure.

Just looking at the science and not coming from a place of judgment, smoking has been shown to cause lung disease because it damages your airways and the small air sacs (alveoli) in your lungs. Chronic bronchitis, emphysema, and COPD are all common diseases caused by smoking and tobacco. Smoking also compromises the immune system, leading to many respiratory infections. Smoking can also lead to Crohn's disease and rheumatoid arthritis. The use of tobacco also decreases bone density and can increase one's risk for developing osteoporosis. Smoking heavily increases the risk for stroke, heart attack, and many other preventable diseases and early death. Also, smoking can relate to macular degeneration, cataracts, and optic nerve damage, all of which can lead to blindness. Lastly, smoking can cause more than 18 different types of cancer.

According to the National Institute of Health (NIH) and the National Cancer Institute, tobacco use is the leading cause of preventable death. Smoking cessation, or the process of quitting tobacco smoking, greatly reduces the risks of developing smoking-related diseases. It is crucial to quit smoking as nearly half the people who do not quit will die from smoking-related diseases.

Soon after quitting, circulation will begin to improve, blood pressure will start returning to normal, sense of smell and taste will begin to return, and it will be easier to breathe. In the long-term, giving up tobacco can help you live longer as it greatly reduces your risk of getting cancer. Overall, it is crucial for smokers to quit as they are putting their life in jeopardy with the risk of cardiovascular diseases or cancer.

There are many ways to quit smoking, some more natural and others not as much. While quitting can be extremely hard, some techniques include quitting "cold turkey," step-by-step manuals, meditating, or counseling. Of course, there are medications, patches and gums, but I would recommend for the person who really wants to quit, try guided meditation (*see Ch. 6-9*) and visualization first. Do not go to just anyone, but someone who specializes in smoking cessation. If done correctly and with the right attitude, you can actually quit smoking within 1–3 visits!

A study in the *Journal of Adolescent Health* concluded, "The present findings indicate that parent smoking contributes to the onset of daily smoking in their teenagers even if parents practice good family management, hold norms against teen tobacco use, and do not involve their children in their own tobacco use."[4] Additionally, it was found that children between the ages of 13 and 21 whose parents smoked were more than two times as likely to begin smoking cigarettes than children of the same age who did not have a parent that smoked cigarettes. If you do not want to quit for yourself, I beg you to consider to at least do it for you kids.

E-cigarettes and vaping are two popular alternatives to cigarette smoking, neither of which I recommend for a multitude of reasons. The deleterious health effects may vary and are still uncertain, but if a life filled with health and wellness is a desire of yours, neither of those will bring you any closer.

BONUSES & RESOURCES *Quit Smoking in 30 Days or Less Guide*
WORKBOOK ACTIVITY *Talking to Your Teen about Smoking and Vaping Action Sheet*

5-8

USE HYPOALLERGENIC PRODUCTS

♫ I'VE GOT YOU UNDER MY SKIN

I personally live a very healthy lifestyle, yet I still had reoccurring skin issues that developed as an adult. I even tried to clean up my diet even more, which drove my wife crazy! I did different cleanses. I even ruled out mold, air pollution, parasites and different fungi. With all of that, I still had a few patches of skin that would itch like crazy, no matter what I did.

Food allergy and sensitivity testing measures the amount of IgE antibodies to determine if a person will have issues with certain foods. Tests will reveal certain foods that range from low to high reactivity within your body.

It is important to have food sensitivity testing done as not everyone knows they may be allergic to certain foods. Even if it is a small or mild allergy, it can cause headaches, stomach pain, fatigue, itchy skin, joint pain, and more.

I was convinced that at least one food item that I was consuming was the culprit, but once I was tested, I learned it was not the food.

I then looked more closely at my household products. I always used the most natural, but now I started to look at every ingredient and realized that I needed to only use hypoallergenic products.

Generally speaking, hypoallergenic products center around skin care. However, they can also include household items such as air purifiers, duvet covers, dehumidifiers, shampoos, pillows, sheets, clothing and even the bed you sleep on.

These products claim to cause significantly fewer allergies than other mainstream products. They can be great for people with dermatitis, eczema, rosacea, psoriasis and autoimmune problems. People with sensitive skin can be comforted knowing that their risk for flare ups and irritations are greatly decreased. Using hypoallergenic products reduce the risk for acne or infections as they don't contain allergens that irritate the skin's pores. Hypoallergenic products decrease the risk for dark spots and blotches.

After going through a series of examinations and a patch test, I learned that I had developed an allergy to fragrance. I did not realize that even naturally occurring fragrances in essential oils could cause problems for some people. Once I changed my detergent, soap, shampoo and pretty much everything else in my life, the rashes stopped returning.

You and your kids are constantly being bombarded with allergens and pathogens floating in the air you breathe and sitting on surfaces you touch, including the clothes you wear. It is important to understand that even if you don't have any of the conditions above, it is recommended to utilize as many hypo-allergenic products as possible in daily life and to have a good air purifier at home and work.

Some of the most common products that can increase your toxic load if not manufactured with very clean and pure ingredients include household cleaning supplies, detergents, cosmetics, beauty supplies, body cleansers, soaps, shampoos, lotions, toothpaste, bubble bath, sunscreen, diapers, tampons, nail polish, nail polish remover and insect repellent.

Anything you to do reduce the toxic load will help reduce stress to the nervous system.

BONUSES & RESOURCES Lists of my favorite brands that provide non-toxic ingredients in their products.
BONUSES & RESOURCES *Toxic Items in the Home Blacklist Guide*
BONUSES & RESOURCES Significant discount off my favorite air purifier

5-9

REDUCE DRUG USE . . . PUSHED OR PRESCRIBED

♫ I WANT A NEW DRUG

All I want to convey about recreational drugs is . . . if you are taking them . . . please get the appropriate professional help if you cannot stop on your own. You know how bad they are for your health, and they likely negatively affect your work, your relationships and ultimately your very existence (if not now, they likely will in the future). If you use drugs on rare occasions and like to "party," just think about the fact that most people addicted to drugs started by taking them here and there. Also remember, your kids are watching you and they are counting on you to be present and available to them all of the time.

Recreational drugs increase heart rate, body temperature and blood pressure and can cause dental problems, anxiety, nausea, paranoia, trouble sleeping and kidney failure. They can also cause physical and psychological dependencies. Physical dependence comes when someone shows withdrawal symptoms. Psychological dependence comes when someone believes they rely on the drug to be happy.

Drug use also weakens the immune system. Recreational drugs tamper with the brain by sending abnormal messages, which can lead to problems with memory, attention, decision making, mental confusion, and permanent brain damage. Recreational drug use can also cause personality disorders and antisocial characteristics. Lastly, absolute dependence on drugs create addiction, which leads to anxiety disorders and depression.

Drug use during pregnancy has led to premature and undeveloped babies and withdrawal symptoms within the babies and can cause the children to develop the addiction as well.

One of the most common chemical stressors that can be found in your bathroom cabinet are medications. Whether a medication is purchased over the counter, by prescription or illegally, it is designed to alter your body's chemistry in an artificial way.

As mentioned earlier in this book, the United States makes up 4% of the world's population, yet we spend more than 50% of the world's healthcare dollars. The medical system in the U.S. is probably the best in the world when it comes to saving lives in crisis situations. However, we rank very low when it comes to keeping our people healthy. Again, that is because we have a sick-care system, not healthcare.

Imagine if a jumbo jet crashed every other day for an entire year, killing everyone on board. Do you think that would make the news? How many deaths would that be? Let us do some math. If a 747-passenger airplane transporting 450 people crashed 4 times per week, that would be 1800 deaths per week. Now multiply that by 52 weeks and we would see the unfortunate deaths of 93,600 people each year.

According to a study published in the Journal of the American Medical Association, the authors found that adverse drug reactions (ADRs) from properly prescribed medications in hospitals kill an estimated 106,000 Americans each year.[5]

According to the CDC, the top 10 causes of death in the U.S. in 2019 were:[6]

1) Heart disease: 659,041
2) Cancer: 599,601
3) Accidents (unintentional injuries): 173,040
4) Chronic lower respiratory diseases: 156,979
5) Stroke (cerebrovascular diseases): 150,005
6) Alzheimer's disease: 121,499
7) Diabetes: 87,647
8) Nephritis, nephrotic syndrome, and nephrosis: 51,565
9) Influenza and pneumonia: 49,783
10) Intentional self-harm (suicide): 47,511

As you can clearly see, there is no mention of these deaths in that list, yet they would fit between Alzheimer's and diabetes, making it the 7th leading cause of death in America. The 106,000 deaths do not include nearly 30,000 additional deaths caused by hospital errors and improperly prescribed medications. Add those in and "death by medicine" becomes the 6th leading cause of death in the U.S.

While medications often relieve symptoms, kill unwanted pathogens and save lives, abuse or long-term use can cause many potential problems. The opioid crisis in America is a perfect example of how a drug that can do some good can destroy so many lives. Most people do not realize that of those addicted to opioids started out as healthy, law abiding citizens . . . they weren't "druggies." Good, everyday people that had injuries that may have occurred at work, in an auto accident or a sports injury were prescribed an opioid to deal with the pain and recovery. Opioids (and many other medications) are highly addictive and cause ordinary people to lose everything good in their lives. It only takes a few days on opioids for your brain chemistry to change and create dependencies. I often hear people say that they are strong willed and would never get addicted. What they fail to understand is, it does not matter how strong-willed you may be, the chemical changes in the brain are difficult for almost all people to overcome.

I am in no way suggesting that you should not take or give your child medication. That is a decision between you and your healthcare provider(s). Even when medications are taken at appropriate times, however, they are still chemical stressors on the body. It is important to explore the risks and benefits and discontinue use as soon as possible.

If you decide to use medication to handle a health issue, the least you can do is follow up with ways to restore the body back to balance.

If your house is on fire, you will obviously call the fire department. The firefighters will arrive to your home, break windows, knock down doors and fill the house with water and nasty foams. Your house is now a mess, but at least it is still standing.

Once the fire fighters have left your home, what is next? Would you call the fire department back and ask them to repair all the damage they caused?

It is now time to call a contractor to have the house put back together. Here comes the cool part . . .

When the house is being repaired, you now get to choose the type of tile, carpet and other flooring you want, the look of the cabinets and even the wall colors. And hopefully you will put in more safety measures to mitigate damage in the event of a future fire. Heck, you may even like your rebuilt home more than the original.

After the medical doctors put out the fire using medication, you should consider doing a purification program and anything possible to reset your gut and microbiome (*see Ch. 5-2*) as well as your nervous system (*see Ch. 8-2*). This is a great time to reflect on what caused the "fire" in the first place. Consider what lifestyle changes you could make to not only avoid similar problems in the future but to also build health for a lifetime.

The "contractor" you hire should be a guide (whether it is a person or this book) to help you and your family live your DREAM, every day. Even if the DREAM lifestyle does not prevent future "fires," it can certainly help diminish the severity and damage if another "fire" were to light up.

BONUSES & RESOURCES: Links to websites that provide information about effects and side-effects of every medication.

5-10

ORGANIC/NON-GMO

♫ OLD MACDONALD HAD A FARM . . . N-O-N-GMO

I remember very clearly in the early 2000s when organic produce began to hit the store shelves. I was a new doctor who recently learned of the potential dangers of pesticides and GMOs, but there was not much I could do about it. We did not have many choices back then.

I frequented Whole Foods and local farmers markets, which were barely even a thing back then. I remember seeing apples that looked like they were hit with a nuclear bomb. Tomatoes that appeared to have been under attack by distorted looking hairy cucumbers. I wondered how they ended up on the shelves in these fancy produce aisles; and they cost twice as much as the pretty stuff that was shiny and immaculately waxed.

After much inquiry and learning about organic farming, I began to purchase these grotesque looking vegetables. Believe it or not, they tasted incredible. In fact, they tasted like the produce we used to grow in the family garden when I was a kid.

I remember family members telling me that they would not eat any of my organic produce. "Gross! I'm not eating that. Don't buy that stuff for me, no way!" If they were coming to my place for dinner and they knew I used organic produce in the meal, they would politely say, "No thanks, I'm good!" It was a fight to try to get them to taste these items, but I do understand. The food looked bizarre, and the word organic in this context was new and quite frankly, odd.

Throughout this book, anytime you read about a recommended food or product that enters the body, including touching the skin, the recommendation is that it be made with organic and/or non-GMO ingredients whenever possible. Currently in the United States, anything that is certified organic is automatically, by definition, also non-GMO, because certified organic products do not allow using genetically modified organisms in them. However, the reverse is not true . . . not everything that is non-GMO is also organic.

Organic farming is done without the use of artificial pesticides and fertilizers to keep away unwanted pests. Instead, those farmers will use natural repellents to protect the crops, such as insects including lady bugs. Organic products do not use irradiation during the process, and they avoid using synthetic food additives.

Aside from organic produce seeming to have more antioxidant content, which is extremely important in terms of general health and potentially avoiding cancers than non-organic (conventional) produce, there is not sufficient evidence that it has more vitamins and minerals. You would be choosing organic because of the potential harmful effects of the many toxins found in conventional produce. Also, just because something wears the organic label, it does not automatically make it healthy. Any processed food is still processed, which is less than ideal. And if it has potentially harmful ingredients, it is still not good whether it is organically derived or not.

When you are reading a conventional (non-organic) product label and you see "natural flavors," that is often a time to run away. You would not believe what some of these companies get away with when using the word natural, like beaver anal gland for vanilla flavor (look it up)! Maybe these additives occur in "nature," but they are not from the source that you would expect for that product, and it would completely gross you out if you knew where they actually came from. Of even greater concern, many of the ingredients that claim to be natural may originate from natural sources but go through processes that are anything but natural.

Organic products, on the other hand, have higher standards. When you see natural flavors in their product labels, it is more likely that the flavor comes from the essential oils of a particular source (such as a plant, root, fruit, herb, vegetable, spice or animal) after heating, extracting or other natural process such as fermentation. Unfortunately, even companies selling organic products do not always disclose the source of these ingredients for proprietary reasons, but generally speaking, they are a safer bet.

Genetically modified organisms (GMO) are a little more difficult to understand and discern. Ultimately, a GMO does not occur naturally by nature or recombination according to the Food and Agriculture Organization, the World Health Organization and the European Commission. Essentially, they are artificially manipulated in a laboratory. You will often find GMOs in conventional products that contain sugar, canola, soy and corn (*see Ch. 5-13*).

There are benevolent arguments for the benefits of using pesticides and genetically modified organisms, including keeping food prices down, better looking produce and helping feed people around the world where food is scarce. While these are noble efforts by those not strictly looking at profits, the question remains, At what cost to your health?

Manufacturers of conventional products will try to convince you that their goods will have no detrimental effect on your health. On the contrary, many of these manufacturers are being sued for millions of dollars for contributing to various health conditions. While there is more independent research that needs to be done, there is evidence that GMOs have been contributing factors in the development of certain cancers, auto-immune issues, severe allergies, skin conditions, respiratory distress, diabetes, neurological disorders (such as Parkinson's and Alzheimer's) and even infertility. Additionally, the environment is no fan of them either.

There will be times that you will not have access to organic products. However, there are certain items that you should consider avoiding if possible when organic is not an option. According to the non-profit the Environmental Working Group (EWG) (an activist group that specializes in research and advocacy in the areas of agricultural subsidies, toxic chemicals, drinking water pollutants and corporate accountability), there are 12 food items in particular referred to as the Dirty Dozen. In 2019, they deemed the Dirty Dozen to be: strawberries, spinach, kale, nectarines, apples, grapes, peaches, cherries, pears, tomatoes, celery and potatoes.

These are singled out mostly because of how they contain the most pesticide residue. While it would be nice to have all fruits and veggies be organic, it is not always available or affordable. Other produce that has hard shells or thick skins are often safer from pesticide residue, such as avocados, pineapple and melons. However, I would recommend trying to find non-GMO versions of these when possible if organic is not an option.

My wife, Brooke, and I keep our household almost exclusively organic and non-GMO. We explained this to Zion before he was 2 and even taught him how to identify it on the labels. There are few cuter things to see in a supermarket than a 2-year-old saying we can't get something because it is not organic!

If you want to learn more about GMOs and how special interests deceive the public regarding GMOs and other health matters, I recommend watching the documentary, *Bought* by Jeff Hays . . . that is, if you can still find it. Your family will thank you for it!

5-11

FRUIT AND VEGETABLES

♫ EAT YOUR VEGGIES!

I will never forget the photo texted to us from a friend when Zion was attending her daughter's birthday party. In the photo you see all the children indulging in birthday cake and Zion munching on a cucumber. He was not even 3-years-old at this point. The mom asked Zion if he wanted a piece of cake and he said, "No thanks, I have these that my mommy gave me." This was not a one-time occurrence by any stretch of imagination. Sure, Zion now has sweets on occasion, but he eats fruits and vegetables like they are going out of style (*see Ch. 5-3*). Not only does he love the taste of them, but he knows that they make him "Big and strong," and that is a value to him, even today. He knows this because not only do we tell him but also he sees what we eat.

Fruits and vegetables contain important vitamins, minerals, fiber, antioxidants and plant chemicals. Eating fruits and vegetables each day can reduce the risk of chronic diseases, such as cancer, diabetes and heart disease. Produce also contains phytochemicals, which are natural compounds in plants, which maintain proper cell growth and health. Along with these health benefits, eating fruits and vegetables help make weight management easier.

All calories are not created equally. Many famous "weight loss" programs focus primarily on the number of calories consumed. While the quantity of your caloric intake is extremely important, the quality is equally crucial.

When it comes to food, a calorie is a unit to measure the amount of energy stored in food. It is important to eat high-quality foods in appropriately sized portions. High quality foods are unrefined and minimally processed if at all. The notion of "a calorie is a calorie" should not be paid attention to, as certain foods such as chips, potatoes and sugar-sweetened beverages will likely cause weight gain and other health issues, even if they have the same amount of calories as healthy foods.

The number of calories in a particular food item can essentially be determined by the amount and weight of its macronutrients, the structural/energy-giving caloric components which are carbohydrates, fats and proteins. One gram of carbohydrate and one gram of protein each contain four calories and one gram of fat contains nine calories.

Macronutrients fuel the activities of every physiological system and are important to function properly. While macronutrients are essential for all vital physiological functions, it is important to understand that not all macronutrients are created equally, and the source and quality can significantly impact one's health, energy and body-fat composition.

5-12

CARBOHYDRATES/SUGAR

♫ POUR SOME SUGAR ON ME

All carbohydrates are actually sugar. However, the way they impact your health and weight can be determined by several factors, including whether they are simple or complex, refined or whole and naturally derived or genetically modified. The nature of each sugar will have an impact on the glycemic index, which determines how quickly the food item raises the blood sugar levels. Low glycemic foods have a rating of 55 or less, whereas high glycemic food rate at 70 or higher.

Simple carbohydrates are essentially simple sugars (monosaccharides), which include glucose, fructose and galactose, or double sugars (disaccharides), which include sucrose (table sugar), lactose and maltose. Aside from the temporary energy they provide, they are considered to be "empty calories" because they offer no nutritional value. These are used to sweeten the foods we like to eat. Whether the sources of these simple sugars are from fruit (which is a combination of sucrose, fructose and glucose) or sugar cane (sucrose), they have high glycemic values and both cause blood sugar (glucose) levels to spike. This spike can lead to issues with the pancreas and the production of insulin, energy level fluctuations, hyperactivity, decreased immune function and weight gain.

There is so much that people should be aware of when it comes to sugar, and I could never do it justice as a small part of this book. This book will cover different types of sugar and alternatives, but if you want to know more about sugar, the potential harmful effects of sugar and how to avoid it in a healthy diet, I recommend the books, *The Virgin Diet* and *Sugar Impact Diet*, both written by my friend JJ Virgin.

Complex carbohydrates (polysaccharides: three or more sugars) are starches that take a bit longer to break down because they also contain fiber and various micronutrients (*see Ch. 5-3*). If you recall from earlier in the book, micronutrients are the vitamins, minerals and antioxidants that are essential for good health and they play a part in the production of hormones and proteins that are critical to body and brain function. Complex carbohydrates tend to have lower glycemic indexes and do not cause your insulin levels to spike quite as quickly as simple sugars, but that doesn't mean that they are all good.

Every carbohydrate affects blood sugar differently, so looking at the glycemic index of each food item can help determine the effect it will have on your blood sugar fluctuations. Major determining factors of a food's glycemic index include the amount of fiber it contains, the micronutrient content, the ripeness of the fruit, fat content and whether the food is refined or not. A refined food is essentially something that does not contain all of its original nutrients. In terms of breads, refined breads have the bran and the germ stripped away unlike the whole food versions.

Lower glycemic foods include bran cereals (with no sugar added), chickpeas (including hummus), peanuts, cashews, lentils, black beans, kidney beans and cashews. Middle range would include your whole grain breads and pastas, oatmeal, bulgur and brown rice. The high glycemic foods are really too numerous to name, but some common foods that are very high on the glycemic index that would surprise some people include fruit juice (even unsweetened, but especially sweetened), baked potatoes, white rice, white pasta, white bread . . . etc . . .

The "white foods" are typically the refined and highly processed foods. The process of refining certain foods, especially in relation to grains, removes the germ and bran, which are the important and nutrient rich parts of the grain. Once that germ and bran are removed, almost all the redeeming qualities go out the window. This is one of the major reasons why food manufacturers enrich and fortify many of their products. Fortification adds back many of the essential nutrients and minerals that were removed during the refining process. Refining is done for a few reasons, including look, taste, consistency and shelf life. In my opinion, none of these are worth losing the natural vitamins and minerals in order to artificially replace them.

I would also like to bring your attention to fruit juice. Many parents love to give their kids apple juice to sip around for the day. The kids love it, and the parents think it is good for them because, heck, apples are good for them, with lots of nutrients, so what can be bad about apple juice? If you are one of those parents, hopefully by now you are starting to see a pattern and realize what is wrong with that thinking.

What is the difference between an apple and apple juice? Well an apple is crunchy, and juice is not. That stuff you bite into that makes an apple go crunch is the plant material that is composed of fiber (and other cells of course). That fiber helps absorb the sugar that is in the apple and causes the fruit to have a lower glycemic index than just the juice. While the juice does contain vitamins and minerals, it is still mostly sugar. Kids that drink a lot of fruit juice are more likely to deal with hyperactivity issues, weight gain, diabetes and dental cavities.

A common question I get is, "Should I juice my fruits/veggies or blend them?" This is a very controversial conversation with strong opinions by the experts on both sides. I take a commonsense approach, which I combine with my intellect and experience. One of the main benefits of juicing is, it enables a person to consume a large quantity of important vitamins and minerals. In fact, one glass of juice will contain many more times the amount of micronutrients than one piece of fruit. The reason is, once you remove the pulp of the fruit or vegetable, there is nothing left but liquid enabling you to consume more. The problem is, the pulp contains the fiber. Without the fiber, the sugar in the fruit or vegetable can cause a spike in glucose levels. If you want a nutrient boost and a quick snack, juicing can be the perfect fit when done right. Be sure to prepare it with lower sugar containing veggies and fruit, such as kale, spinach, cucumbers, celery and if you must have an apple, make it a granny smith, because studies have shown that they contain the most antioxidants and promote the growth of healthy bacteria in the colon.

If you are looking for a complete meal, I recommend blending your shake, and make it nutritious, including proteins and healthy fats. I personally start approximately 340 mornings per year with a healthy shake for breakfast (*see Ch. 5-16*).

Keep in mind that the heart can be heavily affected by sugar, which can lead to cardiovascular disease. Sugar can also lead to liver problems and yeast infections within the gut and, of course, type II diabetes. The risk for type II diabetes increases 1.1% for every 150 calories of sugar consumed a day. Children who consume sugar, especially before school, tend to have difficulty concentrating in class and often get labeled as hyperactive. As a final standing, if you want your body and that of your kids to look and function optimally and prevent avoidable diseases, eliminate as many sugars from your diet as possible . . . especially the refined, highly processed and simple ones!

So how much sugar is acceptable? As you read earlier, zero grams of sugar is acceptable for children under the age of two. For kids between the ages of 2 and 18 and adult women, the American Heart Association recommends no more than 25 grams of added sugar, which is equivalent to approximately six teaspoons. For adult men, the recommendation is no more than 36 grams (nine teaspoons). It is my recommendation, however, to avoid added sugar whenever possible. And when you do consume food with added sugar, choose items that use the sugar in its most natural form (organic and unrefined) and with the lowest glycemic indexes possible.

When reading labels, you will see many different types of sugar used to sweeten certain food items, including coconut palm sugar, coconut nectar, raw honey, agave, maple syrup, date paste, date syrup and blackstrap molasses. While many of these have a lower glycemic index than table sugar, you should be reminded that they are still sugar and should be consumed in moderation, below the recommended daily allowances mentioned above.

Quite possibly one of the most destructive forms of processed sugar is high fructose corn syrup, and it seems to be in everything! Well, not everything, but it sure seems like that, especially in the United States. High fructose corn syrup (HFCS) is derived from corn (as the name states) and is just as sweet as table (cane) sugar but much worse for you. So if it's so bad, why is it everywhere?

Did you know that the United States government pays farmers approximately $100 billion to grow corn? Because corn is a subsidized crop, it makes the production of HFCS much cheaper than cane sugar, and therefore, less expensive to sweeten processed foods, which leads to much higher profit margins.

"So why is HFCS so bad for me? I thought fructose is good. Isn't that the sugar in fruit?"

Fructose is in fruit, but it is one of three sugars in fruit, the other two being sucrose and glucose. When fructose is consumed in large amounts (especially when not bound with sucrose), it can have very harmful impacts on your health. According to a 2013 article, risk of metabolic syndrome, type II diabetes and cardiovascular disease are increased.[7]

Additionally, HFCS is inherently genetically modified because two of the enzymes are used to make it more stable; that is, in addition to the fact that most (and arguably all) of the corn is genetically modified (*see Ch. 5-10*).

Another issue with HFCS is that it easily converts into fat, because fructose is metabolized in the liver, which in turn stores it as glycogen (stored carbs) but with a limited capacity. This can lead to fatty liver and obesity more so than consuming sugar cane. Also, HFCS does not satiate the person's appetite like cane sugar, thus having people consume much more than what would usually be eaten.

Much like Zion only "allowing" us to buy foods that are organic, he is the same way about corn syrup. He never, ever asks for candy or food items that have HFCS. I am extremely blessed that I never have this battle with him. When he sees something sweet, he actually asks if it has corn syrup. If we tell him it does, he says, "Yuck," and moves on.

BONUSES & RESOURCES Shopping and recipe lists for yummy foods that are sugar conscious.
BONUSES & RESOURCES My complete breakfast smoothie recipe.
BONUSES & RESOURCES Sugar Avoidance Affirmation
WORKBOOK ACTIVITY *Sugar Addiction Checklist*

5-13

AVOID ARTIFICIAL SWEETENERS

♫ HOW SWEET IT IS

Is there a case for artificial sweeteners? Anyone who writes about the potential negative effects of artificial sweeteners should be prepared to be sued as the manufacturers of these products have tons of money and resources and do not like being called out. So, if you would be so kind, please tell everyone you know to purchase this book because I will probably need the money to defend myself in court because I do not plan to hold back on this one!

Let's start with the redeeming qualities of these non-caloric artificial sweeteners, which should take less than 10 seconds to read. We learned that sugar in general, especially in large quantities is not good for you. If you have a sweet tooth and do not want the extra calories or blood sugar fluctuations, an alternative would be in order. Artificial sweeteners are an alternative to sugar. Okay done with the good stuff.

That said, artificial sweeteners are not a good alternative to sugar. In fact, I would argue that if you needed to choose between sugar itself or an artificial sweetener, I would choose the sugar in a heartbeat. Even refined sugar, which I avoid as much as possible would be chosen over the artificial sweeteners. Just the word artificial should raise red flags while reading this book. (In the case of diabetes, consult your healthcare provider about your options as sugar is not advised, but I never advise artificial sugars.)

So why are they so bad? Well, if you read most of the literature on them, you would think I was crazy and they are the best thing since sliced bread . . . which they are if you think bread is good for you! Okay, I digress . . . let's get into the science . . .

First off, because artificial sweeteners have no nutrients in them (or calories), they can cause you to eat and drink more of the food or beverage that is being sweetened. While calories are partially responsible for weight gain, they also give energy and allow us to satiate ourselves, which means, we get "full" when we consume them. Food and beverages without calories can cause us to consume much more than we normally would which could easily lead to weight gain and metabolic syndrome.

Additionally, when you consume something sweet, the brain thinks you are consuming sugar, which in turn causes the pancreas to produce insulin to breakdown the sugar. However, when there is no actual sugar to breakdown, the pancreas gets confused and works in overdrive. These are not technical terms; I'm simplifying the process so that you understand what is happening. What do you think happens if the pancreas is working, producing and releasing insulin into the bloodstream when it doesn't need to?

This is like having your car engine on, the car in neutral and you are stepping really hard on the gas pedal for an extended period of time. Do you think that is good for your car? When your pancreas is working when it does not need to, it begins to stop working . . . just like your car would eventually run out of gas. What happens when your pancreas stops working? That's right, type II diabetes results.

Sucralose (Splenda) for example is 600 times sweeter than sugar . . . think about how much work the pancreas will think it needs to do when the brain thinks it needs to breakdown that much sugar.

The most common artificial sweeteners we see today are aspartame (Equal and NutraSweet), sucralose (Splenda) and saccharin (Sweet 'n Low). Aside from the effects these artificial sweeteners can have related to insulin production, there is also widespread concern that some of them may be carcinogenic. There is much more research that needs to be done, and it must be done by independent parties not related to the companies that manufacture them.

Combined, the potential side effects can include headaches, migraines, dizziness, cancers, digestive problems, mood swings and more. Additionally, pregnant and breastfeeding moms should be aware that studies show that consuming artificial sweeteners during those times can potentially cause harm. According to an article from 2014, there is evidence that exposure to these sweeteners can predispose the fetus/baby to metabolic syndrome and obesity later in life.[8]

The most unfortunate aspect to artificial sweeteners, aside from the deleterious health effects, is that they are found in so many alleged "health food" products, such as protein powders, children's chewable vitamins and even toothpaste.

Then there are sugar alcohols, including xylitol, sorbitol, maltitol, mannitol and erythritol. These sugar substitutes are not synthetic, they do not seem to negatively affect blood glucose levels and some even have positive health benefits, including helping prevent tooth decay. However, some can cause minor issues and symptoms, including belly aches. Because the body cannot digest most sugar alcohols, they end up being metabolized by the gut bacteria in the large intestine. I would recommend only using sugar alcohols in moderation as there is still much we do not know about them, and there could be potential health issues down the road.

Now that we know that both sugar and artificial sweeteners are not wonderful, how do you get around them and still enjoy life?

I would say that the first step is to find a way to enjoy life (food) without the need for something sweet, too often. There are plenty of natural spices, herbs and flavors that wet the palate and make our foods tasty and enjoyable. To "need" something sweet is a sign that something else is lacking. I can tell you with certainty that no one was born with a tooth that requires sweetness . . . or a "sweet tooth." If you have a well-balanced diet, your hormones are in check and you are living a wellness lifestyle, your cravings should be minimal if at all, and they usually will pass within a short period of time. Additionally, palates do change over time, so the less sweetness you consume, the less you will need.

If you must go for something sweet, here are some options on the healthier side. I personally like (organic) stevia. Some people do not like the taste of it and others claim to have a sensitivity as well, but it is certainly worth trying. As of the latest research that I have evaluated, there is no real downside to stevia in moderation. It is a naturally occurring herb (plant) and can be purchased as an extract. While the potential is there to have a similar impact on the pancreas as other non-caloric sweeteners mentioned, this natural sweetener is not as sweet as those, so it would take a ton of stevia to have a similar effect. Stevia is the sugar substitute found in the protein powders that I drink. Another similar option to stevia without any score on the glycemic index because it has no sugar is monk fruit. Other natural sweeteners may include organic raw local honey, dates and even apples. Those do have sugar, but because they are not processed sugars and have a lower glycemic index, they are better choices than table sugar.

5-14

TYPES OF FAT . . . THE GOOD, THE BAD AND THE UGLY

♫ LET'S GET FAT TOGETHER

I always love the reaction when I tell a crowd to eat more fat. That gets their attention!

It is important to understand that *fat* in general is not all bad. In fact, fat is essential for survival. However, it is important to understand what types of fats to consume, why it is important to consume them and why it is important to avoid the bad stuff, at least in large quantities.

For simplification purposes, think of fat in two categories . . . saturated and unsaturated (monounsaturated and polyunsaturated). Saturated fats are typically solid at room temperature (like butter) and unsaturated are usually liquid (think olive oil).

Saturated fats are found in foods such as lamb, beef, chicken skin and cheese. While some of those foods are very tasty and contain a lot of important nutrients, the risks associated with the saturated fat content may outweigh the benefits if consumed in large amounts.

That said, not all saturated fats are created equal. Coconut is an example of a saturated fat that offers health benefits in the form of medium chain triglycerides (MCTs). The body does not store MCTs as fat but rather burns them for additional energy. If you are going to choose to consume saturated fats, the coconut family, including coconut butter, coconut oil and coconut milk, offer a much healthier option than the saturated fats hiding within those pre-packaged foods lining your supermarket aisles.

Cholesterol in and of itself is not the enemy. Cholesterol is a fatty substance (in the lipid category) found in your blood that has a waxy-like texture. We need cholesterol in our blood to build the structure of cell membranes, and it also helps in the production of hormones, including those from the adrenal glands as well as testosterone and estrogen. Interestingly, approximately 20% of your body's content of cholesterol is found in the brain. Cholesterol in the brain is essential because it helps the nerves send better signals. However, a deficiency of cholesterol in the brain can cause brain activity to diminish considerably, which of course can affect mood, memory and overall learning.

So why is everyone so afraid of cholesterol? Because too much of the wrong stuff can kill you! When cholesterol (lipid—think "lipo") travels through your blood, it attaches to proteins. This is where the word *lipoprotein* comes from.

Low-density lipoproteins (LDL) build up fatty deposits (plaque) onto the walls of arteries, making them hard and narrow, causing atherosclerosis. This is why LDLs are referred to as the "bad cholesterol." High-density lipoproteins (HDL) on the other hand, clean up and remove excess cholesterol, taking it back to your liver. And this is why HDLs are referred to as the "good cholesterol."

It is recommended to not allow more than 5% of your caloric intake to come from saturated fats, according to the American Heart Association. Among other potential health issues, saturated fats have been shown to increase LDLs, as it can lead to cardiovascular disease.

Trans-fats are a form of saturated fat that is either naturally occurring (typically within the gut of an animal) or artificially created by processors of food by adding hydrogen to liquid vegetable oil, making them solid. (Naturally occurring trans-fats may not be as unhealthy as artificially created ones, though more research is warranted. Remember, they are still saturated, so you want to limit the intake.)

The reason why manufacturers create trans-fats is ultimately to enhance taste, texture and consistency—and increase profits by decreasing production costs. Not only do trans-fats raise your LDLs, but they also lower your HDLs.

It is my recommendation that you and your family avoid any product that has "hydrogenated oil," with or without the word "partially" on the label. These trans-fats are found in a wide variety of fast-food items and many common products likely in your home. Common culprits are margarine and shortening, fried foods (think chicken fingers, French fries and potato chips), baked goods (think cupcakes, donuts and pies), and even frozen pizza. Take a look in your pantry right now and pick any snack you have for your kids and look at the label; it's very likely you will find at least one item in your house. Then you can get some exercise when you walk (or jog) to your garbage bin and promptly throw it away.

Foods containing trans-fats are one of my dealbreakers (*see Ch. 5-1*) you read about earlier in the book. Sometimes manufacturers get sneaky in the labeling process and change the order of words (or add additional words in between), but do not let them fool you. These are bad for your health and should be avoided at all costs! Not only can they lead to cardiovascular disease, but they also raise blood sugar considerably and can potentially lead to type II diabetes. Trans-fats are in *many* processed food items that are found in almost every aisle of the traditional supermarket. While 5% of your caloric intake of saturated fats may be acceptable, this expert (me) recommends that the amount of artificial trans-fat in your diet should not exceed 0%! Get my point? None! Zilch! Zero! Hint: Read the food labels of every product you buy . . . period.

Unlike saturated fats that you want to avoid 95% of the time, the reverse is true for unsaturated fats. Obviously, you don't want to overload on these fats, but they should be plentiful in a healthy diet. These are the fats that are found in nuts, seeds, olive oil, fish and more. This is also where you find your omega-6 and omega-3 fatty acids that are essential for a healthy you. (Note: it is recommended to have a ratio of 4:1 or less of omega-6 [think nuts and seeds] to omega-3 [think fish].) Unsaturated fats raise your HDL and lower your LDL and have been known to reduce the risk of heart disease and strokes.

High cholesterol is a term often used but not widely understood. A lot of factors go into determining whether someone's cholesterol is within safe limits by using a lipid panel. A lipid panel will measure the amount of LDLs and HDLs, as well as a triglyceride level, which is a type of fat in the blood. Triglyceride levels should be below 150 in adults and under 75 in children. For HDLs, ideally you want to see above 60 for adults and above 45 for children; and for LDLs, you want to see below 100 for adults and 110 for children. To determine your cholesterol ratio, divide your total cholesterol number (HDL plus LDL) by your HDL number. Ultimately, if your ratio of LDL to HDL is higher than 4:1, then you may be at risk for heart disease and need to make some serious changes to your diet and lifestyle!

Have you ever gone to a fancy Italian restaurant and you see on the menu "Chicken Parmesan fried (or baked) in extra-virgin olive oil"? Most people would look at that and be excited. "Yay, I love olive oil . . . and it's healthy! This place must really care about flavor and health." If you thought that, you may be dead wrong.

When it comes to cooking with oils, it is very important that you use the proper oil at the proper time. Extra virgin olive oil (EVOO) for example is an oil that is extremely healthy and has the benefits of the unsaturated fats we talked about earlier. That is, until you cook it![9]

The smoke point of EVOO, which is when it becomes rancid and releases potential cancer-causing free radicals, is only 375°F. Therefore, be sure to not fry or bake above that temperature. Avocado oil, on the other hand, can withstand heats of up to 520°F if refined or 480°F unrefined (virgin). In the middle, you can use coconut oil for cooking at 450°F or 350°F based on whether it is refined or not respectively. So, if you want to enjoy the benefits of EVOO, keep it in your salads, dressings or sautéing at very low temperatures.

5-15

PROEINS

♫ NO EASY "WHEY" OUT

Simply stated, proteins are made from amino acids and are the building blocks of muscle. Some amino acids are made on our own and some we get from what we ingest. The typical person should consume around seven grams of protein for every 20 pounds they weigh. This can vary based on their individual body type (*see Ch. 7-7*), daily activities and goals, but this is a general recommendation. So someone who weighs 160 pounds should be consuming around 56 grams of protein daily.

Be mindful that not all protein sources are equal. For example, if you wanted to build up more muscle and eat steak every day, remember that the steak also comes with a considerable amount of saturated fat (*see Ch. 5-14*). While protein from animal sources are easy to come by and measure, proteins from plant sources are typically much leaner and cleaner, and come chock full of healthy nutrients.

Whey protein is one of the two proteins that come from milk (the other being casein that we addressed earlier). Whey protein contains nine essential amino acids. While there are quite a few positive benefits to whey protein (assuming you are not a vegan), many people who have milk allergies complain of stomach pains, nausea, fatigue and headaches when consuming in large amounts. Also, it is considered a milk product, so all the potential issues with dairy come along, though whey does have low lactose content (*see Ch. 5-3*).

Some of the best sources of plant-based proteins include chickpeas, beans, lentils, peas, nuts, seeds (quinoa, hemp and chia in particular), wild rice and oats. If you insist on animal proteins, healthier options include poultry, eggs and seafood. While grass-fed beef does have its share of health benefits—including antioxidants, Omega-3 fatty acids and conjugated linoleic acid (CLA), which has been shown to reduce body fat, contains anti-inflammatory properties and helps the immune system—not all the benefits outweigh the potential health risks that come with consuming them in large quantities.

I would be remiss to not acknowledge the humane and environmental justifications to consider a diet that does not include animal products. That said, this is not the conversation I choose to have in this book based on everyone's unique makeup and philosophical views. There are many articles, books and documentaries that cover this concern in much greater detail, and I could not do it justice to even try. A vegan (or even vegetarian) lifestyle is a noble endeavor and worth considering for all people. Even those who choose to consume animal products can do their part at the very least by purchasing products from animals that were humanely raised, free-range and handled with love and care throughout their lifetimes.

BONUSES & RESOURCES List of my favorite protein powders.

5-16

A REAL BREAKFAST FOR CHAMPIONS

♫ SHAKE, RATTLE AND ROLL

I know firsthand how difficult it can be to get your kid awake, dressed, fed and off to school on time. Zion loves to take his time eating. It is a process that seems to never end. However, we have lots of healthy, quick options for breakfast on school days. Healthy cereal or granola with fresh berries and coconut milk; hard-boiled eggs; and even gluten-free pancakes (without added sugar) are all staples in our home that ensure he is properly nourished and does not miss assembly.

Personally speaking, prior to discovering breakfast shakes, I went through a period of time in my young adult life when I did not eat breakfast. (Breakfast shakes really weren't a thing prior to the mid-1990s). I just was not hungry in the morning, and honestly, I typically found it difficult to eat healthy breakfasts since most breakfast items are loaded with carbs, saturated fats and sugar.

Think about your favorite breakfast place . . . that's right, you are probably visualizing the decadent pancakes/waffles/crepes with the fruit preserves only to be topped with sugar and syrup (usually corn syrup, not even the real maple stuff); the scrambled eggs with bacon, cheese and sausage (nice and greasy); and of course the white potatoes to go on the side.

Now I no longer skip breakfast. In my Vitamix, I blend a combination of veggies (typically spinach, kale, chard), a half of banana or apple; some fresh or frozen berries; some form of healthy fat, such as hemp seeds, chia seeds, coconut oil or half of an avocado; and I add a scoop of plant based protein powder (sweetened with stevia or monk fruit only); and sometimes I add a scoop of a green "superfood" to ensure I am getting the most vitamins and minerals possible.

Consuming a healthy breakfast has been shown to provide energy to start the day and has many long-term health benefits, such as reducing obesity, high blood pressure, and diabetes; improve concentration, creativity, and strength/endurance; lower cholesterol; prevent heart disease; boost metabolism; and reduce morning crankiness.

There are healthy ways to eat breakfast in restaurants, but it takes a lot of discipline! It is much easier to make breakfast healthier in your own home. My shakes have a ton of nutrition in them and they keep me filled and energized for hours.

My son loves the shakes we make at home. While we do not serve him a full-size portion, the shakes he consumes provide a ton of nutrition that he may not otherwise get throughout the day.

BONUSES & RESOURCES My complete breakfast smoothie recipe.

5-17

AVOID JUNK FOOD AND TOXIC CONTAINERS

♫ CAN YOU CAN CAN?

Eating "traditional" fast food, what I refer to as junk food, can create a multitude of nutritional deficiencies and weight gain, which can lead to obesity and diabetes.

These fast foods usually contain high amounts of cholesterol, saturated fat, and salt, which contribute to many cardiovascular health problems, including atherosclerosis. Most of my dealbreakers (*see Ch. 5-1*) are found in junk food. People who eat fast food often are 51% more likely to develop depression than those who do not. Regularly eating fast food increases your risk for developing type II diabetes. Some people may even become addicted to eating fast food. Eating fast food also can contribute to acne, headaches, shortness of breath, insulin resistance, bloating and even dental problems.

Fast food, however, has changed quite a bit from years ago. Today, there are many more options that are less processed and use fewer preservatives. In the past, if you could order your food and have it served to you within 10 minutes, that would be considered fast food. Healthier restaurants are popping up in certain geographic regions that cater to the more health-conscious person; yet because the food is prepared quickly, it falls under the category of fast food. If you decide to eat at a restaurant, there are some questions you can ask to determine what is on the healthier side to consume.

Here are some things you want to look for when choosing a "fast food" option:

- Is the food made fresh daily?
- Do they prepare food in microwaves?
- Are they using organic, non-GMO ingredients?
- What type of oil do they cook with?
- Where do they source their meats from (if not vegetarian)? Are they free range/ grass fed?
- Do they offer more wholesome complex carb options? (Whole grain breads/buns, brown rice, etc . . .)
- Are they using canned items?
- Do they have "clean" condiments? Did you know that most tomato ketchup and mayonnaise contain high fructose corn syrup and pickles have yellow #3? In fact, most condiments surprisingly include loads of destructive ingredients and preservatives. Sour cream and many dressings are often loaded with hydrogenated soybean oil (genetically modified to boot). BBQ sauce has many of the destructive ingredients listed above along with a litany of food colorings such as red 40, yellow 6 and blue 1.

Historically, fast food restaurants prepare food that is canned, processed, preserved and barely even food. If you are going to eat food that is not prepared at home, look for restaurants that tout that they do not use cans or microwaves. That is typically a tell-tale sign that they are aware of the potential dangers of processed foods and are more conscious when preparing meals. Of course that is not a guarantee that the food you will purchase is the healthiest or highest quality, as this is just one of many qualifying attributes you want to look for when eating out.

Eating canned foods can have negative effects on the brain, behavior and prostate glands, and has been linked to an increased risk of diabetes and cardiovascular diseases. Aluminum cans can leak aluminum and contaminate the food within them, and studies have shown that accumulated aluminum can be a causative factor in Alzheimer's disease. Preservatives are typically also found in canned foods and most contain high amounts of salt.

By now, you have probably seen aluminum cans and plastic bottles with labels that read "BPA Free." Bisphenol A (BPA) is a chemical compound that is used to line plastic and aluminum containers. It has been linked to many health issues, including cancer, birth defects, heart disease, obesity, asthma, type II diabetes, infertility and behavior/neurodevelopmental disorders, including but not limited to ADD/ADHD.[10]

If you are buying canned foods and it does not have a "BPA Free" label on it, do not purchase that item. In a 2017 report, "Kicking the Can, Major Retailers Still Selling Canned Food with Toxic BPA" produced by the Center for Environmental Health (CEH), they found that 40% of the cans they tested contained trace amounts of BPA.

That is down from 67% found in a 2015 study . . . but it is still way too risky!

So what about cans that claim to be BPA free and even have the fancy label? There have been independent studies (none of which I have personally verified) where cans that have been labeled as "BPA Free" still had some trace amounts of BPA found in them. Additionally, there are other can linings in these BPA free cans that are also considered to be potentially harmful, including acrylic and polyester resins and polyvinyl chloride, better known as PVC.

Your best option to avoid unwanted chemicals potentially leaching into your kid's lunchbox is to prepare the meals using fresh ingredients whenever possible. When it comes to packing their lunches and storing the food items, do your best to avoid plastic. If plastic containers are your only option, be sure that they are at least BPA free; avoid storing acidic foods (such as tomatoes); do not heat in them or add hot foods; never expose them to direct sunlight; and be sure to handwash them. Glass jars are by far the safest storage option, but of course that can be risky when dealing with young children because of potential breakage. Fortunately, there are now many outer layers that can be placed on glass products that can prevent them from shattering when dropped. Other storage options that are better than aluminum or plastic include silicone, beeswax wraps and cotton produce bags.

Now that you better understand the potential dangers of canned foods, it should make you think twice about eating at many restaurants. You are literally putting your health in someone else's hands, so I recommend that you choose restaurants that you trust and that provide transparency regarding their ingredients when asked.

When you prepare meals at home, you should know exactly what is going into your recipes and what quantities. When preparing your own meals, think fresh and natural. The first question that should come to mind when purchasing your groceries is, "Does this food item show up in nature similarly to the way I see it here?" If the answer is not a yes, then you should consider what process it went through to make it to the grocery store and whether there is a better option.

Preparing meals at home not only saves money, but it can also be much healthier than eating out at restaurants. It also allows you to avoid food allergies and food sensitivities. Additionally, it is easier to control appropriate portion sizes. It can also bring family together as it allows members to sit down and talk about their day.

5-18

REDUCE ALCOHOL CONSUMPTION

♫ RED RED WINE

Okay, I am not going to be all high and mighty and say, "Never drink alcohol." That would make me not only a hypocrite but also out of touch with reality for most people. That said, if you choose to consume alcoholic beverages, you should do so responsibly and understand the way it affects your body. I also recommend that if you drink alcoholic beverages, you do so in a controlled, safe environment. Also, be mindful of how much you drink when your children are around. Not only is there a risk of them not being protected appropriately if they need you when you are intoxicated, but also remember that they are watching your habits. Think about the impression you make on your kids and other people when you drink too much and the message that gives your children.

There is a body of evidence that demonstrates the benefits of certain alcoholic beverages on the human body when consumed in moderation. Red wine in particular has been shown to have various health benefits by acting as an anti-oxidant, reducing cholesterol and decreasing the risk of strokes. The chemical compound that provides wine with those health benefits is called resveratrol, which is found in the skin and seeds of grapes. So yes, eating grapes will provide the same benefit!

While moderately drinking red wine can have health benefits such as the ones mentioned above, as well as aid in relaxation, which may serve you well in certain social settings, I wouldn't necessarily recommend drinking it solely for those potential health benefits. There are so many other ways to receive the benefits mentioned above without consuming alcohol.

There are healthier options when picking a wine if you so choose to consume them. I recommend selecting wines that are organic, have no sulfites added, do not use commercial yeast for flavoring, minimal (if any) filtering, no chemical additives and no added sugar during the fermentation process. I also recommend trying to find wines that are biodynamically farmed, which is, "a spiritual-ethical-ecological approach to agriculture, gardens, food production and nutrition," according to the Biodynamic Farming and Gardening Association. These farms look at the entire ecosystem in which the grapes are grown and wines are produced.

Alcohol in general interferes with the brain's communication pathways, altering the way the brain looks and works. This changes one's mood and behavior, making it harder to think clearly and move with coordination. Drinking a lot over time or a large amount in a short period of time can damage the heart. Drinking also takes a toll on the liver as it can lead to inflammation as well as a lot of other problems, including fibrosis, stenosis, alcoholic hepatitis, and cirrhosis. Alcohol consumption causes the pancreas to produce toxic substances, leading to pancreatitis, a dangerous inflammation and swelling of the blood vessels which prevents proper digestion. Additionally, drinking alcohol, especially within 4 hours of bedtime, can adversely affect one's sleep.

Drinking large amounts of alcohol can even cause cancers of the mouth, throat, liver and breast. Lastly, drinking weakens the immune system and slows the body's ability to ward off infections. And if you drink too much alcohol and get behind the wheel of the car or operate heavy machinery, you are putting yourself and others in serious danger that can have life altering consequences!

BONUSES & RESOURCES Information about organic, biodynamically produced wines.

5-19

REDUCE COFFEE AND CAFFEINE CONSUMPTION

♫ COFFEE TALK

Caffeine is a funny one . . . this is where I get tomatoes thrown at me for my opinions . . . especially when I speak about coffee. It is not that a cup of coffee is evil, but to me it is more about what it represents. I take no issue with the pleasure someone receives from sipping on a nice cup of joe, as drinking coffee is a pleasant past time for many. My issue with coffee is regarding the vast amounts of people who cannot start their day without it on a regular basis. Americans in particular have become addicts, and they do not even know it. I doubt that any of us were born with too little caffeine in our bodies, so to think that it is "normal" to need caffeine is way off point. Remember, if your kids see you starting every day with a cup of coffee to make it through the morning, you are programming them to believe that they too will need to rely on a substance to make it through their days.

Caffeine is without a doubt a chemical stressor, which often leads one to sympathetic dominance (*see Ch. 8-4*). While there are some (few, but some) health benefits to caffeine, consuming caffeine has been shown to cause insomnia, nervousness, restlessness, irritability, indigestion, fast heartbeat and muscle tremors.

Excessive amounts of caffeine are linked to higher chances of smoking, poor fitness, and even earlier death. Caffeine consumption even increases blood pressure and the risk for heart attacks in young adults. Overuse of caffeine is linked to headaches and migraines. Caffeine consumption can lead to depression, anxiety and dependence on anxiety medications. Large amounts of caffeine can even lead to rhabdomyolysis, a disease that causes skeletal muscle to breakdown.

In conclusion, I'm not saying that if you drink coffee that you're not healthy. I am saying that if you need coffee, then you are not healthy! If you need to start every day with a cup of coffee, please read this entire book again and put my recommendations into action. You should be doing everything you can throughout the day to live your DREAM, which should prepare you for the best night's sleep possible. If you sleep enough hours, you should wake up well rested. Unless there is something limiting your ability from getting a good night's sleep, where you don't wake up well rested (*see Ch. 6-2*), you should try and determine the cause, because I would put any amount of money on it, that your issue is not a lack of caffeine!

BONUSES & RESOURCES *Waking Up Without Coffee & Freeing Yourself from Caffeine Dependency Made Easy* Action Sheet

5-20

AVOID SOFT DRINKS

♫ POPROCKS AND COKE

I remember as a kid I was told that if you poured cola on a car, it would rust the paint; boy was my dad livid when I tested that theory on his car!

While drinking soft drinks is bad for the waistline as well as the teeth, regular consumption of soda is linked to diabetes, heart disease, asthma, COPD and obesity. Drinking soda can place fat in weird places, but most commonly, the stomach. The caramel coloring in many soft drinks can cause cancer as it is an artificial food dye. All sodas (diet or regular) contain phosphates which can lead to heart and kidney failures, muscle loss and even accelerated aging. The phosphoric acid in soda can lead to osteoporosis (bone density loss) because it messes up the calcium/phosphorus buffer system in the body, making it more difficult to absorb calcium in the body. Heck, if the acidity in soda can rust paint, what do you think it will do to your insides?

Brominated vegetable oil, found in many sodas, is known to cause memory loss and nerve disorders. The BPA in many soda cans (*see Ch. 5-17*) can also cause hormone imbalances and other issues previously mentioned during the canned conversation.

For regular sodas with sugar, keep in mind that there is an average of 10 teaspoons of table sugar in every can . . . and that is if you're lucky! Most soda manufactured in the United States these days uses high fructose corn syrup . . . which is much worse (*see Ch. 5-12*)! For additional adverse effects of diet soda with artificial sweeteners, read my diatribe in the chapter on artificial sweeteners (*see Ch. 5-13*), or if you do not want to read it, my advice is to just avoid all of them! If you are drinking soda with caffeine, we just discussed all the health concerns there (*see Ch. 5-19*).

People ask me about whether or not they should drink non-flavored carbonated water. It appears that current research does not support the notion that it poses any health risks. That said, carbonated water is more acidic (pH of 4.5) than tap water, which is regulated at a more alkaline pH, ranging from 6.5 to 8.5. Research also indicates that consuming acidic beverages will not affect the body's internal pH, which hovers around 7.4 because the kidneys and lungs help regulate pH levels. While I do not have the research to back up my "gut" feeling on this, I prefer to consume water in its most natural form and not require my body to work any harder than it needs to. After all, it is understood that disease thrives in acidic environments, so why take the chances? All in all, I do not think that drinking plain carbonated water regularly will cause anyone harm. However, if it is the predominate form that water is consumed for an individual,

I would raise a caution flag for that person and recommend non-carbonated water as well.

BONUSES & RESOURCES *7 Strategies to Help Break You Free from Soda Addiction Guide*

5-21

ORAL HEALTH

♫ CAN'T SMILE WITHOUT YOU

It has been said that the mouth is a window into a person's health, for kids and adults. Most people that practice good dental hygiene do so for aesthetic reasons and to prevent future oral problems. However, they often do not consider the effects that their oral health has on their overall health and well-being. Aside from bringing to your attention that many chemical toxins enter your body through common dental products, the health of your teeth will also have a significant impact on the other *Keys* of wellness, especially how it affects your ability to chew food and your self-esteem.

Periodontal (gum) disease has been linked to not only tooth loss but also cardiovascular disease, stroke and bacterial pneumonia. There is also evidence between premature birth/low newborn birthweight and a pregnant woman with gum disease. Many other systemic health issues, even those in the gut, can be linked to issues arising from the mouth.

Practicing good oral hygiene, which includes brushing and flossing your teeth between meals and rinsing with mouthwash daily is the first step to preventing issues from arising in the mouth. We started teaching our son Zion about dental hygiene before he was two years old—even before he had a full mouth of teeth. We would rub his gums with a baby friendly toothpaste which helped him become comfortable with the feeling as well as create a constructive habit that would help him later in life.

And of course, visiting your dentist at least two times per year for cleanings and checkups is a good practice to avoid the buildup of plaque and to screen for the potential onset of other issues related to or starting in the mouth. Zion's first visit to a pediatric dentist was the same month as his second birthday. While there were no issues we were concerned about, we wanted the experience to be familiar (and fun) for him as he aged. We all know that dental visits are not typically the most comfortable and fun experience for anyone. We understood that if he did not fear the dentist as a baby, he would be less fearful and defiant to go in the future.

It is also important for you and your kids to avoid certain foods and beverages in large quantities that may wreak havoc on your teeth.

Sugar Bacteria breeds rapidly when sugar is present, as well as fruit juice, which I covered earlier (*see Ch. 5-12*), which is loaded with sugar.

Bread Not only does your saliva break the starch down to sugar, but the bread turns into a paste which sticks to your teeth, trapping the sugar, making you more susceptible to cavities.

Citrus and Soda The acidity in lemons, oranges and other citrus fruits, as well as carbonated beverages can erode the enamel on your teeth leading to increased sensitivity and tooth decay.

Choosing the wrong dentist and dental products can add chemical stressors in your life. There is a lot of controversy surrounding many dental procedures and potentially harmful chemicals that are found in dental products, especially toothpaste and mouthwash. I recommend that you have extensive conversations with your dentist and healthcare providers to ask about these concerns, especially because some of the risks may or may not outweigh the benefits based on circumstances.

Holistic dentists, also known as biological dentists, are known for using the purest products and performing the least invasive procedures when possible. Even if you do not use a dentist that primarily practices biological dentistry, you should still have these conversations with your conventional dentist as many are trained in the alternative options as well. This can be especially important when bringing your baby or toddler to the dentist, even for routine cleanings.

Jaw alignment is also very important to be mindful of. Many people suffer from a condition called TMJ dysfunction, which can lead to difficulty chewing, headaches, mouth pain and toothaches. Sometimes TMJ dysfunction is associated with a clicking or crackling sound when opening and closing the mouth.

Another overly common disorder of the mouth is grinding and clenching of the teeth, known as bruxism. Both children and adults clench during the day, but most often while sleeping. Bruxism, often caused by stress, can lead to tense jaw muscles, headaches and untimely wearing of the teeth. Unfortunately, most people do not even know they are doing it, which is another argument for regular dental checkups.

For both TMJ dysfunction and bruxism, there are appliances your dentist can recommend. Also, chiropractic care, particularly adjusting the upper cervical spine has shown to correct these issues naturally, safely and effectively. Additionally, many chiropractors are trained in realigning the jaw when needed, and they will work closely with your dentist to achieve best clinical outcomes. Other services to consider when dealing with TMJ dysfunction and bruxism include massage, manual therapy, cranial sacral therapy, physical therapy and occupational therapy.

BONUSES & RESOURCES *Startling Facts about Dental Hygiene* Fact Sheet

* * *

Everything you have read so far regarding DIET are physical elements that enter your body from the outside. However, we have not even scratched the surface on the immaterial (meaning, not physical in this context) and those effects. All of those will be found in the Mental Wellness section, except for the next two below to set the example.

5-22

APPROPRIATE SCREEN TIME

♫ VIDEO KILLED THE RADIO STAR

While electronic devices with screens are extremely useful in all walks of life, too much exposure can be quite harmful. We all know that both kids and adults spend way too much time on these devices daily, which can lead to mental, emotional, social and physical problems.

In this day and age, kids are spending anywhere between five and eight hours each day in front of a screen. These screens may include computers, televisions (watching or playing video games) and handheld devices, such as smartphones and tablets. When so much time is on these devices, they are spending much less time outdoors or socializing with friends, which is estimated to be less than one hour per day according to multiple research studies.

We all have those moments as parents when we are in a store or at an appointment and the only way to get our kids (especially toddlers) to cooperate is to hand them the tablet or smartphone. You pop on their favorite video or game and go about your business. In small quantities, that is not the worst thing in the world. However, if you do not set ground rules for yourself, you may unwittingly be creating a "screen junkie." Screens are not nannies. At best, they should be used as learning tools, short-term entertainment or very temporary soothing devices.

According to the Mayo Clinic, children under the age of two are much better off in a setting of unstructured playtime than using electronic media for their developing brains. Children under two learn and retain information better when it is in person, as opposed to on video.

The Mayo Clinic also states that by the age of two, programming with music, movement and stories are acceptable forms of screen time, but of course, it still should be limited. Importantly, this passive screen time is not a replacement for reading, playing or problem solving.

Other than video chatting, the American Academy of Pediatrics discourages the use of digital media for children under the age of 18–24 months. Between the ages of two and five, they recommend limiting screen time to only one hour per day.

Here is a summary of how too much screen time can impact your child's health, which is based on research and anecdotal information available today:

Mental/Cognition: Children under the age of three learn to communicate much better with two-way communication in the form of back-and-forth conversations, rather than just hearing and watching it on a screen. This also provides the benefits of real-time facial expressions so the child can observe the impact of the words being spoken. Screens do not provide real life opportunities for dialogue, which can delay a child's speech abilities. Excessive screen time during development has also shown to cause delays in reading, impaired motor skills and language problems.

A small study done on pre-teens by the National Institute of Health revealed that the cerebral cortex of the brain, which is responsible for critical thinking and reasoning, may become thinner in kids who spend more than seven hours using screens each day. With so much education being done at home, it is important to be mindful of breaks and other creative ways to spend less time on a computer.

It has also been shown that children who have televisions in the bedrooms do not perform as well on academic tests as their fellow classmates without their own television sets.

Emotional/Social: Children who spend multiple hours per day on screens tend to become less social and often disconnect from their friends and family. They do not want to join the family during mealtimes and other special moments when the family gathers. They enter a different world and, unfortunately, become addicted to this alternate reality. This also may hold back a child's imagination, as information is being "spoon-fed."

When children are exposed to violence on their screens, whether it be television, videos, movies or video games, this can lead to desensitization and violent behavior of their own (*see Ch. 9-8*). Children between the ages of six and ten who are exposed to more than two hours of daily screen time are more likely to have social, emotional and attention problems.

Physical: The physical impacts that excessive screen time can have on your children are plentiful. For one, it can lead to obesity. Kids that sit around all day on their devices are not moving as much. This sedentary lifestyle does not only lead to lack of movement and exercise to burn calories but also misses opportunities to build cardiovascular health.

Sleep is another common issue for children (and adults) who are on screens too much, especially at night (*see Ch. 6-2*). Much like sunlight, screens emit a combination of red, green and blue lights. It is the blue light emitted from the sun during the day that regulates your circadian rhythm. At night when the sun has set and the blue light is no longer present, the body produces melatonin (a hormone that regulates the circadian rhythm). This is what helps you and your kids feel tired at night and fall asleep. However, the blue light emitted from electronic devices has been shown to decrease melatonin production.

Other physical impacts that screen time can have on your children include eye strain, headaches, neck and back pain and blurred vision. It can even lead to permanent damage to vision with prolonged excessive screen time.

As a parent, it is important to set rules and boundaries as to what is an acceptable amount of screen time for everyone in your household and when it is appropriate. You must set an example for your kids, so you need to be mindful of when you are on your device. While different ages may have different needs, guidelines can come in handy, not only for everyone's health and safety but also for a harmonious home.

BONUSES & RESOURCES *Reduce Screen-Use for Kids, eBook & Digital Detox for Parents,* Workbook

WORKBOOK ACTIVITY *Reduce Screen-Use Worksheets*

5-23

POSITIVE INFLUENCES

♫ GOOD VIBRATIONS

It is extremely important that you surround yourself with positive people and bathe yourself in constructive behaviors as much as humanly possible. Happiness is contagious, spending time with positive people creates a positive environment. Surrounding yourself in this environment will help you create and share happiness with others around you, and it is a very constructive behavior for your kids to witness.

Laughter can also heal physical pain as well as mental stress. It releases "feel-good" endorphins and can express a great positive influence on surrounding people. Laughter decreases stress hormones and increases immune cells along with infection-fighting antibodies that improve the body's resistance to disease.

Hanging around people that do not complain is good for everyone. It lifts one's spirits to spend time with others who choose to look at the positives in life. On top of this, people can learn great coping strategies by taking inspiration from those around them. People tend to mirror those who they spend the most time with. Through admiration and respect of positive people and the environment that is encompassed, people can gain a more positive outlook on life.

BONUSES & RESOURCES *I am drawn to positive people & situations* Affirmation
BONUSES & RESOURCES *Dealing with Negative People* Action Guide

* * *

As mentioned at the beginning of this section, everything in your life has an impact on all 5 Facets of wellness. Many of the choices you make in terms of what you choose to receive into your body through your diet (material or immaterial) will impact the other facets significantly, especially your *mental wellness*; and there we will tackle the impacts of media, gossip and drama.

It is nearly impossible to have a perfect diet, but it is a noble goal to do your best and be very conscious of what you choose to allow in. It is also worth considering that if you choose to avoid something that is not very wholesome and you get a sense of guilt as a result, that may impact *mental wellness* negatively. That is why it is important to understand completely *why* you chose to avoid something; ensure that it is in *alignment* with your beliefs, values and desires; and allow that decision to be one of empowerment rather than deprivation (*see Ch. 9-10*).

REFLECTION OPPORTUNITY

What is your fruit and vegetable intake compared to other foods? How about your kids?

How much of your food & beverage consumption is Organic/non-GMO?

Are you conscious of food that you consume that may have corn syrup or artificial sugars in place of sugar?

Do you consume a nutritious breakfast daily?

Do you drink adequate supplies of purified water?

What percentage of your meals are prepared at home?

If you look in your refrigerator/pantry right now, how much soda would you see?

Do you need to start your day with coffee?

Do you need or desire alcohol to calm you at the end of the day?

Do you surround yourself with positivity?

If you have school age children at home, what are they seeing in the fridge and pantry? What habits are they seeing from you? Do you they observe you starting everyday with a cup of coffee to make it through the morning and/or ending each night with a glass of wine? Are they breathing in your second-hand smoke, even from your clothes? Are your habits the example you want to set for your progeny?

How much time do you spend on your handheld devices? Are you texting or using social media during family time or meals? How about your kids?

What can you and your family do outdoors today in lieu of being entertained by an electronic device?

What are three changes you can make today that will improve your *diet*?

KEY 2
RELAXATION

6-1

SHARPEN YOUR AXE

THE WOOD-CHOPPERS CONTEST —ANONYMOUS

Once upon a time there were two men in a wood-chopping contest. They were tasked with chopping down as many trees in the forest as they could from sunup to sundown. The winner would be rewarded with both fame and fortune.

From morning till noon, both men steadily chopped and chopped. By noon they were neck and neck, but then one man took a break and stopped chopping. The other man saw this and thought to himself, "The lazy fool, he's probably taking a break for lunch. He's given me a chance to get ahead of him and I will without doubt win this contest!"

A while later the man who took the break got back to work. As the day continued, he chopped more trees than his hard-working (and hungry) competitor, and by mid-afternoon he had taken a clear lead.

When sundown came, the man who had taken the break at noon had chopped almost twice as many trees as the other man, who was drenched in sweat, hungry and exhausted.

"How did you beat me?" he asked puzzled. "You were lazier than I and even took a break for lunch!"

"Ah," said the other man, "I did take a break, but it was during that break that I sharpened my axe."

When I ask people if they get enough relaxation, I know that I am giving them a loaded question. That is because most people really have no idea what relaxation really is. Remember, relaxation is a physical, emotional and spiritual mind-body connection in which each and every cell gets a chance to call timeout for repair and regeneration. Everything you do for relaxation will have a positive impact on the autonomic nervous system and help relieve sympathetic dominance (see Ch.8-4). Then you get all the benefits of being back in balance.

When some people think about what relaxation means to them, many visualize themselves on a beach chair on a remote desert island. Others think about their quest to just get a good night's sleep. While vacations and sleep are both essential for many to practice relaxation, there are a vast number of activities you can engage in on a regular basis that promote relaxation as well. Additionally, it is important to consider how every single activity and stimulus (as referenced within the other facets of wellness) will impact one's relaxation.

As a parent, you probably have trouble finding time to relax. Or worse yet, you feel guilty relaxing when you know you can be doing something for your children, or you feel you should be organizing the house when they are finally asleep. It is important to take time for yourself if you want to be a good parent and role model. Just like the airlines tell the parents to put the oxygen mask on themselves before the child during an emergency, the same is true here. And do not think that children do not need time to relax also. You can instill hardworking values and differentiate between relaxing and being lazy.

People ask me how much coffee I drink every day. When I tell them zero, they look at me like I am lying. They then ask, "How do you have so much energy? You're never tired? Do you take other forms of caffeine or stimulants? You must sleep 10 hours per night!"

While it is true that I have a ton of energy and rarely feel tired before bedtime, I chalk it up to my lifestyle. Yes, that pesky DREAM lifestyle that I keep talking about! People that know me really well know I don't sleep very much. I have never had a need to sleep more than 6 or 7 hours per night. Of course, I don't recommend that for everyone, or most people for that matter. I sleep fewer than 7 hours per night because that is what my body requires. I go to sleep when I'm ready and I wake up when I have had enough sleep, and I don't wake up tired. In fact, I probably use an alarm clock once per year and that would be typically for times that I have a meeting or a flight to catch in the wee hours of the morning when I want to ensure I don't oversleep. In fact, my body is so well trained that most of the time when I know I must be awake at a certain time and set a clock, I often wake up before it goes off. I know others can relate to that!

6-2

ADEQUATE SLEEP

♫ FRÈRE JACQUES

Many people do not remember what it feels like to be "truly rested" due to the lack of sleep that they have been getting for years. Stimulants like coffee, energy drinks, alarm clocks and external lights all interfere with our circadian rhythm, or the natural sleep/wake cycle. This can have detrimental effects to their health, energy and overall quality of life.

Because everyone is different, it is important for people to determine how they run on the amount of sleep they get. Some are productive, happy and healthy on seven hours of sleep, while others need at least nine hours to feel functional. Generally, recommended hours go as follows:

- Newborns (0–3 months): 14–17 hours each day
- Infants (4–11 months): 12–15 hours
- Toddlers (1–2 years): 11–14 hours
- Preschoolers (3–5 years): 10–13 hours
- School age children (6–13 years): 9–11 hours

- Teenagers (14–17 years): 8–10 hours
- Younger adults (18–25 years): 7–9 hours
- Adults (26–64 years): 7–9 hours
- Older adults (65+ years): 7–8 hours

It is so important to get adequate sleep, as sleep is involved in healing and repairing your heart and blood vessels. Ongoing sleep deficiency is related to an increased risk of heart disease, kidney disease, high blood pressure, diabetes, stroke and even depression and suicide.

While sleeping, your brain is preparing for the next day by forming new pathways to help you learn and remember information; therefore, a good night's sleep improves learning and memory. Sleep also helps you pay attention, be creative, and make decisions. Sleep regulates and maintains the levels of hormones such as ghrelin or leptin, which make you feel hungry or full. Sleep affects the level of insulin in the body, so the less the sleep, the higher the risk for diabetes. Also, sleep supports healthy growth and development. It triggers the hormone that promotes normal growth in children and teens. This hormone boosts muscle mass and helps repair cells and tissues. The immune system also relies on sleep to stay healthy.

Having been a healthcare practitioner for more than two decades, I can tell you the two most common reasons why people have chronic sleep issues comes down to either not having enough time or not having the ability to sleep through the night.

Time constraints may include a job that includes night shifts or long shifts that make it impossible to sleep more than eight hours because there are only 24-hours in a day. Also, caring for another person in the home, whether it be a baby who cries and needs to be comforted or nursed or any individual who needs your attention. If you have a time constraint on your sleep, it is important to understand that until you make a change to your lifestyle, you will continue to deal with this issue. While many of these situations are temporary, if modifications are not possible, then hopefully reading the remainder of this chapter (and book) will provide you with tools to compensate for the lack of time, rather than using artificial stimulants, especially long-term.

The inability to sleep through the night can be caused by a variety of reasons. If it is caused by a partner snoring or other loud noises such as car and sirens in big cities, you need to find a way to overcome that issue. Whether it be earplugs, white noise machines or changing the location of where you sleep, something must change. If the temperature of your bedroom is not comfortable, try to find a way to fix it. If your pillow or mattress is not comfortable, that is an easier fix, but one you do not want to delay.

More commonly, however, people do not have the ability to sleep because their mind does not shut off; they are hopped-up on caffeine, sugar, alcohol or other drugs, or something else is keeping them awake, such as health issues or an issue they are stressed or excited about. Therefore, it is extremely important to understand and put the DREAM lifestyle into action.

Regardless of the reasons why you or your family members are not able to get adequate sleep, it should be a goal to find ways to do your best to modify as many daily routines as possible.

My friend Dr. Catherine Darley is a leading naturopathic doctor in sleep medicine. She is driven to help people sleep well by structuring their lifestyle in ways that support their natural sleep ability. For Dr. Darley, the sleep health of kids is especially important as it is a basis of setting up healthy sleep for life. Whenever she works with children, she also addresses the whole family sleep system. We had the opportunity to talk about circadian rhythms, our "body clock," and how to strengthen those rhythms which in turn promote healthy sleep.

"When we talk about sleep, one piece of the puzzle that can't be left out is the circadian piece. This had been particularly challenging during the COVID-19 pandemic and continues to be an issue. As work from home styles change long term, it is helpful for you to purposefully promote strong rhythms. Having a robust circadian rhythm helps you fall asleep easily and sleep deeply at night, then in the day helps you be alert, energetic, and feel good," says Dr. Darley.

According to Dr. Darley, "There are several key time points during the day that influence your body clock. The first is when you first get bright, preferably outside, light in the morning which signals to your body it is time to start your day. This is one of the reasons it is important to avoid bright light, particularly blue light, at night as you do not want to trigger wakefulness right before bed" (see Ch. 5-22). "Other time cues that are important are mealtimes, your main activity whether it be work or school, social interaction, and exercise. Ideally these activities each start at the same time, within 30 minutes, every day across the week."

Dr. Darley adds, "The other key to understanding circadian rhythms is to know that at different ages we are programmed for different sleep-wake times. This programming originates deep inside the brain and can't easily be changed. So, in many ways, a child's sleep hours are not their choice, but what they are biologically set for (in some ways like their height, which is not a choice at all). Young children tend to be more morning people, then at about age 10 that all changes. In the second decade, the body clock swings later so that teens aren't sleepy until later at night and need to sleep later in the morning. Many middle and high schools start before teens are programmed to be awake. In the early '20s the body clock starts to gradually shift earlier over the next decades of life."

In many cases, re-learning how to sleep may also be necessary. Even though I personally do not need many hours of sleep, historically speaking, I used to have an awful time shutting off my mind and falling asleep (and staying asleep). That, however, is no longer the case for me since I have been re-trained and finally learned how to sleep.

I was first introduced to Audio-Visual Entrainment (AVE) back in 2017 when I was a speaker at a conference for The Masters Circle (which happens to be the coaching company that helped shape me into the chiropractor and wellness leader that I am today).

I had taken a red-eye flight from San Diego to New Jersey, went straight to my hotel, left my baggage with the concierge (because my room was not ready yet) and proceeded to the meeting room. I was scheduled to speak in one hour, and I could barely keep my eyes open. I knew when I booked the flight that there was a good chance that I would not get much sleep, but I hadn't counted on not sleeping the night before my flight also.

I went into the exhibit hall, gave the owners of The Masters Circle, Dr. Bob Hoffman and Dr. Dennis Perman a big hug and said, "Where can I go sleep for 30 minutes?" They laughed and pointed me to one of the vendors, BrainTap Technologies. I laughed back thinking they were joking, but they were completely serious.

I went over to the booth as instructed, I always do what Bob and Dennis tell me to do, and introduced myself to Patrick Porter, PhD, the inventor and owner of BrainTap. I told him who I was and why I was talking to him. He said, "It's nice to meet you, Dr. Stenzler, have a seat right here." They did a quick heart rate variability test on me and then put on this strange set of glasses with flashing lights and headphones on me. I then began to hear a guy's voice saying strange stuff into my ears. I began to wonder why I was doing this and then I remembered it was because Dennis and Bob said so.

After what seemed like two minutes, the flashing lights and positive messages stopped. When the glasses came off, I could see the room with a clarity and vividness that was not noticed prior. I looked at my watch realized that 20 minutes had passed, but I felt like I had slept for 7 hours. I had energy and alertness, and just enough time to use the restroom before giving my presentation.

In general, AVE is not just to help someone overcome jetlag (that was just my experience at the time), but it helps get someone into a very relaxed state. This in turn can help with a litany of issues that can improve one's quality of life. For me (after purchasing one and using it daily for several months), it retrained and taught me how to sleep. I now fall asleep easily and quickly. For others, it may be increased energy, reduced brain fog, enhanced memory and reduced bad habits.

People that know how busy my life is and everything I seem to accomplish on a daily basis are dumbfounded by my energy levels. They cannot fathom how I have time to participate in activities that promote relaxation in the middle of a workday. The truth is, if I did not do all these activities, I wouldn't get nearly as many daily tasks done. That at least is how I justify to my wife the need for weekly massages, adjustments, workouts, meditation and so on. She understands, I am just sharpening my axe!

WORKBOOK ACTIVITY *Create a Sleep Healthy Lifestyle Plan* and *Family Sleep Plan*

BONUSES & RESOURCES *Parents' Guide to Teaching Children to Sleep Alone*

BONUSES & RESOURCES *14 Bedtime Rituals for Better Sleep*

BONUSES & RESOURCES Sleep Affirmation

BONUSES & RESOURCES Information on BrainTap and opportunities to access at discounted rates.

6-3

ALONE TIME

♫ DON'T STAND SO CLOSE TO ME

My wife, Brooke, has a need to take some time to herself each day. This is one of the things that was revealed from the Ultimate Life Tool (ULT) test (*see Ch. 9-3*). If she does not get that time to herself each day, she will begin to get stressed, fatigued and eventually wilt like an un-watered flower. Fortunately for us, we took the ULT together very early in our relationship and I knew to expect this. In the past when I was in relationships with women who also had this significant need to be alone, I just thought they were being rude, shy or inconsiderate when they needed to retreat, especially when we were in certain social situations.

It is crucial for everyone to carve out time for solitude and self-reflection because it allows us the opportunity to reboot and relax our mind. Not everyone needs as much time alone as Brooke, but everyone does need some. Encourage your children to spend time by themselves and insist that you create alone time as well.

Alone time improves concentration and increases productivity. Also, it sparks time for reflection and time to discover yourself and your voice. Solitude allows an opportunity for you to think deeply and work through problems more efficiently.

Making time for yourself can improve the quality of your relationships with others. By spending time by yourself and realizing what you value in yourself and others, you can make better choices regarding who you choose to be friends with. Waking up early, before anyone else in the household, allows me to meditate, reflect, exercise and whatever else my inner voice tells me I need.

Alone time also provides for a great opportunity to journal. Journaling is a wonderful outlet to creatively memorialize your activities that have just past and visualize your future. It allows for opportunities of both reflection and growth. Many of the most successful businesspeople write in their journals daily.

Journaling is an important exercise used to release thoughts that we often do not want to verbalize to our significant others, parents, friends, teachers or relatives. It allows us to release any mental burdens or thoughts that may be plaguing us. We often do not realize that they are plaguing us until we sit down to write them out. It is also a great problem-solving tool.

Teaching your children to journal at a young age will provide tremendous benefits for their mental health, ability to express themselves and even their writing skills. It will also be fun for them to look back when they are older to reflect on their childhood. Heck, you never know, maybe one day a book or movie will be made from their journals.

BONUSES & RESOURCES *Journaling: A Powerful Practice to Up-Level You and Your Parenting,* Workbook

BONUSES & RESOURCES After you read about the ULT in Chapter 9-3, you will have an opportunity to test drive the assessment at a significantly reduced rate to see how important alone time is for you and learn creative ways to create more of it.

6-4

ORDER, ORDER . . .

♬ DIRTY LAUNDRY

For me, I do not need as much alone time as Brooke, but the Ultimate Life Tool revealed my need to create order (*see Ch. 9-3*). Being organized helps me optimize my full use of time. Organized people in general also feel more in control of their schedules, so they can remain relaxed even when things go awry or when they are busier than ever. It has been scientifically demonstrated that the more one feels in control of their work, the more job satisfaction they have, which leads to less stress.

Organized people also have more energy, are able to relax more and get better sleep because they do not waste their time procrastinating or worrying that they are going to forget something. This goes for kids also! Organizing gives people flexibility within their life and sparks personal creativity and mental growth. It also sets examples for your children, and it is contagious. Organizing creates self-esteem and improves/enhances family relationships. With a more flexible schedule, people can find more time for their family, feel less rushed and because of the reduced stress, one has a better relationship with others. When I have order in my life, I can focus more on my top priorities.

It is extremely important to prioritize important tasks in the hustle and bustle of life.

You would think that with all the advancements of technology and automation, we should have more time on our hands. To the contrary, we just have more and more to do, and it is driving some people bonkers, overwhelming so many!

Being overwhelmed is a common symptom of anxiety. That is not the same thing as having a ton of things to do on a daily basis. You can be a very busy, productive person with a full schedule of items to accomplish, but still not be overwhelmed. Overwhelm is how you respond to a hectic life.

Being in a constant state of overwhelm will cloud one's mind with negative thoughts and can lead one to a dark mindset. It is not healthy to live in such a state of pain and negative energy, as overwhelmed people often cannot stop and see the positive in their lives. While overwhelming factors can negatively affect one's health, steps can be made to get back on track.

My recommendation is to take a step back, breathe and determine if all the activities and tasks that you are doing are really that important. The first thing to do is look at your life's purpose statement (*see Ch. 9-7*). Which of these tasks are in alignment with living that purpose? Can you remove some of them? Can you pass them on to others? Are you in a position to pay someone to accomplish the tasks that are taking up so much of your time? Consider how much you earn per hour and determine if you can pay someone less than that to get the task done.

Once you determine which tasks that *you* must accomplish, create a list. Some tasks repeat, some do not. Some have a deadline, some do not. Some are high priority, some are not. Categorize your tasks by determining how important they are, and then consider how urgently they must be completed.

Many type A personalities, like myself, tend to fill up our schedules no matter what. It is how we live, how we breathe. We cannot sit around for long periods of time without feeling like we are wasting time (unless we are in *relaxation* mode). Voids in our schedules fill up within moments. That is not an issue as long as it doesn't cause stress and make you feel overwhelmed. You can be an intense individual (like I have been referred to as many times) but still have balance in your life.

I prove that every single day. In fact, I accomplish more tasks in a day than many do in a week. Yet I still make time to live a DREAM lifestyle, every day and live by the advice I give. For me, it is a non-negotiable. I know that I would not be nearly as productive with my required tasks in life if I didn't live the wellness lifestyle that I do.

WORKBOOK ACTIVITY *9 Hacks to Having a More Organized Life* Guide and Worksheet

BONUSES & RESOURCES After you read about the ULT in Chapter 9-3, you will have an opportunity to test drive the assessment at a significantly reduced rate and learn how important being organized is to you and gain access to multiple ways of creating more order in your life.

6-5

AMPLE OUTLETS FOR SELF-EXPRESSION

♫ NEW YORK STATE OF MIND

After a long day at the office, the first thing I like to do (when possible) is sit down at the piano and play one of my favorite Billy Joel or Elton John songs. That is the easiest way to get me into a "Zen" mood, relaxed mind and ready for family time.

In fact, when I was attending chiropractic college in Georgia, my piano was at my parent's house on Long Island and all I had in my apartment was a small keyboard. At the time, there was a huge warehouse music store called Mars. Mars used to sell instruments and sheet music, and they would allow their customers to play the instruments to try them out. When I needed to chill out, I would drive to Mars, grab some sheet music off the shelves and start jamming on the best piano they had for sale. I would sit there and play for hours at a time. The customers loved listening, and the staff sold many of those pianos and even some of the sheet music. Heck, they should have put me on payroll or at least given me a commission for providing free demos! But I was just happy to be able to play.

One day, a customer was listening to me play for at least an hour and kept bringing me different sheet music for her requests. It felt like I was the headliner at a piano bar! When I was finally leaving, she asked me if I could give her piano lessons. I told her that I did not know how to teach piano but thanked her for the job offer. She was very insistent. She asked me what I did for a living. I told her I was a chiropractic student and a personal trainer. She asked what I charged to train people. When I told her, she said, "I will pay you that to teach me piano. Just think of it as personally training me to play the piano." I set the expectations very low, but she still insisted so I agreed. That was my one and only piano student, but I did teach her for over a year, until she moved out of state. Just sitting down with her for 30 minutes per week gave me that music "fix" that I so craved.

Art and music are great forms of self-expression. It is crucial to express oneself through these means to better find, understand and further one's self-development and purpose. Art is a means of expressing one's emotions; this is very important as emotions can become tense if they are not expressed. Whether one's emotions are melancholy or ecstatic, expressing them through art is crucial in self-development and healing. Also, art and music are great ways to calm down and relax, especially if one is plagued with stress and work. Taking at least an hour every day to forget about work or stressful obligations and focusing on other creative outlets is important to relieve one from an anxious mindset.

Parents these days get so caught up in the daily routines to run the household and their own responsibilities that they do not take time to tap into their "artsy" side.

For me, I love to sit down to the piano and have my son listen, sing along, dance or bang on the keys with me. I'm not very good (or interested) in the crafty stuff, especially glitter, so fortunately Brooke enjoys it more for Zion's sake.

Maybe the next time you go to a music store for your kid's next lesson, check out some instruments and see if you want to take one up or improve on what you may have started when you were a kid. Perhaps you can even take a lesson the same time as your kiddos instead of just dropping them off.

The next time you are at a craft store with your kids, see if there are any crafts that interest you. How does making jewelry sound? How about coloring or painting? Maybe woodworking, sculpting or carving would be more interesting to you. I know for myself I would love to learn to sew, but for me, it's for more practical purposes because being short, my sleeves and pants are always too long! It is never too late to learn these skills, and many stores offer classes for adults. These are great opportunities for your "younger self" to work on interests that you never fully developed or experienced.

These are some examples of activities you can do with your children and create more bonding and intimate moments that also keep you away from technology. You can also do these activities on your own and get some more alone time.

Either way, focusing on these types of relaxing outlets can transport one from a stressful day to a fun, positive environment. Creativity is key to increasing and renewing the brain's function, cultivating a social life, and relieving stress. It can even help prevent memory loss.

Pursuing creative outlets is crucial for self-expression, development, and prosperity.

BONUSES & RESOURCES *8 Hobbies that Support Your Physical & Emotional Health* Factsheet

BONUSES & RESOURCES After you read about the ULT in Chapter 9-3, you will have an opportunity to test drive the assessment at a significantly reduced rate and learn what forms of expression you can tap into that will bring you more joy and relaxation.

6-6

MASSAGE

♫ FOOTLOOSE

I mentioned earlier that I get regular massages; it is not something I have time for, but it is enough of a priority that I make time for it. The healing powers of massage have been recognized as early as the 5th century BC, and even children benefit greatly. Various forms of massage were employed by ancient cultures in China, India, Rome, Greece and Egypt. It was in the last century that the ancient healing art has been embraced by the New World and transformed into modern day massage.

It has been demonstrated that massage is an effective service for reducing stress, pain, and muscle tension. Many recipients also suggest that massages help anxiety, digestive disorders, headaches, fibromyalgia, joint pain and enhanced immune function. Holistically, clients of massage claim it allows them to feel cared for, comforted, and connected. Massage promotes circulatory function, improves lymphatic flow, "loosens" tight muscles and joints, and promotes endorphins to be released within the brain. Massage is commonly used in conjunction with chiropractic care and other natural wellness services to relax the musculature surrounding the spine, allowing for optimal flow of nerve and spiritual energy throughout the body.

Some of the more popular massage therapy techniques include Swedish, deep tissue, sports massage, prenatal massage, trigger point therapy, reflexology and myofascial release.

Lymphatic massage is not as widely known but very important for the immune system. The lymphatic system is a component of the circulatory and immune systems and lymphatic drainage massages (a.k.a. manual lymph drainage, or MLD) increase the flow of lymph throughout the body and has been known to reduce toxins. Aside from the relaxation qualities of lymphatic massage, it has also been shown to increase immune function and help with certain conditions, including lymphedema, headaches, pain relief, skin issues and even cellulite. Not all massage therapists are trained the same in this technique, so I recommend you find someone who specializes in MLD.

All massage techniques mentioned above have been found to be beneficial and serve different purposes and people of all ages, including children. Be sure when choosing a massage therapist that you know which technique you desire and hire a therapist who specializes in that technique!

BONUSES & RESOURCES Access our provider directory for a massage therapist near you.

6-7

CRANIAL SACRAL WORK

♫ LOVE ON THE BRAIN

Approximately an hour following Zion's amazing homebirth, he started to cry non-stop. The midwife noticed that he had not been nursing and looked at Zion's mouth and saw he had tongue-tie. She said that Zion was likely to have a difficult time latching and that we should schedule an appointment to have it corrected as soon as possible. Given that it was a Sunday evening, we knew we would need to wait until the morning to schedule an appointment.

We thought that there was no way Zion could go that long without consuming food and did not know what to do. It just did not make sense to me. Every single cell of Zion was coordinated in such a divine way, we did not want to accept the possibility that he would be in need of medical attention this soon. After 30 minutes of constant crying, the midwife went home (as there was nothing else she could do for us). Brooke continued to try nursing, but Zion seemed to have no interest.

Brooke went into the shower, and I was in the bed with Zion on my chest. I began to pray and thank God for the wisdom to know what to do next. I then received inspiration and thought, "As a pediatric and family chiropractor, what do I do when practice members bring their newborns to me?" I had already adjusted Zion as soon as he was born, but then I thought it would be wise to try a technique I use on almost all newborns.

Knowing all of this, I began to perform SOT on Zion. Within minutes, he went right for my nipple and tried to get his first meal. I called for Brooke and asked her to get out of the shower to try to nurse him. He latched on and essentially did not let go for three years!

Craniosacral Therapy performed by massage therapists and Sacral Occipital Technique (SOT) by chiropractic doctors are techniques that use light touch to gently realign the synarthrodial joints of the cranium and base of the spine (sacrum). These joints connect bones by fibrous tissue and allow only little or no movement. While both practices are not identical, they have common purposes which have been known to regulate the flow of cerebrospinal fluid, relieving symptoms of stress and tension by stimulating the parasympathetic nervous system (*see Ch. 8-4*). (SOT has a complete chiropractic analysis and adjusting protocol that complements the craniosacral aspects.)

With both techniques, the provider lightly palpates the client's body, focusing on the communicated movements. As a result, many people describe feeling deeply relaxed during and after the session. Looking at these techniques through a holistic approach, they can help improve the entire well-being of an individual as it connects healing and the inter-connections of mind, body and spirit. They are an effective form of care for many illnesses, and are suitable for people of all ages (babies through the elderly), and can be effective in both acute and chronic situations.

Not only do these techniques calm babies, assist with nursing, sleep and digestive issues (colic included), but they also help with asymmetrical head shape (deformational plagiocephaly) which may have resulted from fetal positioning within the uterus or during childbirth.

BONUSES & RESOURCES Access our provider directory for a therapist that does cranial sacral work or SOT near you.

6-8

ACUPUNCTURE

♫ NEEDLES AND PINS

As a holistic healthcare provider, I was naturally curious about acupuncture, though initially hesitant to try it because I do not like needles. Acupuncture is a system of complementary medicine that involves pricking the skin or tissues with fine needles. It has been shown to be an effective tool for alleviating pain and helping various physical, mental, and emotional conditions.

Much like craniosacral work, acupuncture helps stimulate the parasympathetic nervous system (*see Ch.8-4*), which increases relaxation and all the benefits associated with it. Acupuncture is also often utilized for decreasing post-surgical pain. Other benefits reported from acupuncture include reduction in headaches, migraines, improving chronic and arthritic pain, overcoming insomnia, improving cancer and chemotherapy recovery, preventing cognitive decline, and supports fertility, pregnancy, labor, and postpartum health. Acupuncture is also very safe and effective for children and can be quite useful for issues mentioned above, as well as improving concentration and general relaxation.

Acupuncture is a service that we have offered at various locations of DREAM Wellness throughout the years, and I have had the opportunity to receive quite a bit. I can say with certainty that I rarely feel more relaxed than when I am on the table. In fact, some of my best meditations take place while those needles are stuck in me!

BONUSES & RESOURCES Access our provider directory for an acupuncturist that cares for the entire family.

6-9

MEDITATE, DON'T MEDICATE!

♫ LITHIUM

I have already mentioned in many instances throughout the book that there is a time and place for medication, but its use should be limited when possible. Rarely does medication get to the root of the problem and it often just serves as a temporary solution. Perhaps if people did more meditation, there would be less need for them to take so many medications.

Meditation is the action of thinking deeply or focusing one's mind for a period of time in silence or with chanting, for religious or spiritual purposes. For the goal of this book, I am suggesting it be used as a relaxation technique. Meditation makes your mind calmer and more focused. It can help you to overcome stress, as well as find inner peace and balance. It can help us learn how to transform our minds from negative to positive. As a spiritual person, I like to say that prayer is when I speak to God and meditation is when I listen (*see Ch. 9.20*).

Meditation reduces stress, improves concentration, and encourages a healthy lifestyle. Some say it helps them eat better, quit smoking and reduce alcohol and drug dependency. It promotes self-awareness, causing people to recognize their thoughts and emotions and detach themselves from the negative ones. It increases happiness and acceptance, and even slows aging.

I especially love that my son's preschool even teaches meditation to the children. It is a great way to get them to control their emotions better, calm down, rest more easily and create good habits.

I recommend everyone get into a daily meditation routine, even if it is only 15 minutes per day, regardless of age. Even starting small with sitting for 5 minutes is a great place to begin. When I meditate, I typically start by focusing on the things I am grateful for and my internal chant always starts with thanking God for three things in particular; first for this awesome thing we call life; second for my wife, Brooke; and third for our son, Zion. After I share many of the things I am grateful for, I then quiet my mind and listen.

The beautiful thing is, there is no right or wrong way to mediate, so just start. You will be glad you did.

BONUSES & RESOURCES *How to Meditate* Playbook
BONUSES & RESOURCES Learn about my favorite online meditation courses for adults and kids; and other meditation videos and guides.

6-10

YOGA

♫ EVERY BREATH YOU TAKE

I never did much yoga prior to moving to San Diego in 2006; now I'm hooked!

Yoga's origin is traced back to Northern India more than 5,000 years ago. It includes breath control, simple meditation and the adoption of specific body postures. It is widely practiced for health and relaxation, with the goal of harmony between the human mind and body, as well as humans and nature. Yoga is the *union* of the individual consciousness/soul with the Universal Consciousness or Spirit.

While there are still many traditional yoga studios in America, most are more "non-denominational" and have few elements of its religious, philosophical and spiritual origins. For most Americans, it is a form of exercise that keeps them grounded, flexible and relaxed.

Yoga is touted for its ability to increase flexibility, balance, muscle tone and strength. It improves respiration, energy and vitality, as well as helps people maintain a balanced metabolism. It also helps with weight reduction and cardio/circulatory health. Meanwhile, it can improve athletic performance and protect athletes from injuries.

Along with physical benefits, yoga helps the mind tremendously as well. Yoga can help people manage stress. Yogis report experiencing less stress, which can help reduce neck/back pain, sleeping problems, headaches. It also improves the ability to concentrate. Therefore, yoga can be very effective in developing coping skills and in reaching a more positive outlook on life. All in all, yoga creates mental clarity and calmness, relieves chronic stress patterns, centers attention and increases physical and mental awareness.

Rhythmic breathing is a breathing technique that has a repeating cycle of inhalation, exhalation and retention of air. Rhythmic breathing involves observing your breathing and simultaneously conditioning of inflow, outflow and retention of breath in a rhythmic pattern.

By practicing rhythmic breathing, the respiratory rate slows down to a relaxed state. This relaxes the body and reduces the wear and tear of internal organs. It is very good for relaxing the entire nervous system, and it is helpful in the letting go of the emotions and calming the mind. Rhythmic breathing is a tool I use often when sitting in traffic.

While a long daily commute can offer one solitude and alone time to reflect, it generally can be detrimental to your health and waistline. With longer commutes, anxiety and stress increases, and life happiness and satisfaction decreases. During a long commute, especially in traffic, your blood temperature temporarily spikes, and over time, rises overall.

For many that spend many hours in a daily commute, cardiovascular fitness also drops, and as a result, heart health declines over time. Your blood sugar and cholesterol rise, leading to the risks of diabetes and heart disease. Depression risks rise and quality of sleep declines. Also, back pain and aches become common after spending hours slouched in a confined seat. This places negative consequences on one's neck, back and posture. If you have a long daily commute, make sure you are taking the necessary steps to mitigate the potential negative health consequences. Yoga and deep breathing exercises are just a couple of helpful tools that mitigate the detrimental impact of long commutes.

Brooke and I would teach yoga moves to Zion when he was a baby, and he really learned to enjoy doing them. It was always fun to watch our two-year old in downward dog and other poses. That is one way to create a happy baby!

BONUSES & RESOURCES *The Power of Conscious Breathing to Transform Your Life* Guide
BONUSES & RESOURCES Learn about my favorite online yoga classes and other resources.

6-11

ESSENTIAL OILS

♬ LOVE POTION NO.9

Essential oils are concentrated hydrophobic liquids containing volatile aroma compounds from plants. Plant roots, leaves, stems, flowers, or bark are distilled by steam or water. The oils will have the characteristic fragrance and properties of the plant from which it was extracted, and it contains the true essence of the plant it came from. Not only does it contain the smell of the plant, but it also contains the plant's healing properties and other characteristics.

While the oils are still in the plant, they provide the plant with protection against predators and disease, which can translate into the properties of the oil. Therefore, essential oils can benefit the body in many ways. They have been shown to help cold/flu symptoms; relax the body and soothe muscle aches; help heal skin conditions; alleviate pain; balance hormones; and improve digestion. Some essential oils have even demonstrated the ability to help anxiety, by calming and soothing the nervous system. Some can also have antimicrobial properties that can help purify the air and kill pathogens. Used correctly, they can also help put your little one to sleep in no time.

It is important to note that because the oils have natural fragrances, many people tend to have allergies and sensitivities to them (*see Ch. 5-8*). Also, these oils used in high concentration can be potentially harmful, especially for babies and young children.

There are many people who distribute essential oils through various companies, and numerous distributors state that the oils can cure numerous health issues. While there is evidence to back up many of these claims, it is important to make sure you are receiving your health advice from a professional who has studied the human body and the effects of these oils extensively. Using the wrong oil on the wrong person at the wrong time can be disastrous. Conversely, using the correct oil at the correct time on the correct person can be magical.

BONUSES & RESOURCES *Essential Oils and Common Uses* Guide
BONUSES & RESOURCES Dive deeper into the importance of essential oils along with proper use from some of the leading experts in the field.

6-12

BIOFEEDBACK AND NEUROFEEDBACK

♫ FEEDBACK

Biofeedback is a technique used to learn how to control your body's functions, such as heart rate. With biofeedback, you are connected to electrical sensors that receive information about your body's biology. It enables people to influence their heart rate, blood pressure, muscle tension, brain waves, etc. Biofeedback is a therapy used to treat or prevent conditions including migraine headaches, chronic pain, high blood pressure and more. The idea behind biofeedback is that through harnessing the power of your mind and becoming aware of what is happening inside your body, you can gain more control over your health.

Biofeedback promotes relaxation, which can relieve several conditions related to stress. It can help people gain more control over their involuntary actions. According to research from the Institute of Psychiatry at King's College London, biofeedback has been found to treat conditions such as anxiety, autism, depression, and eating disorders. Biofeedback helps many of these chronic stress related conditions because it is effective as a natural stress relieving therapy technique.

Neurofeedback is a type of biofeedback that uses real time displays of brain activity, most commonly electroencephalography (EEG), to teach self-regulation of brain activity. While biofeedback relates to physical functions within the body, neurofeedback focuses on specific brain waves. Neurofeedback can assess the functioning of the brain and where it is not functioning properly. It is important to remember that anxiety is the symptom, not the cause. Neurofeedback looks for the cause, such as what specific pathways are under activated. Once this type of assessment locates the cause of the symptom, then a wide variety of methods and equipment can be chosen based on what is the best one specifically for your needs and neurological issues. Neurofeedback has been shown to help a variety of issues, including anxiety, panic attacks, stress, worry, fearfulness, sleep disorders, depression and learning problems.

* * *

REFLECTION OPPORTUNITY

It is extremely important to consider your living situation when it comes to proper relaxation. If you are not able to find moments of relaxation at home, think about what you can do to make changes. We all have tasks we must do at home as well, but in general your home should be a place of peace. If you live with others, whether it be family, friends or roommates, have a conversation with the others to see what you can do differently to create a calmer home.

Just like the woodchopper, it's okay to be very busy as long as you take care of yourself and remain productive. If you are generally a social person but feel burdened when you get invitations for activities and events, consider what is important in life. It's okay to say no to events or invitations if you need to recharge or alone time. Some seasons in life require you to say *no* more than *yes*. Think about whether your daily activities are wearing you down so much that you forget to enjoy life, friendship and relationships. Always remember to sharpen your axe!

How often do you wake up in the morning feeling rested? Is there anything you can do to improve the quality and quantity of your sleep?

How often do you feel like there just is not enough time to get everything done that needs to get done? Is there something you can do to prioritize your daily tasks?

What is the last thing you do before going to sleep for the night? Is it calming or stimulating?

What do you do to express creativity?

What are you teaching your children and how are you helping them get proper relaxation? Do they see you relax?

Are you experiencing conflict at work?

Are your children experiencing conflict at school?

Do you have frequent misunderstandings with your children? How about your spouse/partner?

Are you able to spend adequate time with your family?

KEY 3
EXERCISE

7-1

GET MOVING

♫ BURNING HEART

We do not stop exercising because we grow old—we grow old because we stop exercising. —Kenneth Cooper, MD, MPH, author of the best-selling book, Aerobics.

Not to compare myself to Rocky Balboa, the fictional boxing character created and portrayed by Sylvester Stallone, but we do have a lot in common. Okay, well maybe not a lot, but when I think about my first gym experience, I am reminded of the Rocky IV training scene in snowy Russia.

It was a typical cold New York December in 1988, and I had just gotten my driver's permit. My days started with me dropping my father off at the train station before 5:30 in the morning and then heading straight to the gym before school. The air was cold and the roads were icy. I knew that if I wanted to transform my scrawny body into something more substantial, I would need to start training like the *Italian Stallion*.

I would arrive at the gym before 6 a.m. and wait for the manager to open the doors, which sometimes was not until 6:15 or even later. There were days that we had to wait outside for so long that my workout partner and I began to train outside in the snow. Pushups, sprints, using backpacks as kettle bells; you name it, we did it. Over time, I became such a fixture at that gym that the owner eventually gave me the key so I could let myself and the other members in when the staff was late.

When I was growing up, however, I was always the last kid picked on any team. Sure, I played on soccer, baseball and other sports teams, but I was always the smallest and skinniest. And quite honestly, I was not very coordinated and therefore, not very good. My lack of confidence did not help either. The closest I got to being on the football field at this point in life was playing trumpet and baritone in the marching band.

When I turned 15 years old, there were two pivotal events that changed the trajectory of my life. First, I joined a martial arts studio. This is where I began to move my body, build confidence and gain coordination. It is also when I began to understand the importance of being disciplined and how that quality impacts every aspect of one's life. This was the beginning of an entirely new mental attitude. Second, my physical transformation began after being inspired by Arnold Schwarzenegger's first book, *Arnold: The Education of a Bodybuilder*.

It did not take long before my physique began to change, as did my attitude about myself. What also changed was the way others perceived me. I was still short, as I always will be, but I was no longer a "skinny little twerp." If not for this new appreciation for health and fitness, I truly believe that I would not be the healthcare provider I am today.

Once I "hit my stride," everything changed.

In my junior year of high school, I joined the wrestling team and won the very first tournament I competed in. Before my second match came around, I advanced to the varsity team where I had great success for Syosset High School.

Physical fitness went from something I was hiding from others when I first started to it becoming part of my identity. When I started at college, my fellow classmates did not know me as the unconfident horrible athlete, but as a fit guy who beamed of certainty. I was no longer last to be picked and people did not sigh out of disappointment when they got stuck with me on their team, unless it was basketball!

I began to help my fellow fraternity brothers in the gym, and I would out "bench" most of them, even the ones twice my size. Pound for pound, none of them could compete with me. When I was in chiropractic school, I helped pay my tuition by working as a personal trainer, and I helped transform the bodies, minds and overall health of hundreds of other people.

Who would have thought that this once "small, scrawny space cadet" would become a doctor of chiropractic, hold a master's degree in sports health science and author a book that would help countless of other people live their DREAM?

Never underestimate the importance that exercise and fitness can have regarding your health, your confidence and your entire life. During the COVID-19 pandemic, my son Zion would watch me workout at home, and I would even have him engage with me. At his young age, he is already aware of the importance Brooke and I place on physical activity and exercise. Like Zion, I was blessed that I learned about physical fitness early in life. However, it does not matter *when* you start, as long as you start!

7-2

MENTAL EXERCISE

♫ MIND GAMES

When people think of exercise in general, they think about physical activity. However, I want to emphasize the absolute need for mental exertion to also help curb the impact of premature aging.

I think we all know people in life who checked out prematurely; both physically and mentally. We see it all too often . . . people reach the retirement age and if they do not replace that void with other activities and relationships, it is not long before they expire. Whether it is their mind or body that goes first, the other is not far behind.

It is extremely important to remain physically active while on this planet, until your body is no longer able. There is usually something you can do until your very last breath. It is equally important to remain mentally sharp throughout your existence and to constantly input new information and stimulus daily.

Did you know that crossword and jigsaw puzzles release dopamine in the brain? Most people only think of dopamine as the feel-good hormone. However, it is also a neurotransmitter, which means it helps send messages between the nerves. Among many other roles, dopamine is responsible for learning and memory. Therefore, puzzles are a great way to create new pathways in the brain. Also, jigsaw puzzles help develop hand-eye coordination as well as fine motor skills. Zion has been doing puzzles since before he was two years old, and I know with certainty that it has aided in his development in so many ways.

Activities that stimulate one's mind also develop attention and concentration. Additionally, they develop thinking skills such as recognizing, matching, and problem solving. Playing board games has been shown to train the hippocampus and prefrontal cortex, which are the areas of the brain responsible for learning, memory, behavior, speech, planning, problem solving and reasoning. This is one of many reasons why it is very important for young kids to engage and actively participate in board games to develop the brain at a faster rate.

Reading books and magazines is also a great way to stimulate the brain. For example, reading in general reduces stress, stimulates the mind, and expands one's vocabulary. Any activity that engages and stimulates one's mind is advantageous for the present, and more importantly the future, whether a toddler or retiree!

7-3

PHYSICAL EXERCISE

♫ LET'S GET PHYSICAL

Physical exercise improves the quality of one's life. While the list of benefits from exercise is tremendous, a few are highlighted here. Consistent exercise controls weight by increasing metabolism and burning calories. The more skeletal muscle you develop, the more calories you will burn at rest. Exercise also combats health conditions and diseases by improving cardiovascular health and through the release of high-density lipoprotein (HDL) (*see Ch. 5-14*). This protein boosts good cholesterol, as well as decreases the amount of unhealthy triglycerides. Exercise also improves mood through the release of endorphins. It also increases energy and helps promote better sleep.

Physical exercise is an activity that requires effort, carried out to sustain or improve health and fitness. This includes any movement that works the body at a greater intensity than its usual level of daily activity. Exercise increases the heart rate and works the muscles.

When people think of exercise, they generally think of one or two things; huffing and puffing from cardio workouts or banging and thumping heavy weights from strength training. While both forms of activity are important, it is very common for certain people to enjoy one form of exercise and have incredible disdain for the other. There are a multitude of reasons for that, including a person's body type (*see Ch. 7-7*).

Physical activity, first and foremost, must be enjoyable. This is especially important when being active as a family. While physical fitness is a huge value for both Brooke and me, she would not be caught dead in the weight room of a gym. Conversely, while Brooke has successfully climbed more than 30 "Fourteeners" in the Colorado mountains (with more to come), my one hike above 14,000 feet was enough to give me tremendous respect for those who do that level of hiking, but also to know that I'm happiest in the gym.

Brooke and I are built very differently and enjoy different types of physical activity, yet we still find a way to create a culture of movement in our home as we raise Zion.

We all know of the typical cardiovascular equipment that one can use at the gym or home. The treadmills, ellipticals and rowers are examples of good ones. Then there are the aerobic type classes and activities that increase cardiovascular health.

When it comes to muscle strengthening, there are numerous options in the weight room that I enjoy, whereas Brooke prefers to take Barre, yoga and Pilates classes for strength and tone (which also incorporate cardio activities). In fact, many of these classes can now be done at home while streaming them for free or with a low-cost membership.

But what if you don't want to spend your time on a piece of equipment or in a class, especially since you can't do that with your kids?

The age of your children (and your current fitness level) will determine the types of activities you can do as a family. For some families, walking around the block is enough. Perhaps you can build up to an area with hills. If you have a child in a stroller, that extra resistance will do you some good. The more adventurous families can take hikes together, just be mindful of the terrain. It does not matter if the hike is long or short, as long as you do it together.

Play at the park with your kids. Kick the soccer ball, throw a frisbee or play tag. Heck, I never realized how good of a cardio workout you can get from flying a kite when there is not much wind. The sprints required to launch the kite and keep it in the air can do wonders for your heart rate!

Zion began balance biking at three years old thanks to advice from our friend Barrett. His son was pedaling on two wheels by his third birthday, and within a year, Zion was as well. We enjoy biking together on a regular basis. Biking is a healthy, exciting and enjoyable outdoor activity.

Exposing your children to physical activity at a young age will help set them up for life, especially if the activities are fun. If they are active in their youth, they will more likely be active adults. Enrolling them in activities they enjoy such as martial arts, gymnastics, dance and even parkour will teach basic skills of movement, flexibility, coordination and discipline. And then of course there are the typical sports so many children play, such as soccer, baseball, tennis, basketball and even water polo that build solid skills, teamwork and healthy competitiveness.

While many families do not have the financial means to enroll their children in some of these activities, many are offered through afterschool programs, local YMCA facilities and other community recreational centers that make it more affordable if not free. And then there are always pick-up games at the local parks where kids can participate. If the desire is there, there is usually a way of making it happen.

In the next sections, I will detail the different types of exercise to put the "science" behind it, but the biggest takeaway should be to keep moving and do it as a fun family activity. Being active with your family should not be a chore, it should be a blessing.

Staying in shape does not need to be burdensome. There are plenty of modifications that a busy parent can make in their current daily activities that are easy and do not cost money. To set you up for success, I have included my e-book, *Beyond the Gym*, for you to enjoy for free.

Prenatal and post-partum exercise is of vital importance. Most (although not all) of the activities we will be discussing in this book can be done during and after pregnancy with slight modifications. However, it is always important to talk with your trusted healthcare provider to ensure that the exercises and activities you are doing are safe for you.

BONUSES & RESOURCES *Beyond the Gym . . . Fitness Tips to Incorporate into Your Daily Life* E-Book

WORKBOOK ACTIVITY *Beyond the Gym* Worksheet

WORKBOOK ACTIVITY *Beyond the Gym Weekly* Checklist

WORKBOOK ACTIVITY *Designing a Health-Focused Workout Plan* Action Sheet

BONUSES & RESOURCES *What Parents Need to Know about Physical Activity and Their Teen*, Action Guide

BONUSES & RESOURCES *Top 10 Fitness Tips for Beginners* Action Sheet

BONUSES & RESOURCES *Family Fitness: Staying Healthy Together* Activity Guide

BONUSES & RESOURCES Access videos and handouts on specific stretches and exercises for adults and children.

7-4

CARDIOVASCULAR TRAINING

♫ HEARTS ON FIRE

Whether it's in a fitness class, on a machine or as a family activity, you should aim to do at least some form of cardiovascular activity at least 4–5 times a week. It is important to continuously partake in cardio activity as its benefits are short lived and it must be kept up. People start to lose its physiological and psychological effects after only a couple days.

These activities stimulate the heart and respiratory (breathing) rate to increase in a way that can be sustained during the session. Aerobic exercise is a great way to improve cardiovascular health as it requires the pumping of oxygenated blood by the heart to deliver oxygen to the working muscles.

A key element to properly doing aerobic exercise is to know your heart rate through the workout. I know this is not practical in most cases, but it is valuable to be aware of. The magic happens within certain zones of your maximum heart rate, so having a heart rate monitor when doing cardio is highly recommended. For cardio exercise to be most beneficial (in most cases), you want to remain in the zone of 55%– 80% of your maximum heart rate. A quick and easy formula to determine your maximum heart rate is by subtracting 220 minus your age. Once you have that number, multiply it by the percentage you want to exercise at to get your zone. Exercise aficionados will actually increase and decrease the intensity of their activity throughout the workout to sometimes be at the higher range (closer to 80%) and then at the lower range (closer to 55%) when needed; but they make sure not to go above or below for any substantial period of time.

It is important to not go over 85% of your maximum heart rate as it becomes stress inducing at that point. At more than 85% max heart rate, your adrenal glands can start to produce the stress hormone cortisol, which can lead to chronic inflammation and even cause you to breakdown muscle tissue, leading to fat gain around your belly, a decreased libido and negatively impact fertility. Additionally, all the negative effects of being sympathetic dominant (fight or flight, *see Ch. 8-4*) can come into play if you get to a point of long-term cortisol production.

Aerobic activities vary in their level of intensity, which is why it is important to know your heart rate. Generally, you should aim to aerobically exercise for 10–30 minutes each interval (depending on the type of activity you are doing), no more than 60 minutes or that too can cause cortisol levels to rise. You should gradually increase your aerobic exercise durations and/or intensities over time as you build up endurance; however, remain within the proper target heart rate zones. For example, if you never swim, then doing 3 laps at a moderate speed may cause you to be at 75% max heart rate. However, after doing that weekly for 3 weeks, you may be able to do the same number of laps at the same speed and only be at 50% max heart rate. This is where you would either want to increase the number of laps, the speed of your swim or a combination of both.

Examples of cardiovascular/aerobic exercises that keep you within 55%–85% max heart rate include (but certainly not limited to) a brisk walk, slow jog, moderate swim and dancing.

High intensity interval training (HIIT) is a very popular form of aerobic activity. HIIT is a cardio session that contains short bursts of intense workouts. Each set is typically 20–90 seconds long and people should be pushing themselves to their full potential/max limit. (The high intensity portion of the set is commonly a 30–60 second burst, followed by a short rest until the next set.) Because HIIT consists of using one's own body weight most of the time, it improves both endurance and strength development. It is the perfect combination of working your "show muscles" (the muscles that make your physique look good) and your "go muscles" (the muscles that provide for strength and stamina). Rest periods within each interval/set are crucial because they are used to prep the body again for the next interval and to keep your heart rate within the proper zones. You can get the benefits of a HIIT workout in as few as eight minutes if done properly.

Many exercises that often fall into the HIIT category include sprinting, biking, running stairs, pushups, jumping jacks, jump rope and more. HIIT is both a muscle-building and fat-burning exercise. HIIT should not be done more than 3 times a week, as too much can inadvertently harm one's health; going overboard on HIIT can increase cortisol production, weaken the immune system and tamper with strength gains.

While it may not be appropriate to put a kid on a treadmill, cardiovascular activity is just as important for them. Make sure your child has plenty of time to go outside and play. Kick a ball, ride a bike, run a lap or just play tag.

If you want your child to be more active, it helps to let them see you being active. If you are sitting on a couch or computer all day, that is what they will mimic. Too many kids are inside playing video games and not getting the physical activity they need. Teach your kids the value of activity and let them see it firsthand.

BONUSES & RESOURCES Access our provider directory for a personal trainer near you.

BONUSES & RESOURCES Check out online personal training courses at a reduced rate.

BONUSES & RESOURCES Visit our online store for cardiovascular training equipment to purchase at a reduced rate.

7-5

RESISTANCE/STRENGTH TRAINING

♫ PUSH IT!

Resistance exercise is any form of exercise that requires one's skeletal muscles to contract. External resistance with weights, for example, is done to cause contractions that lead to an increase in muscular mass, strength, and definition, as well as stimulate bone strength. It is done to improve, sculpt and increase the size of skeletal muscles. Resistance training strengthens muscles because it makes them work against a force or a weight.

Choosing the right type of resistance exercise is important, not only for your enjoyment but also for optimal results. I also recommend changing up your routine on a regular basis to continually "shock" the muscles and encourage continued progress.

Not only is the type of equipment you use an important factor in your results, but also the amount of rest time between sets, the number of repetitions in each set, the type of muscle contraction during that set and the rest time between sets.

Personally speaking, my routine contains a combination of free weights using barbells and dumbbells (bench press, military press, squat racks, curls); weight machines (hamstring curls and extensions, calf raises, chest press); and body weight exercises (sit-ups, pull-ups, chin-ups, push-ups). As mentioned earlier, my wife prefers Barre style classes.

Regardless of the way in which you choose to partake in resistance training, it is important for the routine to include certain types of movements and contractions. The typical concentric type of contraction is where the muscle that is shortening is the one with greatest resistance. This generally builds size in the muscle. You also want to add eccentric contractions, where the concentration is on elongating the muscle and done at a slower speed. These are referred to as *negatives* and typically increase strength as opposed to size. (These also create the most amount of muscle soreness the next day.) Then there is the isometric contraction where the body part remains still. Think of this as the type of contraction you would do if holding a squat position for many seconds, or if you were showing off and flexing your muscles. These contractions are good for maintaining strength but will not usually increase strength or size. Those are especially great to do when you do not have access to a weight room and do not want to lose muscle when unable to do a full workout for a period of time (such as when traveling).

Rest periods depend on the goal of the routine at the time. The more you rest between sets, the more weight you should be able to lift. The less you rest, the lower the weight you will be able to lift. However, with shorter resting periods, you will gain the benefit of more cardio fitness. It is important to clearly know your goal before starting your routine so you get the best results. Also, goals can and should change frequently so your exercise program should never get stale.

Details of these are easily available with a quick internet search. I do recommend that if this is new for you or you are looking for different results than you achieved in the past, hire a personal trainer for the best results and for safety. If you are experienced, there are a lot of great apps that have programs you can subscribe to and go to the next level.

In general, you should train with resistance exercise at least 2–3 times a week to reap the most benefit. A good workout routine can be accomplished within 20 minutes each time.

Aside from looking good, resistance training has a ton of health benefits, including maintaining optimal body weight through increasing metabolism, increasing strength and stability of the spine and body, and it also helps get the most out of your cardiovascular exercise.

Strength training can start at any age for children, but of course you do not want to use heavy objects that would be too strenuous before they are teenagers. You do not want to injure growth plates that can stunt the child's growth or injure their joints and ligaments that have not yet fully turned to bone. At first, building value is more important than building muscle. Explain to your child why you are exercising and what value it brings to your life and health. Many of the activities mentioned earlier will lay a foundation for increasing strength and muscle tone.

As your children develop and gain coordination, start teaching them how to do lunges, squats and other functional movements (with only their body weight at first) to develop balance and lower body strength. Make it fun for them. Then teach them planks and sit-ups for developing their core muscles if they seem interested. They can push against an exercise ball to simulate the push-up exercise and modified chin-ups to work on upper body muscles.

Once your children reach 7 or 8 years old and they have better body awareness, add a little more resistance so they can start to build a little bit of muscle tone. It is extremely important to make sure your children are using perfect form and technique as the habits they create now will be with them for years to come.

If your child cannot perform at least 15 repetitions of a set in perfect form, then the weight should be decreased. I am not recommending your pre-teen become a bodybuilder. They just need to enjoy the process and understand the value.

BONUSES & RESOURCES Access our provider directory for a personal trainer near you.

BONUSES & RESOURCES Check out online personal training courses at a reduced rate.

BONUSES & RESOURCES Visit our online store for resistance training equipment to purchase at a reduced rate.

7-6

STRETCHING/FLEXIBILITY TRAINING

♫ STRETCH IT!

Other elements of a well-rounded exercise routine should include proper stretching, stabilizing and balance activities. This is also important for parents and children alike.

Every workout, whether its cardio or strength training, should start with a brief warmup to get the muscles ready for a light stretch routine and should finish with a cooldown and stretching. The activities for kids mentioned earlier, such as dance, martial arts and gymnastics, will automatically increase a person's flexibility. Regardless of what you are training on a particular day, you should at least do a few minutes of light stretching of the neck, shoulders, hips/low back and legs. Each stretch should be held for at least 30 seconds for the cold muscles to be oxygenated properly by getting the blood flowing, which will give you a burst of energy. Take your muscles through their proper and complete range of motion to increase flexibility, and you can even do this with resistance. Depending on the workout you are about to do would determine exactly which body parts you should stretch and how to stretch them, but the areas mentioned above should be done no matter what.

While stretching may not focus primarily on endurance or strength, stretching regularly helps decrease muscle pain and soreness, provides additional freedom of movement, increases flexibility and prevents avoidable injuries. Stretching should be done for at least 15 minutes each time, no fewer than three times per week—the more, the better. Your fitness routine should also include exercises that work on stability and balance. Most core and abdominal exercises fall into this category, but it can also include motions that require standing on one foot, heel-to-toe walking and many yoga poses (*see Ch. 6-10*). If you started and/or finished every workout with 15 minutes of various yoga postures, you would be way ahead of the game as yoga incorporates stretch, balance and stability exercises.

It is easy to do yoga at home, especially with all the online classes. Invite your children to join you and start teaching them the benefits that come with it. Zion loves to do yoga with us, and it is especially fun when he takes it seriously. Other activities that will complement your workout routine include Pilates, Tai Chi and many forms of martial arts, as well as movements referred to as somatic techniques, which include Rolfing/structural integration, Alexander Technique and the Feldenkrais Method. Balance training maneuvers help improve not only your balance but also your core strength and stability.

BONUSES & RESOURCES *Increase Your Flexibility in 30 Days or Less* Activity Guide
BONUSES & RESOURCES Access videos and handouts on specific stretches and exercises.

7-7

BODY TYPES

♫ BORN THIS WAY

We are all unique and perfect in our own way. However, a person's body image can either break them down, leading to low self-esteem and depression, or it can do the opposite, as it did for me as a teenager. In recent years, "Hollywood" has become more aware of this and its impact on society and has made tremendous efforts at celebrating people of all shapes and sizes. Without getting into the psychology and its impact on an individual's mental health, whether a child or adult, it is important to understand that because we are not all born with the same type of body, the food we consume and the exercise we do should vary.

While some people gravitate to one or two of the types of exercise mentioned in the previous sections, all are important to incorporate into your routine. However, based on your body type, it is likely that you should focus more on certain types over others, even if they are not your favorite or in your wheelhouse. Not knowing your body type is one of the most common reasons why people who are committed to an exercise regimen and meal plan do not get the desired results.

Most people do not realize that there are three different body types . . . all of which burn fat, metabolize food and build muscle differently. Everyone has elements of the three body types in them, but ultimately fall more within one category or another.

Ectomorph: If you are an ectomorph, you are probably slender and have trouble gaining weight, no matter what you eat. You need to focus more on weight training and less on cardio, as the cardio activities will cause you to burn the protein and carbohydrates you consume. You do not want to avoid cardio exercises altogether, as it is important to keep the heart, lungs and other organs healthy. You just need to not overdo it.

Endomorph: The endomorph reading the paragraph above wishes they had those problems. It is very likely you cannot keep weight off, no matter how hard you try. While you typically put on more muscle than the others, fat often accompanies it. You will need to do more cardio exercises along with some weight training. The muscle is important to build because muscle burns fat while resting and aids in metabolism, but you do not want to overdo muscle building. Too much cardio for the endomorph, however, can be deleterious because if you work too hard, you can cause your adrenal glands to fatigue and release cortisol, and this in turn can actually cause weight gain, particularly around the belly.

Mesomorph: The mesomorph fits between the two. You "mesos" get the best and worst of both worlds, but being fit for mesomorphs definitely comes easier. You should do a relatively equal combination of both weight training and cardio activities. When weight training, mesomorphs should lift moderate to heavy weights and keep their heart rate at a moderate pace.

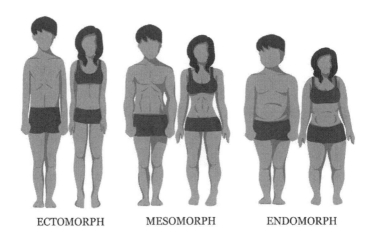

ECTOMORPH   MESOMORPH   ENDOMORPH

(It is important to note that most people do not fit squarely into one of the categories. Most people are a blend of two. The body type that is most prominent would be listed first and the less prominent would be second. For example, someone who is both meso and endo but a bit more mesomorph, would be a meso-endomorph.)

As someone who paid his way through chiropractic college as a personal trainer, I am an advocate for everyone to consult with a personal trainer at least once every few years. While not everyone can afford one-on-one training, many trainers offer small group training, which not only lowers the cost but also may increase motivation and accountability. Also, many trainers are now offering individual and group session via video, which became very popular during the Covid-19 pandemic.

I would not personally consult with a trainer who does not consider your specific body type from the start. While you can visually see what someone looks like, there are various questions that should be answered in a survey/questionnaire form that will confirm your actual body type. The trainer will then know exactly what he/she is working with and create an appropriate fitness and possibly meal plan for you specifically. Generalizations are good guides, but specifics will help you reach your goals much more easily.

The amount of physical activity that you engage in on a regular basis is truly a choice (excluding people with actual physical limitations). Not all exercise has to take place in a gym or on a track. Our daily activities play a huge role. Are you choosing to take the stairs or take an elevator/escalator? Do you park close or further away from your destination? Even when you are on vacation, staying in motion is essential for the growth and sustainability of your overall health.

The bottom line is, you need to be training and stimulating your mind and body every single day, even if for only 30 minutes!

BONUSES & RESOURCES Take the online survey to determine your body type, FREE!

REFLECTION OPPORTUNITY

What kinds of activities do you participate in to keep your mind sharp?

How often do you exercise and stretch? Is it enough to be your best self, or could you do more?

Do you eat and exercise appropriately based on your body type?

What can you do differently starting today to get more exercise?

Do you set a good example for your children when it comes to physical activity? What physical activities do they engage in (if age appropriate)?

What type of physical activities do you and your kids enjoy that you can all do together?

KEY 4
ADJUSTMENT

8-1

STRAIGHT TALK

Throughout this book, I hope that I have made it abundantly clear that the purpose of the DREAM lifestyle is to avoid and neutralize chemical, physical and emotional stressors. Whether it is a newborn baby or a retiree, all who do not adapt to these stressors will likely have problems, whether the signs and symptoms are obvious or not.

Because your nervous system controls and coordinates the function of every other system in your body, it is essential to be in *adjustment* to experience optimal health. The same goes for your kids.

Perfect health is not possible when the brain-body communication is interfered with. There are many dimensions to being in *adjustment* (as discussed earlier) that impact your life physically, mentally, emotionally and spiritually. Remember, two components of being in *adjustment* include *alignment* and *atonement* (*see Ch. 4-1*), both of which have strategies covered within the other four keys to ensure their optimization.

When you are consciously living and have appropriate balance within *diet*, *relaxation*, *exercise* and *mental wellness*, ultimately you should remain in *adjustment*.

This next section will delve deeper into the nervous system's role in your health and quality of life.

8-2

NEUROSPINAL WELLNOLOGY

♫ MORE THAN A FEELING

As one of my mentors, Dr. Patrick Gentempo would say, "You live your life through your nervous system." What he means by that is every organ, every muscle, every gland, every tissue and every cell in your body knows exactly what to do, when to do it and how to do it because the brain tells it so. Your digestive system, reproductive system, musculoskeletal system, endocrine system, cardiovascular system, respiratory system and your immune system are all examples of systems in your body that are under direct control of your nervous system. Every flower you smell, every book you read, every kiss you feel, every treat you taste and every emotion you feel is processed through the nervous system.

For example, if your brain wants your lungs to pump oxygenated air throughout your body, simply put, the brain sends electrical messages down the spinal cord, out the phrenic nerves (found in the neck) and tells the diaphragm (which sits just below each lung) to contract so you can inhale. The diaphragm then relaxes to allow you to exhale. If the phrenic nerves were cut, what do you think will happen to your ability to breathe?

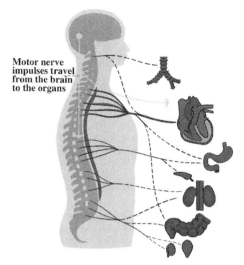

Motor nerve impulses travel from the brain to the organs

That's right, the lungs will eventually stop pushing fresh air to your body.

Do you think that is good or bad for your health? Yeah, really bad!

Now, instead of *cutting* the nerves that go to the diaphragm, what if something put stress on those nerves? Do you see how that would affect your health negatively as well?

Your body consists of a combination of both motor and sensory nerves. Motor nerves do not feel any pain and only a portion of the sensory nerves transmit information related to pain. Therefore, if there is tension in the nervous system at any location, it can affect your health negatively and ultimately your expression of innate intelligence (*see Ch. 3-1*) will be diminished, whether you *feel* it or not.

8-3

THE IMPACTS OF STRESS

♫ KILLING ME SOFTLY

We have all heard that stress is a silent killer. I believe that stress is not just a silent killer but also the primary killer. When we learned about the 10 leading causes of death (*see Ch. 5-9*) in the United States, with the exception of a congenital, genetic, or accidental origin, most deaths can be related to the inability to adapt to some form of a chemical, physical or emotional stressor.

Some indications of stress impacting your life can be demonstrated as sleep difficulties, insomnia, fatigue, lack of energy and anxiety, depression, overwhelm, memory fog, forgetfulness, high blood pressure, low resistance/weakened immunity, digestive issues/irritable bowel, weight gain/belly fat, chronic achiness, food cravings/addictions, headaches, feeling judgmental/negative/picky, cold hands or feet, hormonal imbalances, poor concentration, racing mind, mood swings and accelerated aging.

These signs and symptoms are typical manifestations of the autonomic nervous system being out of balance.

The autonomic nervous system (ANS) is the part of the nervous system comprised of motor nerves that functions *automatically* to control your organs and glands. The ANS has two parts: sympathetic which is known as "Fight or Flight" and parasympathetic, known as "Rest and Digest."

If you were to sit quietly reading this book and you heard a loud explosion, how will your body respond physiologically to the unexpected noise? Or how about your kid taking an exam at school?

The heart will beat quickly, lungs will pump air more rapidly, pupils will dilate, digestion will slow (if not completely stop) and the adrenal glands will produce adrenaline.

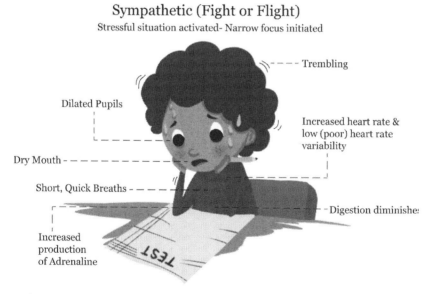

Sympathetic (Fight or Flight)
Stressful situation activated- Narrow focus initiated

Trembling

Dilated Pupils

Increased heart rate & low (poor) heart rate variability

Dry Mouth

Short, Quick Breaths

Digestion diminishe[s]

Increased production of Adrenaline

Is this reaction a good thing or bad thing?

The reason that this reaction is called "fight or flight" is because your body is physiologically preparing to fight an assailant (which in many cases is equivalent to taking an exam) or flee a situation. Those physiological changes mentioned above happen because if you are fighting or fleeing, you need have more blood to pump through the body, more bursts of air, better visual acuity and more immediate energy, and of course, you don't want to waste time breaking down food. Those are completely normal and important reactions to a stressful situation.

The problem is, too many people are stuck in fight or flight when they are not supposed to be or when at rest. This is referred to as being *sympathetic dominant*. If the parasympathetic nervous system is not allowing the body to rest, repair and digest as illustrated below, then a litany of issues may arise, such as the ones above.

Parasympathetic (Rest and Digest)
Calm situation activated- Broader focus enabled

Stimulates flow of Saliva

Normal heart rate & high (normal) heart rate variability

Normal Breathing Patterns

Adrenaline Secretion Normalizes

Digestive activity normalizes

I find more and more adults and kids stuck in sympathetic dominance (*see Ch. 8-4*) than ever before, and it is not typically caused by a lack of Ritalin, Adderall or other psychotropic medications in their bodies.

Here is what you and your family can do to ensure proper ANS balance:

1) Avoid as many stressors as possible that were previously mentioned and illustrated in this book (see opening of Part II, Wellness Wikis)

2) Find out, regardless of how you feel, if your ANS is out of balance. There are different types of tests out there that help determine balance within the ANS. Some tests measure blood pressure while doing particular activities and positions. There are sweat tests and various reflex tests. My absolute favorite marker of autonomic balance, and probably the easiest and quickest to perform is heart rate variability (HRV). This technology is used in DREAM Wellness centers and thousands of chiropractic offices and wellness centers around the world.

The next section will provide greater insight into the ANS balance.

8-4

BALANCING THE AUTONOMIC NERVOUS SYSTEM

♫ VIVA LAS VAGUS

Medicine has been trying to catch up with scientists' knowledge of sympathetic dominance for decades. Sympathetic dominance, or paroxysmal sympathetic hyperactivity (PSH) is a syndrome of increased sympathetic nervous system activity, causing the individual to essentially be in "fight or flight" more often than not. In fact, a vast majority of medications currently prescribed for disorders affect the autonomic nervous system in one way or another.

One common medical treatment for sympathetic dominance is the use of a vagal stimulator. Vagus (or vagal) nerve stimulation (VNS) is a treatment that involves delivering electrical impulses to the vagus nerve. The vagus nerve is the longest nerve of the ANS and controls parasympathetic function to the heart, lungs and digestive system, to name a few. VNS is used to treat dozens of conditions, many of which were mentioned earlier. The general idea behind VNS is essentially to stimulate the vagus nerve to activate the parasympathetic nervous system, which in turn would calm the sympathetic nervous system.

Another more recent medical treatment is the use of Botox; yes the same stuff used to iron out the wrinkles for those who have not discovered the natural fountain of youth. Botulinum toxin is a neurotoxic protein produced by the bacterium Clostridium botulinum and related species. It prevents the release of the neurotransmitter acetylcholine from axon endings at the neuromuscular junction and thus causes flaccid paralysis. Essentially, the goal of the Botox with this treatment is to paralyze and shut off the sympathetic neurons in order to bring the parasympathetics to the forefront.

While there may be some benefits from both treatments above, it is important to note that all medical interventions come with some form of risk of adverse reactions and side effects. Additionally, I question the need for some people that undergo some of these treatments and how the doctor is determining why the person is sympathetic dominant.

One of my colleagues, Tony Ebel, DC, puts it in a really easy way to understand. Is the person sympathetic dominant because he/she has the foot stuck on the gas (over stimulation of sympathetic nerves) or because the brakes do not work (an issue with the vagus or other parasympathetic nerves)? Either cause may require a different course of care.

In the chiropractic world, for example, we determine where the subluxation(s) exist and adjust accordingly (see Ch. 8-5). Sometimes we only adjust the spinal areas of the upper cervical and/or sacrum by the parasympathetic nerves, and sometimes we adjust in the midback where the sympathetic nerves live. Sometimes we adjust both based on the subluxation pattern. By knowing this, the chiropractor can determine the appropriate areas and make corrections to help restore ANS balance, in a natural way!

In an article published by one of my mentors Christopher Kent, DC, Kent concluded,

> Vertebral subluxations may result in autonomic dysregulation, compromising the adaptive capacity of the organism. By analyzing and correcting vertebral subluxations, a patient is placed on a more optimum physiological path, potentially Increasing resilience and adaptability. Further research into the effects of vertebral subluxations on mental health, the neurobiological mechanisms involved, and the use of reliable and valid outcomes assessments should be undertaken. It is biologically plausible that vertebral subluxations compromise nervous system function and affect mental health.[11]

In addition to chiropractic care, other natural, non-invasive ways of helping balance the ANS include, but not limited to, cranial sacral work, massage, acupuncture, biofeedback, neurofeedback, sleep, meditation, mindfulness, prayer, nutrition, functional medicine and exercise.

We all know that feeling when something scary or exciting is coming. Your heart starts racing, your palms get sweaty and you can barely breath. For you, it may be a meeting with your employer. For your kid it may be a big test. Whatever the reason is that you have been thrown into a fight-or-flight situation, there are quick "biohacks" you can do to calm down, as it is not likely that you will be able to get a quick chiropractic adjustment. Try any or all of these and please, share these tips with your kids.

- Take a series of eight to ten long deep breaths (five second inhale, ten second exhale).
- Rub your eyes.
- Drink water (or anything that will get you to swallow . . . heck, you can even swallow your own saliva if no liquid is around).
- Shrug your shoulders up to you ears and hold for five seconds. Repeat 3 times.
- Make weird facial expressions (start with smiling), then raise your eyebrows and then squint. Hold them for five to ten seconds.

The reason these seemingly silly acts work so well is because the muscles that are used during these actions are controlled by the cranial nerves that control the parasympathetic nervous system.

8-5

HEALTHCARE'S UNSUNG HERO

♫ COME TOGETHER

It was December 1999 and I was set to open my first chiropractic practice with my buddy from chiropractic college, Dan Matzner, in Great Neck, New York, on Long Island. Yes, I know . . . Great Neck is an awesome place for a chiropractor, just based on the name of the town. In fact, the name of the practice was Great Neck, Better Health Chiropractic. I liked the play on words.

Construction was delaying our opening as it often does, but I already had an advertisement in the local Penny Saver offering a special for the community to see me for a chiropractic examination. Weeks before I was able to start seeing people in the office, I received a call from Mary. Mary told me that she was dealing with upper back pain which started when she was a high school swimmer and wanted to finally get the pain resolved. She also relayed to me that she was a physical therapist and she did not "believe" in chiropractic. I then asked her why she was calling me. (I wondered for a moment if she was just *taunting* me or if maybe this was a prank call.)

She told me that she had done physical therapy and regular *medical* care for it, but nothing helped, and friends encouraged her to see a chiropractor. I then asked her why she did not believe in chiropractic, and she said that during her training as a physical therapist, some of her instructors didn't speak kindly about the chiropractic profession.

I explained to her that our goals may not be in complete "alignment" and that she would need to understand my intention and agree to it before I would consider taking her on as a practice member. (I refer to the people I take care of as practice members because the word patient means to suffer . . . and so I like to use positive words as illustrated earlier in the book.) I told her that while she may be dealing with back pain, my job would be to analyze her nervous system and see if subluxations were present, and if so, I would work to help correct them.

Vertebral subluxations are dysfunctions within the spine, typically caused by misaligned vertebrae, that place stress and tension on the nervous system. This tension essentially prohibits the brain from communicating perfectly with the rest of the body, which ultimately will affect one's health and quality of life.

I also explained that if her spinal subluxations were corrected, my performance would be a success whether her pain was gone or not. I noticed some surprise and even a little hesitation in her voice, but she agreed to at least continue the conversation. Additionally, I had to inform her of one other thing . . .

I told Mary that because the construction workers were behind schedule, I did not have an office to see her in. However, because I had a portable adjusting table and the technology I used to evaluate nervous system performance was rather portable, I could go to her home and do the exam there. While she was a little taken aback by that (after all, doctors rarely make house calls these days), she agreed and appreciated the gesture and convenience.

At her home, I set up my equipment and began to ask her questions about her overall health and health history. She shared a lot, but not everything. Upon palpation of her spine, I felt areas throughout that were not moving the way they should—indicating what we call *fixation* or *stuck* vertebrae—some where she had pain and some where she did not. I then ran a couple of tests on her and gained further insight. In fact, the technology used is called the Insight Subluxation Station, and at the time I was able to do a thermographic test and a surface electromyography (sEMG).

The thermal scan reads heat temperatures along the spine. Normal body temperature should be around 98.6°F and so it should be 98.6° on both left and right sides. If there is a significant difference on one side versus the other, that informs me that something unhealthy is going on with her autonomic nervous system.

The sEMG reads how much nerve energy (measured in voltage) is flowing from the brain, down the spinal cord, out the nerves to the muscles alongside the spine (paraspinal). Much like an ECG/EKG reads nerve activity of the heart, sEMG reads nerve activity of the muscles. (Note: It's not that I care a ton about the muscles themselves, but the nerve roots that contain nerve fibers that are feeding those muscles with the information may also contain nerve fibers that are feeding other body parts with information.) If there is too much voltage going to a particular muscle, it will likely over contract, tighten or spasm. Not only was I interested to see where there was too much or too little voltage (intensity), I also wanted to determine if there was more voltage on one side versus the other (balance).

All of the clinical findings during Mary's exam revealed that the greatest amount of nerve tension was actually in her upper cervical region at the base of her skull and her lumbar region (lower back), even though her symptoms were in the mid-upper back. Telling someone that their symptoms are not necessarily the problem is not always an easy conversation, especially for someone who, from the very beginning, does not believe in what you do. Somehow after all of this, she still wanted to receive her first adjustment.

I performed a very specific and gentle adjustment, and when I was done, I said, "Power's on." That is a phrase that many chiropractor's and I say after every single adjustment. That phrase is a reminder that "the power that made the body . . . heals the body." It is also a metaphor for a fuse box. When a circuit blows because of too much input (stress), it shuts off the power to protect against a fire. The way to know which fuse to switch back is simply to look at the fuses and see which one is out of alignment. (Next time you put a fuse back into place, say, "Power's on," and see how good it feels.) I want to make one thing clear; the power is never actually off in a living human being. The power is always on; it's just that the adjustment is now helping that person express the power more fully. I am reminding them of their perfection.

Following the adjustment, Mary got up and thanked me. She said she would think about everything I told her and decide if she would continue with *corrective* care and work toward long-term correction of her subluxations. This was not exactly the way I thought practice would be. I thought that I would make recommendations, they would accept and follow the care plan that I recommended, they would pay cash and refer all their friends and family. I was not prepared for the reality of subluxation correction not being everyone's priority! I was gracious and told her that I was here for her when she was ready if at all.

Two days later I received a call from Mary telling me that she wanted to start on a corrective care plan. I asked her what brought her to that decision. She told me that her pain was still there, but she actually got two of the best nights of sleep she'd had in years. I didn't know that she had trouble sleeping, but I went with it. I told her that I was thrilled that she was going to make a commitment to correcting her issues and that now the only other hurdle was where we would do the adjustments since the office was still not open. Because she was taking classes not far from where I lived, she would go to my home for some of the visits and I would go to hers for the others. This went on for almost two months until the office opened.

After receiving several adjustments in the office after it finally opened, I could tell that Mary was getting a little frustrated because her mid-back pain was still there. Some days were better than others, but it was not gone. I kept reminding her of the goal and she would agree. Then, after a few weeks, I got *the* call.

Mary called the office and asked for an extended appointment time so we could chat. She had to talk to me about something important. "Uh oh, what could this be about?" I thought to myself. Of course, I made up all kinds of stories in my head wondering what that could possibly be about, mostly imagining that she was still frustrated about her pain not going away. She came into the office with her husband

and, surprisingly, it was the first time I had met him. Remember, I adjusted her at their house several times, but he was always at work.

Before she could say anything, I said, "Mary, I understand you're frustrated. If you want, we can take X-rays and see if there's something else causing your symptoms or something that I am missing." She informed me that X-rays cannot be taken on her at this time. When I asked why, she said, "Because I'm pregnant," and then she proceeded to cry.

I stood there for a second like a deer caught in the headlights . . . eyes and mouth as open as you can imagine not knowing what to say. My heart was pounding, body was shaking and I was in total fight or flight because I could not understand why she was crying and why she brought her husband. The only words I could conjure up at that point were, "Mary, I had nothing to do with that and please make sure your husband knows!" The two of them looked at each other and then at me and started laughing hysterically. They then gave me a big hug.

Mary proceeded to tell me that she believed I had a ton to do with her pregnancy. She continued to tell me that she was informed years earlier that she was not going to be able to conceive a child. Apparently when I showed her the initial scan of her spine and told her what organs the areas of interference control (combined with her understanding of anatomy and physiology), a glimmer of hope arose for her, unbeknownst to me. She never told me about her fertility issues. Mary then let me know that after that first adjustment, "Something felt like it turned on," and that the only thing different in her life that could have impacted her fertility was her adjustments.

There are many morals to this story.

First, the goal of chiropractic care is not to get rid of pain. It is to improve function in your body and nervous system. If dysfunction is causing your pain or related to the cause, the pain will typically go away when the function improves.

Second, it is important to see a chiropractor who uses objective measures to determine what needs to be adjusted if anything. A good chiropractor does not need to know your symptoms to help you or your child. They just need to be competent and precise in the application of chiropractic principles.

Third, never lose hope when you are in the hands of a qualified chiropractor. Because there is no human function outside the realm of the nervous system, it is always worth ensuring that you are subluxation free, whether you have a symptom or not. It does not matter what *condition* you may have. If an issue is caused or complicated by vertebral subluxations, there's a good possibility that correcting them can help.

People hear stories like this all the time and ask, "Can chiropractic cure XXXXX?" My answer is always the same. We do not treat or cure any disease or condition. We help correct tension in the nervous system, and if that issue was caused by the tension, then the issue should resolve.

Then I hear, "So if that's the case, are you saying that someone with cancer should go to a chiropractor?" My answer again is pretty much the same. If someone has cancer, is he/she better off with or without nerve interference? It is not about treating cancer; it's about helping someone who has cancer. There is a big difference!

One of my favorite passages that sums up the chiropractic profession and how we can help humanity is summed up beautifully in the poem "This Inner Power Speaks" by the developer of chiropractic, B.J. Palmer, D.C., Ph.C. (1949) in *The Bigness of the Fellow Within*:

> We chiropractors work with the subtle substance of the soul. We release the prisoned impulse, the tiny rivulet of force that emanates from the mind and flows over the nerves to the cells and stirs them into life. We deal with the magic power that transforms common food into living, loving, thinking clay; that robes the earth with beauty and hues and scents the flowers with the glory of the air. In the dim, dark, distant long ago, when the sun first bowed to the morning star, this power spoke and there was life; it quickened the slime of the sea and the dust of the earth and drove the cell to union with its fellows in countless living forms. Through eons of time it finned the fish and winged the bird and fanged the beast. Endlessly it worked, evolving its forms until it produced the crowning glory of them all. With tireless energy it blows the bubble of each individual life and then silently, relentlessly dissolves the form and absorbs the spirit into itself again. And yet you ask, 'Can Chiropractic cure appendicitis or the 'flu'?' Have you more faith in a knife or a spoonful of medicine than in the innate power that animates the internal living world?

Doctors of chiropractic are the only licensed and trained healthcare providers that determine the presence or absence of subluxations and how to help correct them.

There is a lot of confusion and misinformation about the chiropractic profession as a whole and its uniqueness in the healthcare world. The next wiki was designed to help bring clarity to an often-misunderstood practice. It is my hope that after reading it, you will better understand how chiropractic can support you and your family in living the DREAM lifestyle.

8-6

A BRIEF HISTORY OF CHIROPRACTIC

♫ A STAR IS BORN

For a brief historical perspective of the profession, it is important to understand that its founder was not necessarily trying to create a new healthcare discipline. In fact, its founder, Canadian born Daniel David (D.D.) Palmer studied under the founder of Osteopathic Medicine, A.T. Still. Palmer at the time was involved in all types of different healing modalities, including magnetic healing, and he was always trying to find the cause of issues as opposed to just treating symptoms. He was particularly interested in the role that the nervous system played in one's overall health and well-being.

At a school D.D. Palmer was teaching at in Davenport, Iowa, he met a janitor named Harvey Lillard. Lillard was a deaf man who claimed that his hearing loss began after a fall off a horse. Intrigued by the nervous system and its role in all body functions, Palmer palpated Lillard's spine and felt certain vertebrae out of alignment. Palmer thought that if the vertebrae misaligned during the fall, then perhaps by realigning the vertebrae, hearing could be restored. Somehow, on September 18, 1895, Palmer convinced Lillard to allow D.D. to "rack" the bones in place, with the purpose of improving nervous system function. It was on this day that the first chiropractic adjustment was performed.

As a result of this historic first ever adjustment, Harvey Lillard's hearing was restored. Palmer thought that he had found the cure to deafness. He advertised far and wide, "Come to Davenport, Iowa, and have your hearing restored!"

Deaf folks came from all over the country, as they were willing to try anything to be able to hear again. Remember, this was the late 1800s, so getting there was no easy feat. Some of the people that came were deaf and blind, some were deaf and disabled, and some were deaf and had other health ailments.

While very few had their hearing completely restored, some were able to see again, some were able to walk again, and some showed significant resolution of their health issues.

It was at this time that D.D. Palmer realized that he had not found the cure to deafness. He found the cause of most health issues . . . interference to the nervous system caused by dysfunctions in the spine, and the chiropractic profession was born.

From a philosophical context, D.D. Palmer talked about chiropractic being founded on *tone*. He referred to the tone of the organs as well as the nerves. He claimed that a subluxated joint would cause tension to the nerve. This tension would impact the vibration, thus the tone.

From a musician's perspective, I have great appreciation to this concept as I understand that all objects, including every cell in your body, has a frequency at which it vibrates. When an object vibrates at a single frequency, it is said to produce a pure tone. As my friend Dr. Steve Lindner says, "When the tone is off, the chiropractor gives a 'tune-up' by delivering a 'fine-tuned' adjustment. Once tuned up by a chiropractic adjustment, the instrument (or the person) is 'recalibrated.' Tone is restored and the body functions in better harmony. T = the balance + One. T-One When you are in a state of balance you are one with yourself."

Remember, being in *adjustment* entails being in *alignment* and *atonement*. When the vertebrae are in alignment and all cells are vibrating at the correct frequencies, you are now expressing a-tone-ment.

To me, the goal of chiropractic is to help avoid tension in the nervous system thus enabling you to express perfect tone with every cell in the body. When you express pure tone, you can then act in harmony with everything else more easily.

This goes back to my initial definition of wellness . . .

The complete integration of mind, body and spirit affects not only your visible body parts but also the trillions of cells that make up your entire body. It is a proactive approach toward creating physical, mental, social and spiritual harmony.

BJ Palmer, the *developer* of chiropractic and son of D.D. Palmer said it so brilliantly, "While other professions are concerned with changing the environment to suit the weakened body, chiropractic is concerned with strengthening the body to suit the environment."

This is why I believe it is impossible to truly live a wellness lifestyle if you are not in *adjustment*.

CHIROPRACTIC TODAY

Over the past century, chiropractic has grown to be one of the largest non-allopathic form of healthcare in the United States of America.

While there is a wide variety of practice styles and philosophic constructs within the chiropractic profession, the ultimate goal of any chiropractor should be to have their patients/clients/practice members receive a natural way to restore function of the nervous system. Chiropractors analyze the spine and nervous system differently than any other healthcare practitioner and provide a unique perspective on how to care for that individual.

Manual manipulation of the spine and other joints in the body have been around for centuries. There are ancient writings from China and Greece dating between 2700 BC and 1500 BC mentioning manipulation and lower extremities to fix low back pain.

Hippocrates even published a text explaining the importance of manual manipulation. In one of his writings, he wrote, "Get knowledge of the spine, for this is the requisite for many diseases." Manual manipulation was also practiced in the ancient civilizations of Egypt, Babylon, Syria, Japan, the Incas, Mayans and Native Americans.

The difference between a manipulation and an adjustment comes down to the intent, the analysis and the technique.

A manipulation is essentially the movement of bones to increase range of motion, decrease pain and reduce inflammation. An adjustment, however, is a very specific form of manipulation intended to restore alignment and remove tension from the nervous system, ultimately the correction of a subluxation. Additionally, D.D. Palmer was the first to use certain parts of the vertebra (spinous process and transverse process) to realign vertebra to make a precise adjustment.

While some other healthcare providers, such as medical doctors, doctors of osteopathy, and even physical therapists and naturopathic doctors in some parts of the country may legally perform spinal manipulation, none of them can claim to be doing chiropractic. It is only a Doctor of Chiropractic who is duly licensed in his/her state that can refer to their care as a chiropractic adjustment. Additionally, chiropractic doctors use a very specific form of analysis to determine exactly what to move, when to move it, and how to move it.

Be very wary of anyone whether it is a friend, co-worker, massage therapist, personal trainer or other healthcare provider that wants to manipulate your spine, or "crack your back" (a term chiropractors despise for good reason), if he or she is not a chiropractor. It is extremely important to understand that the nerves that exit the spinal cord feed vital information to the various organs, muscles and glands, and by the non-specific movement of bones could actually create nerve tension, spinal instability and even pain. While chiropractors can improve the quality of life for so many people, a non-specific manipulation performed by an untrained professional can be disastrous.

. . . But can chiropractic help . . .?

There are countless chiropractic "miracle" stories, ranging from resolution of ear infections, colic, bedwetting and asthma in kids to infertility, migraines and high blood pressure in adults. There are also a lot of stories out there of chiropractors claiming to cure every disease under the sun. I would like to start by stating that the goal of chiropractic is not to treat or cure any pain, disease or condition. That said, there are few dis-ease processes and conditions that chiropractic care cannot positively impact if they are related to nervous system impairment complicated by improper spinal alignment.

I opened this book with the comical story of my very first patient as a doctor, Rocco the Great Dane (see Preface). You also learned about Mary, the very first patient in my office (*see Ch. 8-5*). I think it would be fitting to share with you my very first toddler I helped when I was a student clinician in chiropractic college.

As you read earlier, I worked at a local health club as a personal trainer to help pay for my chiropractic education. Becky worked at the pro shop of the gym and heard me talking to a club member about chiropractic. The person I was speaking with was raving about his chiropractic experience and how it helped his son overcome chronic ear infections. Overhearing our conversation, Becky asked if chiropractic could possibly help children with eczema and allergies, as her ten-month-old daughter had rashes all over her body for the past nine months of her life. Becky tried multiple treatments and medications with no success and really wanted to get her off the steroids, especially because they were not helping.

I explained to Becky that chiropractic does not treat those conditions (or any condition for that matter), but chiropractors have historically seen these issues resolve under their care, particularly if caused or complicated by subluxations. I invited her to the outpatient clinic at the college to have Laura checked out.

Becky scheduled the appointment but cancelled a day before we were supposed to evaluate Laura. Becky explained that her husband John, a police officer in a suburb of Atlanta, was not on board with his ten-month-old receiving chiropractic care. While Becky was extremely disappointed, she didn't want to create an additional confrontation in an already contentious marriage. After four weeks of additional suffering, Becky decided to make an executive decision and bring Laura, against her husband's wishes.

After the first adjustment, there was an immediate change in Laura's temperament; and after the third adjustment, the red scaly patches on her arms, legs and belly were gone, and her face had a new complexion. I could see that while Becky was elated by the outcome, she showed some concern. I asked her what was bothering her as she seemed conflicted about something. Becky told me that she never told John that she stopped giving Laura the steroids and started to see me. "Oh boy," I thought. I wondered how this was going to play out.

Becky decided to tell John the truth, and it led to another one of their big arguments. While John was happy that Laura was finally healing, this was just another blow to an already strained marriage. John agreed to allow Laura to continue care with me, but he was not happy, he didn't want to hear about it, and he would not step foot near the clinic.

I continued to take care of Laura and eventually Becky for months to follow. After a year of seeing Laura at the clinic, a tragedy was averted by the grace of God.

John was doing some landscaping around the house, removing a bunch of bushes that brushed up against the home. Laura, now almost two years old was watching daddy out of her second-floor bedroom window. I don't know the details of exactly what transpired next, but Laura fell out of the window. What broke her fall was the only bush remaining that John had not yet removed.

Becky and John rushed Laura to the hospital to get checked for broken bones, or worse. She was scratched up and quite shaken. When she got to the hospital, she would not let any of the emergency room doctors touch her. She was kicking and screaming on the gurney the entire time. Then John was finally able to make out what she was saying. She kept saying, "See Brian. See Brian." John and Becky were shocked. The doctors at the hospital were unable to take x-rays of Laura without sedating her, but based on how she was moving and acting, they felt she would be OK to leave. John asked Becky, "Do you think we should take her to see Brian?"

Becky called me right away, and they rushed her to the clinic. When I explained what was going on to the doctors on staff of the clinic, they made sure that everything was safe as they had never experienced anything quite like this with a student clinician.

When the family arrived, there were around ten clinic doctors waiting with me, just to see how this was all going to play out. We could hear Laura screaming from the car and as soon as she got to the entrance and saw me, she got quiet and hugged me. She laid on the table like a perfect angel and got a great adjustment.

John became a patient the next day.

I have been blessed to have many great stories to share from more than two-decades of family practice. There are tens of thousands of chiropractors around the globe with similar "miracles" that have taken place following the correction of subluxations. If this story inspired you and you want more, get a copy of *Chicken Soup for the Chiropractic Soul*, by Jack Canfield, Mark Victor Hanson and Dr. Fabrizio Mancini to read dozens more.

Here is the big takeaway. Not everyone needs a chiropractic adjustment. However, everyone needs a chiropractic doctor on their healthcare team to ensure that they are in *adjustment*. If someone visits the chiropractor, the purpose of that visit should be to get checked for subluxations. If a subluxation is not present, that person should be congratulated and sent on his/her way and invited back for a future check-up.

Technically, it is impossible to get over-adjusted. That is because, as mentioned earlier, an adjustment is a specific maneuver to reduce a vertebral subluxation. If a subluxation is present, it should be adjusted. But if a subluxation is not present, then by definition, an adjustment cannot take place. That would be like having a dentist fill a cavity that doesn't exist. If a person who did not have subluxations were to have their bones moved by someone, then that maneuver was actually a manipulation. It is extremely important to seek the care of a chiropractor who does specific forms of analysis to determine where and when a subluxation is present and then has a way to measure the resulting change after adjustments have been performed.

The cause of all vertebral subluxations can be summarized as the inability to adapt to chemical, physical and emotional stressors.

These stressors are found every day in life. The majority of this book, in fact, is designed to help you live the DREAM lifestyle which enables you to neutralize and avoid as many of these stressors as possible . . . so you can stay in adjustment and live your DREAM, every day!

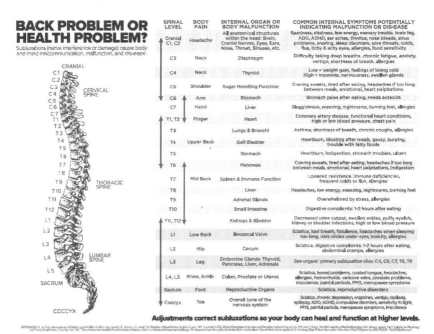

Illustration Credit: Russ Rosen, DC, *The Optimal Health Coaching System, copyright 2000*]

Above are some conditions that can be caused by (or a complicating factor of) subluxations and the respective part of the nervous system that may be compromised.

As mentioned prior, the purpose of chiropractic care is not to treat or cure any disease or condition. The goal is to reduce subluxations, and the causes of the subluxations when possible, so that the body's innate intelligence can express its perfection and let the body do what it needs to do. A saying many of us have in the profession is, "I move the bone, God does the healing."

WHO WOULD SEEK OUT CHIROPRACTIC CARE?

While all chiropractic care is salutogenic (*see Ch. 10-1*), meaning it helps build health, I typically put people into two different categories when it comes to potential recipients of chiropractic care, according to the reasoning of why they have chosen to visit a chiropractor:

- Someone with at least one symptom (migraines, ear infections, colic, back pain, digestive issues, sleep issues, etc.) that they feel chiropractic may help with.

  OR

- Someone without a "known reason" (symptom) for getting checked other than they learned that it is wise to visit a chiropractor for a checkup to ensure his/her nervous system is working optimally. Perhaps this person is a child or friend of an existing patient/practice member or just heard or read about it elsewhere (like this book). At the very least, every newborn baby should be checked by a chiropractor for subluxations as early as possible.

Because the nervous system controls and coordinates the function of every single body part, it should be universally agreed that everyone on the planet would benefit from having this system function optimally. Through the detection and correction of vertebral subluxations, chiropractors play an integral role in nervous system function, as well as that of the immune system.[12]

Therefore, it is vitally important for all babies and children to be checked by a chiropractor as early as possible. Chiropractic adjustments on babies are extremely different from adjustments on adults. In fact, the amount of pressure used on a newborn's spine is less than the pressure that would break the skin of a tomato.

Zion received his first adjustment seconds after entering this world. As he was exiting the birth canal, we saw that the cord was wrapped around his neck. Once I caught him and the midwife resolved the nuchal cord, my hands went right to his atlas (the top bone in the spine). Fortunately for Zion, his dad is a chiropractor. Think about all the children that are born with the cord around their neck, or worse, were in awkward positions for the previous several months. I know apartments in New York City are small, but a womb is tight quarters!

Regardless of how *natural* of a birth one may have, the birth process is still one of the most traumatic experiences in a person's life. Think about all the chemical, physical and emotional stressors newborns experience, just by moving a few inches from being inside the uterus to the outside world. Now throw in the twisting, pulling, pushing, shouting, grabbing, bright lights and everything else.

More than 65% of a person's neurological development occurs in their first year of life, and by the age of five, a child's brain will reach nearly 90% of its adult size. It is extremely important to ensure your children have every opportunity to develop their nervous system without any interference.

Think about the most common stressors your kids will experience.

MOST COMMON PHYSICAL STRESSORS FOR CHILDREN

- Being born (big body exiting a small birth canal with lots of twisting and turning)

- Being carried in inappropriate baby carrying devices

- Frequent falling when learning to walk

- Bumping head and head banging

- Sitting in car seat, swings or chairs for long periods of time

- Asymmetric crawling/scooting

- Sports injuries, including gymnastics, trampoline, frequent falling and "rough housing"

- Heavy & improper backpack usage

- Car accidents and bicycle falls

- Childhood obesity

- Sleeping on the wrong mattress and/or pillow for their bodies

- Footwear that does not support proper alignment

- Lifting improperly

- Sitting cross-legged

- Text (tech) neck

- Computer strain and poor ergonomic setup for schoolwork

- Poor posture & spinal misalignments

- Being swung around by adults

- Rollercoasters and amusement park rides

- Circumcision

MOST COMMON CHEMICAL STRESSORS FOR CHILDREN

• Colorings, additives, and dyes in foods and toys

• Sugar, artificial sweeteners and food items with caffeine

• Toys & objects that babies and toddlers put into their mouths that they pick up off the ground

• Second-hand cigarette smoke

• Air and water pollution & environmental toxins

• Medications and biologics

• Recreational drug and alcohol use

• Poor nutrition (including non-organic & GMOs) and processed food

• Food items that may cause sensitivities or allergic reactions such as dairy, formula & gluten

• Electromagnetic frequencies/broadband cellular networks

• Dehydration

• Heavy metal and chemical toxicity from many household cleaning supplies, plastic containers, aluminum cans, detergents, cosmetics, beauty supplies, body cleansers, soaps, shampoos, lotions, toothpaste, bubble bath, sunscreen, diapers, tampons, nail polish, nail polish remover, cookware, dental amalgam fillings, insect repellent, etc . . .

MOST COMMON EMOTIONAL STRESSORS FOR CHILDREN

- Crying it out
- Loneliness/separation anxiety
- Schoolwork frustrations (homework, tests, applying to college)
- Conflicts with classmates and friends, including bullying and cyberbullying
- Rejection/fear of abandonment
- Fear of parents
- Dysfunction at home
- Too much to do and not enough time
- Not feeling in control
- Time constraints
- Peer pressure
- Disappointment
- Social Media
- Violence or sadness in media (movies, tv, books, magazines, news, etc . . .)
- Puberty
- Dating
- Negative body image
- Gossip
- Lack of self-awareness
- Harboring feelings of guilt, shame or anger
- Fear of failure
- Death of a loved one or pet

Now think about whether you think it would be wise to have a chiropractor check them to ensure the integrity of their nervous systems. If you want your children's brains to develop optimally, when do *you* think would be a good time to take them to a chiropractor to get checked for subluxations?

During the first visit, the chiropractor will do an extensive health history and examine the spinal alignment and its impact on neurological function. On that or a subsequent visit, your chiropractor will report the results to you and make recommendations for care (if subluxations are discovered).

THERE ARE TYPICALLY 3 PHASES OF CHIROPRACTIC CARE

Phase 1 Initial Care: This is where all people with subluxations begin care, whether symptoms are present or not. The doctor will recommend the frequency of visits during this stage based on what he/she finds and what you specifically require. This phase lays the foundation for long-term correction if necessary. After a certain period of time (commonly 12–15 visits or four to eight weeks), the chiropractor will do a re-examination and potentially graduate you into Phase 2 determined by your progress.

Phase 2 Corrective Care: Most people will require several weeks or months to continue with their visits to ensure that the spine stabilizes and begins to hold its adjustment for longer periods of time. The visit frequency (amount of time between visits) during this stage is typically less than the initial phase of care. The length of time in this phase is determined by many factors, including the person's daily lifestyle activities.

Phase 3 Lifestyle Care: This is when the spine is rather stable in proper alignment and adjustments are lasting for longer periods of time. Young children typically graduate to lifestyle care much quicker than adults.

When you are truly in lifestyle care, the only reason you should need to get adjusted is if you have endured a physical, chemical or emotional stressor that you were unable to adapt to. Unfortunately, we all endure these stressors on a daily basis so it is essential to live the DREAM lifestyle to help avoid and adapt to these stressors. If you and your family "master" the contents of this book, you should all be able to go even longer without going out of *adjustment*.

As one of my mentors and author of *The 100 Year Lifestyle*, Eric Plasker, DC, says, "The intensity of your lifestyle care will be determined by the intensity of your lifestyle." In my words, the more constructive activities you do for yourself, the less you'll need to see me. The more destructive activities you do, the more you'll need to see me. My goal is to make the need of a chiropractic adjustment obsolete in the absence of trauma.

For someone seeking corrective chiropractic care, there are essentially only three reasons why complete correction would not take place.

1) Limitation of matter. This is when the practice member literally has a physical reason why complete correction cannot take place. Examples may be a missing limb, a serious injury that permanently changed the structure, a genetic defect, a disease process that has progressed beyond repair, and so on.

2) Poor application of the chiropractic principles. This one is on the doctor. If the chiropractor is not finding (or able to correct based on his/her techniques) the subluxations that need to be corrected, this could limit a person's potential for correction. It is important for a chiropractor to continually measure the progress of the practice member throughout care to ensure subluxations are reducing and the spine is stabilizing in the correct positions, and to refer to another chiropractor when correction is not taking place. It also may be an opportunity to work with other healthcare providers to help support the chiropractic care so the adjustments have a longer lasting impact.

3) Incompatibility with the DREAM lifestyle. If you are constantly bombarded with physical, chemical and emotional stressors, then you will have a difficult if not an impossible time staying in *adjustment* (*see Ch. 4-1*). It is imperative that you take massive action to reduce, avoid and neutralize as many of these stressors as possible in order to stay in *adjustment*!

This is one of the main reasons why it is important to have your nervous system checked for subluxations by a chiropractic doctor on a routine basis, regardless of how you feel. A true wellness lifestyle entails taking proactive measures to ensure your optimal health and well-being, especially prior to experiencing any pain, discomfort or other symptoms.

In review, every family needs a chiropractor on their healthcare team, but hopefully not everyone will need a chiropractic adjustment.

If you follow the recommendations outlined in the remainder of this chapter (along with the recommendations in Diet, Relaxation, Exercise and Mental Wellness), you will increase the odds considerably that you will remain in *adjustment*. Ultimately, most people do not think twice about taking care of their teeth on a daily basis. It is time to start practicing daily "spinal hygiene."

BONUSES & RESOURCES Access our provider directory for a family wellness chiropractor near you if you do not already have one.

8-7

PREGNANCY

♫ LOVED YOU BEFORE

There are few experiences in life that will bring on more chemical, physical and emotional stressors than pregnancy. If you are reading this book, you may have already gone through this process, you are currently pregnant, or you may desire to get pregnant again. Or perhaps you may have lived with someone who went through the most incredible metamorphosis possible, and you should thank that child-bearer every single day.

(If you are considering pregnancy, this entire book provides you with a guide for the lifestyle that best prepares your body for getting pregnant and starts shaping your child's health prior to conception. At the very least, start doing them in the Primester™ (a term coined by my friend Dr. Cleopatra Kamperveen, a scientist, university professor and fertility specialist). The Primester™ is an incredibly powerful time to set your child up for long-term health and success, along with a healthier pregnancy.)

For approximately 280 incredible days, a person's body will go through an immense number of changes and stressors that they need to prepare for, and this entire book will provide information and resources necessary to thrive through the experience that will help parents and the baby.

From a physical standpoint, it is important to understand that as the belly grows, the core muscles will weaken. This will ultimately cause a downward pulling on the low back and cause strain. A modified gait can also aggravate the hip and pelvic joints. Throw in an altered center of gravity, along with an increased low back curvature and breast size (for lactation), and you have a recipe for pain or discomfort in the neck, midback, lower rib cage and, most commonly, low back leading to sciatic pain and possibly "back labor."

Additionally, the endocrine system will produce a hormone called *relaxin*, which loosens the joints of the body so that the pelvis can widen when the baby is ready to exit. However, that hormone will also cause instability in the joints throughout the body, which in turn creates a likelihood that spinal misalignments and subluxations result causing the person to go *out of adjustment*. Therefore, it is exceedingly important that child-bearers do plenty of self-care throughout their pregnancy to handle the hormonal and gravitational changes. Appropriate exercise, massage and chiropractic care, to name a few, are of the utmost importance in handling the physical changes during pregnancy.

In a study by Dr. Joan Fallon, chiropractic care showed to provide for a 25% shorter labor in first time pregnancies and 31% for those who have previously given birth.[13]

I recommend visiting a chiropractor who is proficient and comfortable with adjusting during pregnancy, even though all licensed chiropractic doctors are trained to do so. Also, I recommend working with a chiropractor who is certified by the International Chiropractic Pediatric Association (ICPA) in the Webster Technique during pregnancy, when possible. If you already have a chiropractor you love (who is not certified), feel free to ask the doctor about collaborating with a Webster certified chiropractor during your pregnancy. As per the ICPA:

> The importance of regular chiropractic care vis a vis the Webster Technique during their pregnancy and the evidence pointing toward the potential for safer, easier births as a result of improved neurobiomechanical function may be expressed. The Webster technique is a specific chiropractic analysis and diversified adjustment. The goal of the adjustment is to reduce the effects of subluxation and/ or SI joint dysfunction. In so doing neurobiomechanical function in the sacral/pelvic region is improved. The ICPA recognizes that in a theoretical and clinical framework of the Webster Technique in the care of pregnant women, sacral subluxation may contribute to difficult labor for the mother (i.e., dystocia). Dystocia is caused by inadequate uterine function, pelvic contraction, and baby malpresentation. The correction of sacral subluxation may have a positive effect on all of these causes of dystocia. [14]

BONUSES & RESOURCES *The Ultimate 2-Minute Checklist Scientifically Documented Strategies for Getting Pregnant, Reducing Miscarriage Risk & Finally Having Your Superbaby* Guide

BONUSES & RESOURCES Access videos and handouts on stretches and exercises specific for pregnancy.

BONUSES & RESOURCES Access a provider directory for a Webster certified and pediatric focused chiropractor near you if you don't already have one.

BONUSES & RESOURCES Learn more about The Bradley Method® for a natural childbirth.

BONUSES & RESOURCES Access my favorite online birthing classes.

8-8

PROPER LIFTING AND BACKPACKS

♫ HEAVY LIFTIN'

As a chiropractic doctor, one of the more common, yet easily avoidable physical stressors that I notice in people is improper lifting and carrying. When it comes to lifting objects during everyday activities, it is very important to not lift by bending forward.

Whether you are lifting your toddler, a laundry basket or a heavy box, you should bend your hips and knees (into a squat) to the object, keep the object close to your body and straighten your legs to lift. It is crucial to never lift a heavy object above shoulder level and to avoid turning or twisting your body while lifting or holding the object. Just like when weightlifting, it is very important to focus on breath and to seek balance. Proper form includes moving through the full range of motion in the joints.

Before lifting, it is important to warm up the muscles through any sort of aerobic exercise (preferably 5–10 minutes). It is also important not to rush, overdo it or ignore pain. Lastly, make sure to wear shoes with good support for the arches and with good traction on the bottom of the shoe.

Importantly, make sure you keep an aligned posture while lifting and carrying objects or weights. People ask me all the time if certain exercises, particularly squats, are good or bad for you. I am a firm believer in exercises such as squats because they are a closed chain activity, which means that there is muscle and tendon support on both sides of the joint (the knee in this case). However, if you are doing squats without perfect form or with an imperfectly aligned spinal column, then the load of the weight may be unequally distributed and cause significant problems. Not only might poor spinal alignment cause an unequal distribution of weight leading to instability and injury, but it may also cause a lack of neural integrity (information between the brain and muscle). This in turn can lead to the muscle not contracting and relaxing as it should, thus leading to injury. This is one of the many reasons why it is important for everyone to have a chiropractic doctor on their healthcare team. A chiropractor can check the alignment of the spine and ensure that the nerves are sending the right information to the muscles so they work as they should!

It is very important to use an optimal form when exercising to prevent injuries. When lifting heavy weight, the body may become misaligned, potentially placing tendons and muscles in joints in positions that may lead to strains and even tears. It is better to lift lighter weight with proper form than to lift heavier weight with poor form from a safety perspective. Proper breathing techniques help to ensure correct muscle targeting. It also assures proper breathing patterns and techniques during repetitions and sets. This is essential during weight training exercises as it generates increased force and even reduces the chance of heart problems, aneurysms, and increased blood pressure. In maintaining proper form and breathing, you will be able to lift heavier reps over time and notice increased visible results.

People ask me all the time what I think about different exercise programs that are out there. I won't name any of the brands out there, but I will make a general statement. Any time you compromise your form (whether it be for speed, strength or additional repetitions), you are putting yourself at risk. Period. Yes, many of those programs do increase strength and there is a ton of value to their protocols. However, not every exercise routine is ideal for every person. Not everyone is built like a Navy Seal, nor do they need to train like one. I always tell people that they need to listen to their innate and determine if they think that a particular routine is appropriate for them or not or if they think they should confer with their trusted healthcare provider for advice. Also, as mentioned earlier, training for your body type (*see Ch. 7-7*) will typically garner you the best results.

It is never too early to teach your kids proper lifting techniques as well. The sooner they develop proper habits, the better. Backpacks alone bring up an entirely new challenge. Afterall, more than 5,000 emergency room visits each year are attributed to backpack issues, and more than 14,000 are treated for backpack related injuries. National Public Radio reported that 65% of adolescent visits to doctors are for backpack-related injuries.

While backpacks allow our children to carry all of the essentials they need for school, they also may pose a threat to their spinal heath.

All of those essentials add up, increasing the weight of the backpack dramatically.

Here are some alarming statistics regarding backpacks that every parent should be aware of:

- 55% of students carry more than the recommended guidelines of 10–15% of their body weight.
- 66% of school nurses reported seeing students with pain or injury attributed to carrying backpacks.
- Up to 60% of children will experience back pain by the time they reach 18.

Your child's spine, like yours, is made up of 33 vertebrae (bones) with natural shock absorbers between each one. When a heavy backpack is on a back, a child may bend backwards due to incorrect placement of the bag. Because of this, they tend to bend forward at the hips or arch their backs to compensate, unnaturally compressing the spine. This can lead to discomfort of the spine, shoulders, and hips; poor alignment; and a litany of health issues.

The American Academy of Pediatrics recommends the following guidelines for purchasing the right backpack for your child:

- Lightweight
- Two wide, padded shoulder straps (narrow straps can dig into the shoulders)
- A padded back that provides increased comfort and protection from sharp objects in the backpack, such as rulers or pencils

- A waist belt which helps to distribute the weight more evenly across the body
- Multiple compartments also helping to distribute the weight more evenly across the body

Here is a guide for proper backpack usage.

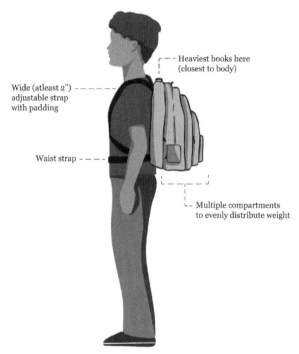

Wide (atleast 2") adjustable strap with padding

Waist strap

Heaviest books here (closest to body)

Multiple compartments to evenly distribute weight

Maximum weight of loaded backpack should not exceed 10-15% of child's body weight.

Wearing it Correctly:

- Make sure your kids always wear both shoulder straps. Tighten the shoulder straps so the backpack rests comfortably in its proper position. The straps should be wide and padded.

- If a front strap exists, use it and fasten it securely.
- Observe your child's posture. If your child leans forward while walking, takes shorter strides while walking or uses his/her hands to protect the shoulders from the straps, it is an indication the backpack is too heavy or being worn improperly.
- The backpack should never hang more than four inches below the waistline. A backpack that hangs too low increases the weight on the shoulders, causing your child to lean forward when walking.

Packing it Correctly:

- Always load heaviest and largest books closest to the back
- If there are side pockets, evenly distribute the weight side to side
- Never place more than 10–15% of your child's body weight worth of books in the backpack

Child's Weight	Backpack Weight
50 lbs.	No more than 7.5 lbs.
80 lbs.	No more than 12 lbs.
100 lbs.	No more than 15 lbs.
130 lbs.	No more than 19.5 lbs.

<u>Lifting it Correctly:</u>

- Place the backpack on a table or an elevated surface so that your child does not have to bend down to lift it.
- Turn the backpack so the straps face him/her, then have your child turn around.
- Slide both arms through the straps while the knees are bent. Make sure that the straps are snug on the shoulders, then with the weight evenly distributed, stand up straight.

Make sure you do your homework when it comes to picking the right backpack for your child and keep backpack safety a top priority. Roller bags are also a great alternative to consider, but those can cause challenges when dealing with stairs. Preparing your children's body is also a key ingredient to ensuring backpack safety. Increase flexibility of muscles by regularly stretching them, perform appropriate exercises to strengthen abdominal (core) and back muscles and have their spine examined regularly to ensure proper alignment and function.

BONUSES & RESOURCES See our recommendations for suitable backpacks.

8-9

PROPER POSTURE WHEN LIFTING, CARRYING & NURSING BABIES

♫ LEAN ON ME

As a pediatric and family wellness chiropractor, there are few moments more exciting to me than new parents bringing their newborn into my office to be checked for subluxations. However, what also comes with this are new aches and pains along with spinal dysfunction for the parents, grandparents and other loving relatives, friends and caregivers.

Everyone is so excited to hold and carry this bundle of joy, but they do not realize that the way they stand and twist can cause more torque on the spine than a Tiger Woods drive off the tee.

As you read in "Heavy Liftin'" (*see Ch. 8-8*), you want to pick up children just as you would any object. It is vitally important to always hold children in a position that does not cause you to lean on one side as it can cause strain on your back and hip muscles and potentially cause sprains to the ligaments surrounding your hips and spine. Especially when carrying a child for extended periods, hold the child in front of you with the child's legs wrapped around your waist. This will help you stand upright.

You also want to be mindful of your wrists, elbows, neck and shoulders to ensure they are in a stable, properly aligned position. Be sure to switch your body around frequently to prevent overuse injuries.

If you are sitting with the child on your lap, make sure you maintain an upright posture, especially when you shift from sitting to standing. As you lift your body, the pressure on the discs between your spinal bones will multiply three to ten times the child's body weight, putting that pressure on your spine.

Another cause of harm when caring for small children is taking them out of the car seat. Twisting your body with both feet outside of the vehicle to remove the child is a great way to injure your lower back, knees, neck and shoulders. Instead, place one leg into the car and face the car seat as you are putting the child in it. This will remove a significant amount of pressure from your spine. If the car seat is in the middle of the back seat, climb in and face the car seat as you lift your child into it or out.

Breastfeeding often leads to complaints of low back discomfort as well as significant neck pain. It is important for new parents to be very cognizant of their torso, head and neck positions when nursing. Also, be mindful to switch sides frequently when possible to prevent overuse injuries to the shoulders, elbows and wrists. Try not to look down too frequently, as it causes additional strain to the neck muscles, though my wife says it is impossible not to constantly gaze at the miracle you are holding. If side-lying is the position of choice, especially following a caesarean section, consider using a pillow for back and neck support and to frequently switch sides as much as possible. Having a chiropractor and lactation consultant on your team is a good way to ensure the best positions for everyone.

There are several products that enhance the comfort and safety for baby wearing and nursing and others that make matters worse.

BONUSES & RESOURCES See our recommendations for comfortable, safe baby wearing devices.

8-10

FOOTWEAR/ORTHOTICS

♫ WALK THIS WAY

Think about your feet for a moment. They take the brunt of every step you take throughout the day. While our feet support our foundation, we do very little to support our feet. While babies do not need to worry too much about what they wear on their feet, as long as it matches and makes them look really cute, once they begin to walk, it can make a big difference.

Footwear that supports the natural stride allows the foot to move naturally. Many people struggling with knee pain greatly benefit from supportive and natural footwear. People, especially runners, run with less effort, more efficiency and less pain. There are many products that encourage the proper form of the foot and greatly contribute to a healthy and aligned body. While some consider very minimalist shoes to be great for running, it is still important to ensure that the shoe has proper arch and foot support.

There are many people who have issues with their feet, including low arches or "flat feet," and this can be detected in childhood. In some cases, custom orthotics can assist with your gait and prevent long-term injuries, whether it be during physical activity or even just walking/standing. Orthotics are inserts placed inside the shoes with the purpose of restoring the natural foot function. I have been wearing orthotics since I turned ten years old. They help correct the over-pronation and help align the foot and ankle bones to their neutral position, restoring natural foot function. The misalignment of the foot and ankle bones can affect the alignment of the knees, hips, and back, leading to bigger issues. Therefore, it is important for some people to wear inserts and correct the over pronation of the foot, in return, alleviating pain and improving foot biomechanics.

Some orthotics are designed to overcome a limitation that cannot be fixed but will provide long-term support, while others help correct the issue. I always recommend ensuring that the bones of the foot are in proper alignment (checked by a chiropractor), especially prior to getting fit for custom orthotics. I also recommend acquiring support by a practitioner who knows the foot and its mechanics very well. Massaging the muscles and working the connective tissue can potentially fix the issue. Practitioners to consider include a physical therapist, massage therapist or Rolfer (structural integration practitioner).

Having been raised in New York, sandals, a.k.a. flipflops, would typically be seen eight weeks out of the year, and typically by a pool or beach. In Southern California, however, I have seen more toes than I care to. Children and adults are wearing flipflops almost on a daily basis, all year round. While they may be comfy and cooling, they are anything but supportive. Some sandals are made with arch supports, but most are not. I recommend that if you spend a lot of time in sandals that you spend a little extra money on good ones; and perhaps even consider purchasing custom sandal orthotics, especially if you have low arches or other issues with your feet.

BONUSES & RESOURCES Learn about custom shoe or sandal orthotics and find a practitioner to fit you properly.

8-11

PILLOWS & MATTRESSES

♫ PILLOW TALK

My personal pillow has traveled to more places in the world than most people. I take my cervical pillow everywhere I travel when spending the night. Cervical pillows can help relieve pain and support proper spinal alignment by providing a natural and correct posture while lying on the back and side-sleeping positions. They are extremely helpful when a person does not have the appropriate curve in the cervical spine (hypolordosis), as they can help restore a normal curve when used in conjunction with proper spinal care, such as chiropractic. It is recommended for everyone to sleep on a cervical pillow to help maintain the optimal spinal curve.

Cervical pillows can positively impact someone's lifestyle by improving tension headaches, whiplash injuries, stiffness, temporomandibular disorders, and in some cases, snoring. This leads users to a full night's sleep, enabling them to wake up feeling refreshed and hopefully pain free.

A question I get almost every week is, "Do you have a mattress that you recommend?" It is important to understand that there is not one mattress that is the perfect mattress for everyone. The mattress you use should provide wholesome sleep while encouraging correct sleeping posture and relaxing muscles. However, not all mattresses benefit all people the same. For example, a medium firm mattress is ideal for people who generally sleep on their back. Meanwhile, a softer mattress is fit for side-sleepers, and a firmer mattress is better for those who sleep on their stomach (which is not a recommended sleeping posture). It is important to find the proper mattress because it will foster a good night's sleep, which is crucial to a healthy lifestyle.

Try and find a mattress that is made with as few toxins as possible and contains mostly natural, organic ingredients. Because technology is always changing and science says different things about certain chemicals that are used in the manufacturing of a mattress, ideally you would purchase your mattress from a company that is environmentally conscious and does not use harmful chemicals, foams and adhesives. You also want to make sure it dissipates heat appropriately. Always purchase a mattress from a company that allows at least 30 days to try it with no return or restocking fee.

It is important to not use your mattress for too long. The shelf life of the average mattress is 10 years (though mine claims 20 years). Sleeping on a mattress beyond the time that it can support your body appropriately can lead to poor spinal alignment and stability, which can lead to pain, stiffness, muscle spasms and vertebral subluxations that affect your health negatively.

BONUSES & RESOURCES Receive discounts on my favorite pillows and mattresses.

8-12

ERGONOMICS AT HOME AND OFFICE

♫ WORKING 9 TO 5

Ergonomic furniture, such as a chair, desk or table, allows someone to use the furniture without suffering from repetitive stress injuries. For example, an ergonomic chair is designed to help someone maintain proper posture. It is especially important to utilize this furniture when computer equipment is involved as all equipment should work in tandem to ensure the safety of the worker.

Whether it is a child doing schoolwork or an adult handling business, ergonomic furniture and workstations are designed to prevent repetitive stress problems associated with the way people sit and spend their days. Certain items such as spine-friendly ergonomic chairs and adjustable desks and monitors help employees avoid work-related aches and pains. It also reduces the risks of neck problems and reduces the amount of pressure placed on the hips.

Whether you spend most of your day working in an office building or home office, or your child in a classroom or at homeschool, it is important to ensure that the workstation allows for proper structure and function and creates the most efficient and safe working environment possible. More and more companies these days are investing in their employee's workstations. However, with more and more people working from home, home workstations are often forgotten about and creating a lot of unnecessary problems. If you are self-employed, it is a worthwhile investment to create an adequate workstation. If you are employed, ask your employer to help cover the costs. You may be surprised as many are willing to spend the money when asked. You can even ask your chiropractor or other healthcare provider for a note to give to your employer explaining the necessity for this investment.

When sitting, the ideal position for your legs is to have your knees slightly higher than the hips to relieve pressure on the back. Problems will likely develop if your feet do not reach the floor. If that is the case, use a footrest, binder or thick book to elevate your feet.

A good chair provides proper support for the lower back and takes pressure off your muscles and joints. A back rest can turn a bad chair into a good chair. If you don't have one, roll up a small towel and put it behind the small of your back. Slouching weakens the spine, creates poor posture and through time will injure your back.

For both sitting and standing workstations, the placement of your arms while working affects your neck, shoulders, hands and back. The best place for your computer keyboard is directly in front of you. The monitor should also be within arm's reach. Proper distance limits eye strain reducing the likelihood of headaches. Arms should be comfortably rested at your side, not reaching for the keyboard.

Proper wrist position is also crucial to avoid injury. Avoid bending your wrists backwards. A flip rest on your keyboard can reduce wrist extension.

Repetitive incorrect use of your hands can result in a painful condition known as carpal tunnel syndrome. One way to avoid carpal tunnel syndrome is to stretch your wrists every hour.

Throughout the day take several "micro breaks" to reduce tension from eye strain that can cause headaches.

Ultimately you want to have your knee joints (when sitting) and elbows at 90 degrees so that your thighs and lower arms are parallel to the ground, your upper arms and lower legs are perpendicular to the ground.

In chapter 7-6, you read about the importance of stretching. Especially when working at a desk for extended periods of time, stretching can increase muscle control, flexibility and range of motion. It can also therapeutically relieve muscle cramps.

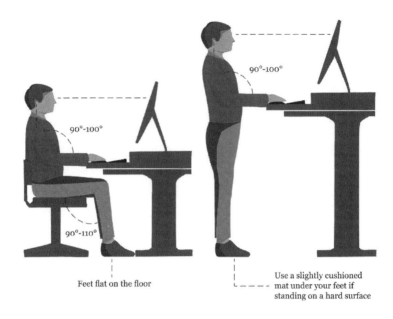

90°-100°

90°-100°

90°-110°

Feet flat on the floor

Use a slightly cushioned mat under your feet if standing on a hard surface

Having flexible muscles can improve daily performance. It increases circulation throughout the body and increases blood flow to muscles. Increased blood flow to muscles can help shorten recovery time if you have had any muscle injuries. Frequent stretching keeps muscles from getting tight which maintains proper posture. Stretching also helps with stress relief and enhanced coordination, helping balance.

BONUSES & RESOURCES *How to Design Your at Home Learning & Working Space* Guide
BONUSES & RESOURCES *Exercises to do at your work desk* Worksheet
BONUSES & RESOURCES Learn about my favorite ergonomic setups.

8-13

FORWARD HEAD POSTURE

♫ STRAIGHT UP

No one wants bad posture . . . not unless you are trying out for the role of Quasimodo. Yet almost everything people do these days would make one think that having a hunchback is the cool thing. Just check out the people in your household, at work or even walking in the streets. Observe your kids when using their electronics. People are not looking up anymore, they are looking at their handheld devices or computer screens. You are most likely guilty too!

Forward head posture (FHP) is all too common and can lead to several health issues with respiration, circulation, digestion and decreased energy.

This used to be an adult issue, but now I see more kids than ever with forward head posture. With all the electronic devices constantly in their hands, there are more opportunities for creating FHP. Just look at a child watching a video or playing a game on a tablet. Or look at yourself while checking your email on your phone. FHP is out of control in epidemic proportions, no one is talking about it and it can lead to all kinds of health problems. This is what we call "Tech Neck."

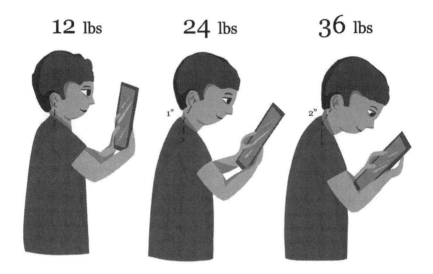

12 lbs   24 lbs   36 lbs

In regard to respiratory (breathing) dysfunction in chronic neck pain patients, a study "demonstrated a strong association between an increased forward head posture and decreased respiratory muscle strength in neck patients."[15]

A common form of analysis used by many chiropractors, physical therapists and personal trainers is posture evaluations. It is very rare these days to evaluate someone without even a little bit of FHP. "For every inch of forward head posture, it can increase the weight of the head on the spine by an additional 10 pounds."[16] Depending on your body size, your head probably weighs between 10 and 14 pounds. If your head is even one inch forward, then your neck muscles are now effectively holding up 20–24 pounds! What do you think that will do to your muscles, your energy levels and your ability to concentrate?

"90% of the stimulation and nutrition to the brain is generated by the movement of the spine," says Dr. Roger Sperry, Nobel Prize recipient for brain research. Dr. Sperry demonstrated that 90 percent of the energy output of the brain is used in relating the physical body to gravity. "Only 10 percent has to do with thinking, metabolism, and healing, so when you have forward head posture, your brain will rob energy from your thinking, metabolism and immune function to deal with abnormal gravity/posture relationships and processing."

According to Rene Cailliet, MD, director of the Department of Physical Medicine and Rehabilitation at the University of Southern California, "Forward head posture (FHP) can add up to 30 pounds of abnormal leverage on the cervical spine. This can pull the entire spine out of alignment. FHP results in loss of vital capacity of the lungs by as much as 30%. This shortness of breath can lead to heart and blood vascular disease. The entire gastrointestinal (digestive) system is affected, particularly the large intestine. Loss of good bowel peristaltic function and evacuation is a common effect of FHP. It causes an increase in discomfort and pain because proprioceptive signals from the first four cervical vertebrae are a major source of the stimuli that create the body's pain controlling chemicals (endorphins). With inadequate endorphin production, many otherwise non-painful sensations are experienced as pain. FHP dramatically reduces endorphin production."

The first tactic in fixing your posture is to stop doing what caused your bad posture in the first place. Once you are aware of the issue, you can now start being more conscious about avoiding it and possibly even correcting it through posture training.

Chiropractic care, massage, Rolfing, physical therapy, stretching, specific exercises along with posture training that can include back braces, belts, ergonomic furniture and workstations will help resolve and avoid FHP. Most posture imbalances develop because of bad habits, and then the muscles that hold a joint in place become imbalanced. Generally, one muscle group will be too tight, and the other will be too loose. Strengthening these muscles through exercise once properly aligned by a chiropractor is a great way to improve overall balance and posture. (Many chiropractors use technology, such as surface electromyography, to measure whether muscle contraction is at the proper intensity and whether or not it is balanced. *See Ch. 8-5*).

Good posture alleviates tension and stress and pain in the neck and back, as well as throughout the body. It can also help alleviate headaches related to tension. While having better posture portrays a more confident human being, it also allows breathing, digestion, and circulation to be easier. Also, it creates the appearance of a slimmer figure and helps muscles and joints by alleviating pressure.

In summary, better habits and exercises along with proper care when needed can help set the stage for better alignment, fewer vertebral subluxations, a better look and a better chance to stay in adjustment!

BONUSES & RESOURCES Learn about devices and clothing that prevent forward head posture and purchase at discounted rates.
BONUSES & RESOURCES Access videos and handouts on specific stretches and exercises
BONUSES & RESOURCES 5 *Easy Posture Exercises for Kids* Guide

REFLECTION OPPORTUNITY

Are you aware of your posture throughout the day? What is your posture right now as you read this book?

Take a look at the backpacks in your house and see if they meet the standards recommended.

If you have children, are you mindful of their posture, especially if they use electronic devices? What is your posture when you are on your devices?

If you spend a lot of time on a computer during the workday, is your workstation set up ergonomically?

When you exercise, are you mindful of your form?

Do you and your kids visit a chiropractor or other appropriate healthcare provider for routine spinal checkups?

How do you go about practicing good spinal hygiene (daily activities that promote a healthy, mobile and well-aligned spine)?

In Chapter 4-1, you learned that being in *adjustment* requires you to also be in *atonement* and *alignment*. (Look back at that section if you need a refresher.) What ideas can you take from that chapter and Chapter 8 to ensure you and your family are living a life that is consistent with staying in *adjustment*?

KEY 5
MENTAL WELLNESS

9-1

THINK ABOUT IT

♫ WHO ARE YOU

Why do *you* do the things *you* do? Why do you do the things you do the *way* you do them?

If you can't answer those questions, you are unfortunately in the same boat as most people.

However, if that is the case, how do you expect to have harmonious relationships with your family, especially your partner, co-parent and your children? What about your friends and co-workers? And most importantly, what about yourself?

To truly be happy, you need to have self-awareness and understand what makes you tick. How do others perceive you? How do you perceive yourself?

Prior to my current blissful marriage with Brooke, I had two significant romantic relationships in my life. There is nothing uncommon about that. In fact, if you think about it, almost everyone in a relationship right now has had at least one preceding relationship that did not work out.

The thing I reflected on after the fact, and something you could consider as well, is answering the question, "Why did the previous relationship(s) end?" Was it because of you, the other person or both? If prior to beginning that relationship, you were both given an operating manual about the other and you both understood the inner workings of one another, could that relationship have worked? If you both had that information beforehand and had been able to "see" one another, would you have even chosen to be with that person in the first place? Would that person have chosen you?

This next section is about learning how to see yourself first, then the others around you. You will then learn how to put your thoughts into appropriate action so that you can truly practice *mental wellness*, the *process* of connecting your inner purpose and passion to your outer goals and tasks in all phases of life.

Understanding this process and putting it into practice will unequivocally lead you to a path of true joy, happiness and fulfillment, with harmonious relationships in all aspects of your life.

9-2

IT'S ALL ABOUT Y.O.U. (BUT FIRST I'M GOING TO TALK ABOUT ME!)

♫ GETTING TO KNOW YOU

A long time ago, in a galaxy far, far away . . . I was 18 years old and it was the first week of my freshman year in college in upstate New York at SUNY Oneonta when I met Lisa. The sweet and cute girl showed interest in me, and I was attracted to her. That is pretty much the depth of it at the inception of my first real romantic relationship.

As we got to know each other over the years, our warmth and caring grew as did our connection. As many college-aged lovebirds can also relate to, we were on again, off again—lots of great times and lots of breakups. How can two loving, caring people constantly be at odds with each other? Well, I suppose that when people begin a relationship without understanding themselves first, it is often going to be doomed from the beginning.

My relationship with Lisa lasted for 15 years, of which we were married for five. I do not regret that relationship in any way as we had some wonderful times and experiences, and I know that the time we shared together helped shape me into the man I am today. During the last year of our marriage, we did seek counseling. The marriage therapist saw two loving individuals, but even for her, it was clear that we were not an ideal match.

The therapist went out on a limb and basically told Lisa and me that I needed to find my June Carter, a reference to singer Johnny Cash's wife portrayed by Reese Witherspoon in the timely 2005 movie, *Walk the Line*. (Watch the movie if you haven't to better understand the reference and to enjoy a terrific film).

Lisa is still today a close friend of mine, and our families even get together on rare occasions. I would venture to guess that we would see each other more frequently if we didn't live so far away, as my wife, Brooke, and she get along very well, and I have a lot in common with her husband.

While Lisa and I were parting ways, I was in a search to find myself and set a vision for my future. While I loved being a chiropractor, I knew that adjusting people my entire life was neither going to satisfy my drive nor would it enable me to impact the world the way that I desired. I knew that being stuck in a single office all day, every day, would prohibit me from spreading the important message that I had to share about the DREAM lifestyle and chiropractic's role in helping all people achieve better health, naturally.

During this time, I had two DREAM Wellness centers on Long Island, each with a different partner. Dan Matzner and I had initially opened a chiropractic office in Great Neck, New York, (in 1999) and five years later we moved to a larger space and turned the chiropractic office into a DREAM Wellness center.

During the initial five years of practice with Dan, I had opened the first DREAM Wellness center in Lake Grove, New York, with my college friend, fraternity brother and first business partner in DREAM Wellness, Gregg Baron. While in college, Gregg and I used to talk and dream about DREAM and what it would look like. I was going to head off to chiropractic college and Gregg was going to law school. I would be the doc and he would be the attorney. It did not take long, however, before Gregg changed course. After a year, he left law school and decided to become a chiropractor. (Instead, we had to hire his brother Jeff as our attorney.) Gregg currently runs a DREAM Wellness center on Long Island. He spends much of his time coaching and doing large corporate talks educating large audiences about the principles of the DREAM lifestyle.

As my relationship with Lisa was coming to an end, so was my time in New York. While I had all of my family and two successful wellness centers on Long Island, I just didn't feel like I was home. Aside from practicing chiropractic at the time, I was also serving in several leadership positions within the chiropractic profession and speaking around the world.

My friend Dr. Matt Hubbard had me speak at his chiropractic philosophy group C.O.R.E. (Chiropractors on the Road to Excellence) in San Diego, California. It was here that I reconnected with my chiropractic college friend Dr. Sandra Castro. She and a few others reintroduced me to a land that I loved as a child, a place that I constantly told my family I wanted to live when I grow up.

In 2006, I moved from New York to California. Soon after settling in San Diego, I opened a wellness center with Dr. Hubbard. Matt introduced me to one of his chiropractic patients, Stephanie (name changed for privacy reasons), who was a Pilates instructor. Stephanie was just recently certified and looking for a place to train students, and Matt and I needed a Pilates instructor for California's first DREAM Wellness center.

Fortunately or unfortunately, depending on how you look at it, there were many delays in getting the wellness center open for business and ready for Pilates. Between office flooding, equipment issues and more, it was months before any classes could begin.

During that time, however, Stephanie and I were spending a lot of hours together. Some were working on getting the business ready and some were hanging out. We shortly found ourselves in a romance that I had never experienced before. (For those in human resources reading this book, don't worry, we were romantically involved before she started teaching any classes, and she was never my employee!)

Stephanie and I appeared to be the perfect couple. We had so much in common. We ate and exercised similarly. We shared views on health and active lifestyles. She loved what I did as a profession. Stephanie appeared to be my June Carter.

It wasn't very long before we were engaged to marry. We even travelled to Greece to consecrate our commitment to one another (though we never had a legal marriage because of a technicality related to proper documents required that we didn't have).

Shortly after our return from Greece, our relationship began to slip. We were arguing more and more, and the things we had in common seemed to not matter as much. Our relationship began to vanish much like a magician's flash paper. Poof . . . and it was gone! I begged

Stephanie to go with me for relationship counseling, but she refused. Stephanie basically blamed me for our issues and said I was the one who needed help. (Oh heck, maybe she was right. I think we all could benefit from some coaching or counseling.)

My friend Sandra told me about her friend Zannah Hackett, PhD. Zannah developed an advanced human assessment called the Ultimate Life Tool (ULT) that would ultimately reveal why people do the things they do . . . the way they do them. Sandra told me that Zannah worked with individuals, couples, families and even businesses. The ULT is administered through the Y.O.U. Institute (TYI, INC.) and other strategic alliances (Y.O.U. is an acronym for Your Own Understanding).

Sandra suggested that Stephanie and I at the very least take the assessment to see what it would divulge. This technology intrigued Stephanie enough to not only take the assessment, but also for us to do a couple's session with Zannah to better understand the results.

Listening to the results of the assessment absolutely blew my mind. Zannah told me things that I didn't even know about myself on the conscious level and could never put into words. I felt that I was being seen and understood for the first time in my life. She explained what drives and motivates me; how I learn and download information; my tolerance toward people, places and things; how I perceive life (cup half-full or half-empty); and how much energy or fuel I have in my "tank" (as if I were a car). Zannah essentially gave me the operating manual that my parents should have been given when I was born!

Zannah also then went over Stephanie's results, which were also spot on. However, it was apparent that Stephanie and I were not a great match. To make our relationship successful would certainly be possible, but it would have required a lot of understanding and work on both of our parts.

If only I had my manual and understood myself beforehand, and Stephanie had her manual and understood herself, then we shared each other's manuals with each other early on, things would have likely been completely different. Perhaps we never would have dated in the first place. Or perhaps we would have known what we were getting into beforehand and agreed to use the information to feed each other's needs to make the relationship succeed no matter how much work it would take. But we did not have it prior and the damage was already done; neither of us was willing to fight hard enough for the relationship . . . so it ended like so many others do.

I vowed to myself that I would never get deep into a relationship with someone without her taking the ULT first. I knew that this information would give us the foundation for a long lasting, honest relationship right from the beginning. We would be equipped with the tools necessary not only to know what makes us tick but to be able to nurture each other through good times and tough times.

The biggest favor that Stephanie did for me was suggest that after our breakup I take the time to work on myself. I took that to heart and heeded her advice. I began to learn more about the ULT and spend time with Zannah and her team. I made the ULT part of my life, which has helped me in every aspect of my being, and now we even make the ULT assessment available through DREAM Wellness.

It took a little bit of time after our breakup to even talk to Stephanie again, but I now see her for who and *what* she is, and I understand

and love her perfection. Stephanie and I are now great friends, and she and Brooke even get along wonderfully.

OUT OF THE ASHES . . .

In the fall of 2010, realizing that at 37 years old I had already had one-and-a-half failed marriages, I wanted to make sure I would not repeat mistakes that I had made in the past. I was also at a low point financially and had to recover from some poorly timed business decisions both on my part and that of former business partners. I needed to take specific, decisive action steps that would enable me to be very clear as to who I wanted to be and who (and what) I wanted to attract to be my partner for life and the mother of my child/children.

Having been through multiple personal development trainings over the years, I learned about vision boards. A vision board is essentially a collage of words and images that depict what your future life would look like if all your goals and dreams came to fruition. I decided to make a vision board "on steroids". I literally created 5 pages of words and images in a document that illustrated my future life with my "DREAM wife." It was very personal, very descriptive and very detailed.

Much like the archer (see Ch. 2-1), once my vision became clear, I drew it up and made it so.

I am going to share the content from this document, which I have never shared before. There were images and photographs that were placed beside each description that really brought home the emotion, but those will not be included as I do not own the rights to them. Feel free to use as much or as little to create your DREAM life, wife, husband, job or whatever you want, and use images that inspire you. Please excuse the corniness and shallowness of some of these.

- ♥ My DREAM wife and I have an unparalleled connection on a physical, spiritual, philosophical and emotional level.
- ♥ My DREAM wife is already "complete," but her mission and purpose are congruent with mine.
- ♥ When I look at my DREAM wife, I am so physically attracted to her that I almost can't believe that she is with me (but of course I believe it because I deserve her and attracted her into my life).
- ♥ My DREAM wife is in great shape and exercises regularly.
- ♥ My DREAM wife is athletic.
- ♥ My DREAM wife eats well, organic and free range. She motivates me to do the same.
- ♥ My DREAM wife is into constant and never-ending personal growth, positively affirms, is happy and loves life.
- ♥ My DREAM wife is intelligent.
- ♥ My DREAM wife is motivated.
- ♥ My DREAM wife is sexy.
- ♥ My DREAM wife is affectionate.
- ♥ My DREAM wife is cultured.
- ♥ My DREAM wife is well traveled.
- ♥ My DREAM wife is energetic.
- ♥ My DREAM wife is easy going.
- ♥ My DREAM wife is loving.
- ♥ My DREAM wife is generous.

- ♥ My DREAM wife is personable.
- ♥ My DREAM wife is fun and playful.
- ♥ My DREAM wife is creative.
- ♥ My DREAM wife is outgoing.
- ♥ My DREAM wife is passionate.
- ♥ My DREAM wife loves me unconditionally, and when I am down, she lifts me up.
- ♥ My DREAM wife is/will be a great mother.
- ♥ My DREAM wife is nurturing.
- ♥ When I am with my DREAM wife, I want to hold her in my arms; when we are apart, I feel her presence.

- ♥ MY VISION FOR MY LIFE WITH MY DREAM WIFE . . .

. . .This is where my document described in great detail what our life together would look like. I included our daily rituals, our vacations, our goals, our dreams, our house and even our family.

I will spare you the extra reading and allow you to be creative and create your own vision of your family if it is not what you currently have.

♫ IT'S A NEW DAWN, IT'S A NEW DAY . . .

In August 2011, I was chatting with my friend Carole who was the personal trainer and nutritionist in my Pacific Beach DREAM Wellness location. She and I were talking about my current dating situation and how difficult it had been for me to find (or attract) someone who fits the descriptions in the vision document I created 11 months earlier. She asked me if I would consider an online dating program. I explained to her that I wasn't interested, and I was actually going on many first dates, but very few were worthy (based on my vision) of a second date or beyond. She then rolled her eyes at me and said, "Well my friend Brooke is on E-Harmony and she's met a few really nice guys, so you never know!"

I then proceeded to interrogate Carole. "Who is your friend Brooke?" I asked. She told me that Brooke was one of her best friends that she grew up and attended camp with. I asked, "Well, how old is she?" Carole told me she was 31. I asked how tall she is (this is important because I'm barely 5'4"). Carole told me that she is *maybe* 5'1". I asked if she was cute. Carole affirmed. I then asked . . . "Where does this girl live?" thinking that maybe she was living in Michigan because that is where they went to camp. Carole said, "She lives right here in in Pacific Beach, a dozen blocks from the office."

I said, "What? This girl lives right here in PB? She's 7 years younger, she's short, she's cute, and she's single? Why is she on E-Harmony and not hanging out with me? You gotta tell me more about her!" Carole began to stutter and basically tried to get me to back off, not even entertaining the thought of introducing us. The more she told me why we would not be a good match, the more intrigued I got.

After a period of convincing Carole to at least tell Brooke about me and see if Brooke would even entertain the idea of meeting me, I broke down Carole's protective shield and she finally caved.

Brooke and I started, like many other relationships, by chatting on the phone, which quickly went from feeling like an interview to besties chatting away. We quickly saw that we had a lot of common values and we were intrigued to meet. By the second date, I learned that Brooke attended a prestigious college, spent time living in China, Chile and other parts of the world, previously taught Mandarin Chinese and Spanish, exercises regularly, eats healthfully, loves to Salsa dance, is extremely spiritual and has a strong love for God, is easy going, lights up a room with her effervescence and is an extremely loving person . . . just to name some of her qualities. It was like I conjured her up out of thin air when I created my DREAM Wife vision document!

♫ THE SEARCH IS OVER . . .

By the third date, we both knew innately that, in the words of the band Survivor, the search was over.

Around a month into dating, I told Brooke, "There is just one thing I need you to do before we go any further in our relationship." "What's that?" she asked. I told her that she needed to take this test that would enable us to each see each other the way nature sees us. I knew it would be a risk telling her this when things were going so well, but I had to stay true to my vow I made a couple of years earlier. I figured that if she was not willing to take the test, then she would not be for me because it would demonstrate that she wasn't into never-ending personal growth . . . one of the conditions within my vision document. Fortunately, she was all about it! She figured, heck, if there is something she needed to know about me, the sooner the better.

We took the test and did a session with Dr. Zannah Hackett and the rest is history. Zannah knew before we even walked through the door of her office that we were an amazing match. It was obvious that we complemented each other incredibly well and the success of our relationship would require much less work than many other couples whose tests reveal different results.

That day, Zannah gave us advice and tools for our relationship that we still use every day in life. At the time of writing this book, we have been together for nearly a decade and have not had a single bad day as a couple. We have never had a fight of any significance. We have maybe made a snide or bickering remark here and there over nearly 10 years, but it was always followed by an apology and kiss. (Yes, me apologizing to her.) This does not mean that we have not had big events or challenges in our lives, including the passing of both of her parents. We just did not let those events negatively impact our relationship. If anything, our challenging times has made us a stronger couple.

People frequently ask me if my previous relationships may have worked if we had operating manuals for each other when we began to date (or even sooner). Of course, I do not know what may have been. But I can say with certainty, there is no better match for me than Brooke. While most relationships can survive with the right knowledge, the relationships with the most compatibilities combined with the knowledge will almost always thrive.

There is no doubt that the foundation Brooke and I built our relationship on has made us incredible role models and great parents for Zion. Not every child has the opportunity to grow up with two loving parents and watch how they interact with each other. I know what Zion observes now will make him an amazing partner for someone special in the future and eventually a great parent (if that is in the cards for him).

Brooke and I became so impassioned by the ULT that in 2013 we both got certified in the technology. I received my certification mostly so I could understand it better and educate others on its value; Brooke did it because she loves helping individuals, couples and now businesses.

Since that time, Brooke has become a Level 5 TYI Certified Practitioner, Corporate Facilitator and Trainer for The Y.O.U. Institute, where she helps teach and certify future TYI Practitioners.

9-3

WHO'S ON FIRST, WHAT'S ON SECOND?

♫ WHO KNEW?

As you just read, one of the best tools that I have in my toolbox that helps me navigate through all relationships in my life is the Ultimate Life Tool (ULT) created by Dr. Zannah Hackett. I referenced how it helped me create the best marriage one could ever be blessed with. While it helped me to attract the right person into my life, it also takes continual work, and it requires me to understand myself as well as I understand Brooke. And vice versa.

The ULT reveals what I refer to as the 5 YOU-tilities. (Remember, Y.O.U. is an acronym for Your Own Understanding). The 5 YOU-tilities help us see each other the way we are seen through the eye's of nature . . . something that our species has lost the ability to do. For some reason, we can see these attributes in everything else on earth. So why not fellow human beings? As Dr. Hackett says, "We have become the blind leading the blind." It is time to open our eyes and renew our ability see each other as perfect human beings.

YOU-tility #1

Nature: How do YOU show up in nature? We have all heard the phrase, structure determines function. Heck, I use it every day in chiropractic practice. But what does that mean? Everything on this planet is structured a certain way to function a certain way.

A Ferrari is sleek, low to the ground and aerodynamically brilliant. A Jeep is rugged with large tires and very spacious. I think that we would all agree that a Ferrari is an amazing specimen of a vehicle. However, if you took it on a camping trip, you would think it was the worst car in the world. Would you blame the Ferrari for being so horrible or would you understand that you did not use it correctly? It just was not built for camping! While the Jeep would be great for the camping trip, would you be angry at it for flipping over the first time it took a curve when racing it at the Indy 500? Sounds ridiculous, I know. However, we do this with people, *all the time*!

Think about trees. If you want shade, you are not going to sit under a cactus, will you? Of course not, you will look for a willow tree. And if you wanted to be in touch with nature and decided to hug the cactus, would you get mad at it when it pricked you with its spikes? If you want a guard dog, are you going to go for the labradoodle or a German Shepard?

With these examples, you can tell the function of each within seconds. How can you tell? Of course, you see them with your eyes.

People are no different. Our physicality (structure) very much determines our best use (function), as well as our strengths and weaknesses. Sure, we can learn to be strong at certain activities, but if they are not natural to us, that extra effort can cause us to drain our energy, fatigue us and negatively affect our entire demeanor. That would be like putting a kayak on top of your Ferrari when you head to the river. You can get away with it once or twice, but eventually your roof will weaken and the foundation will be forever damaged.

If you were a car, what type of vehicle would you be? Are you slender, agile and quick like a Jaguar, or a bulkier car that can carry a heavy load like a Suburban? If you were a bird, would you be lighthearted and fun like a hummingbird? Or maybe you prefer to come out at night and be on watch like an owl. If you were an animal in the wild, would you be strategic, stealthy and calculated like a panther or do you express more regal qualities and lead your pride from the top of a mountain like a lion? We have elements of all these qualities, but some are more pronounced than others. Understanding your true nature reveals *what* you are, as opposed to *who* you are.

Understanding your true nature and that of your kids and their other parent will help nurture those relationships and help them thrive, even if the relationship is somewhat contentious at times.

YOU-tility #2

Drivers: What drives and motivates you? What about your kids? Throughout this book I have woven several examples of drivers and motivators within my anecdotes. For example, I love to entertain at my home, whether it be hosting a pool party or playing the piano for guests—and I admit that I enjoy receiving positive feedback knowing they enjoyed themselves.

I need order and organization in my world. My wife thrives when she has alone time to recharge (whereas I can go on and on for days), and she is very persistent with accomplishing tasks. Optimism is also a quality of hers, and I learned through the ULT that she thrives when she has something to look forward to. Therefore, I know that telling her ahead of time about something she will love will go much further for me than surprising her. In other words, telling her I bought her jewelry (and giving her time to be excited about it and looking forward to receiving it) will score me more points than simply surprising her. Our son, Zion, has this in common with her. Some people need to create protection while others have the burning desire to create a huge empire.

The test also reveals the propensity for one to be violent when angry, steal when in need and others to stray when they get bored or do not have their needs met. The list goes on and on, but knowing an individual's drivers and motivators is an essential key to any successful relationship, whether it is at home, at work or anywhere else in life. Also, it is important to understand how you (and others) will act when needs are not being met. With this understanding, you can "feed" yourself and the ones you care about appropriately to create abundant joy. This will help one another thrive and consequently prevent wilting and toxicity that may otherwise damage the relationship.

YOU-tility #3

Refinement: What is your tolerance toward people, places and things? Have you ever been at a party and just felt it wasn't your atmosphere and needed to leave? The people are nice, there was nothing wrong with them, but you just did not "vibe" with them or the scene. Perhaps the tone was off. Are there people in your life that you can be around 24/7 and never get enough time with them, and others where after 30 minutes you want to get away from them, and maybe even take a shower?

We all have an innate tolerance and threshold to everything in our surroundings, whether living or inanimate. Your home, the clothes and jewelry you wear, the vehicle you drive, the places you visit and even your workspace all have levels of refinement and distinct qualities that you either resonate with or do not. Lack of compatibility with anything around you can cause turmoil and drain you, and it is often the silent killer of relationships.

While *innate* compatibility does not change, the relationships that are stressed can be improved once we bring understanding of this nuance into our lives. For example, couples can survive (and even thrive) even if they lack compatibility, as long as they are aware of the differences and use tools and strategies to handle their differences.

When raising children, refinement differences can get even more challenging. There are more dishes to do, more clothes on the ground and do not even get me started on the toys all over the house! When one parent has a higher level of refinement than the other, understanding the impact and creating appropriate strategies to mitigate incompatibilities is essential to maintain a harmonious home.

YOU-tility #4

Connection: How do you learn and download information? How about your kids? We have heard that some people are visual learners while others are auditory; but that is only scratching the surface.

To learn, we first must connect, which in turn allows us to open up and "download information." Connection with ourselves and others requires some nuance and understanding as to what opens us up. Whether it is connecting with a potential new love interest, a family member, a co-worker or a client, the key to opening the door is always available to us, we just need to know which key will fit in which lock.

For some people, the key is being in motion and for others, it must be enjoyable to their senses. For me, I primarily need to be around living things and my wife needs to have something that stimulates her mind. So, I have learned that if she is the living thing that I want to be around, I better say something interesting!

YOU-tility #5

Perception: How do you perceive life and the world around you? Is the cup half-empty? Or maybe cups are not good enough for you because you only want crystal. Perhaps you come off a bit negative, always seeing what is not working first. Or maybe you're the eternal optimist and it is all rainbows and unicorns. I am one of those positive people who may seem negative at first, but that is because I need to receive all the information, process it, and then react.

There are many useful personality and psychometric tests out there that companies use for hiring and positioning and relationship coaches use for couples and families. However, none of them do what the ULT does. The ULT uses *physiometrics*, which considers physicality, which none of the others even touch on. The ULT can give those other tests a place to live, meaning, make better sense of the results. For example, if a certain test revealed that the person is good at leading, the ULT will confirm whether leadership is natural to him/her or whether it was a learned skill (that may drain and damage him/her over time like the kayak on the Ferrari). Additionally, it would reveal what type of leader he/she is naturally inclined to be. This is just a tiny sampling as to what the ULT has to offer.

The ULT brings the five *YOU-tilities* to life (and so much more) and demonstrates the perfection in all of us. When we see each other through the eyes of nature and appreciate our own perfection, we will automatically find ourselves in harmonious relationships. It takes work, it takes understanding, it takes desire, it takes love, but most importantly, it takes knowledge.

I recommend that all families have a coach to help navigate this world and help express their authentic selves every day in life. My personal preference would be to hire a coach that uses technology like the ULT that reveals your authenticity!

Brooke and her team of practitioners bring this knowledge to help families with:

> ➢ Conflict resolution
> ➢ Teens in crisis
> ➢ Understanding how their child learns and downloads information
> ➢ Sibling rivalry
> ➢ Child behavioral issues
> ➢ Parent-child interactions
> ➢ Chores & activities that help their child thrive

They bring this knowledge to help couples with:

- Marital success strategies
- Parenting as a team (whether they are together as a couple or not)
- Conflict resolution
- Affair proofing the relationship
- Understanding their mate
- Learning how to help and support each other to thrive as individuals and together
- Premarital advisement

They bring this knowledge to individuals with:

- Career discovery
- Dating/attracting the right spouse or partner
- Creating and nurturing lifelong friendships
- Learning what "makes them tic"
- Divorce recovery
- Single parenting
- Overcoming barriers
- Stress management
- Learning styles for education

They bring this knowledge to consult with businesses and organizations to help:

- Bottom line increases, including profit
- Hiring the right person and proper position placement
- Reduced turnover
- Retention of key staff

- ➢ Conflict resolution
- ➢ Improved performance of teams and executives to increase the effectiveness of the organization
- ➢ Improved relationships among peers, subordinates and management
- ➢ Improved communication and focus on customer service
- ➢ Building a foundation of success by utilizing team members' natural talents

BONUSES & RESOURCES Test drive the assessment at a significantly reduced rate so you can learn more about Y.O.U. and your family and how to help everyone in your home thrive on a daily basis.

9-4

BEING INNER DIRECTED

♫ AMAZING GRACE

I will never forget, it was the opening Monday Night Football game, kicking off the 2001 NFL season: the New York Giants versus the Denver Broncos. This was the game to watch, and the Giants were the team to beat. Eight short months earlier, the Giants had lost in the Super Bowl to the Baltimore Ravens. During the off season, the Giants did not lose too many of their top players, and they added a few new great picks. Many predicted them to dominate the National Football League and repeat their appearance to the Super Bowl that season.

That night I had a bunch of friends over to my home to watch the game. We were hoping this would be the beginning of an epic Giants season. Unfortunately, it did not turn out that way. In the first quarter of the game, the Giants were getting blown out by the Broncos, and I was losing it. At half-time, I kicked my friends out of my home because I did not want to even look at anyone. I was that angry.

(When I was a kid, my dad had New York Giants season tickets, and my older brother Scott and I would go to the games with him regularly. I learned at an early age that when you are happy with how your team was performing, you would scream with joy, whistle and applaud. However, when things did not go as planned, it was because the referees were jerks, the coaches were morons or the players were terrible. When the Giants won, we were happy, or at least satisfied because they did what we expected them to do, and when they lost, we were angry. This attitude toward sports carried into my adult life. I know many of you can relate.)

The next morning when I woke up, I turned on my television to watch the "lowlights," because from the Giants perspective, there were no highlights. When my television turned on, it was still on the same channel that the game was on the night before. Only this time, it was not a football game, it was the morning news program.

The very moment that my television screen showed an image, the second commercial airliner flew into the World Trade Center. As I watched in horror, I immediately forgot about why I even turned on the television. At first, I thought I was watching a movie or something. It all just seemed so surreal.

As I was watching the horrific events of 9/11 ensue in real time before my eyes just a few miles away from where I was sitting in my bed, I started to think about all of the people I knew that worked in and around those towers, including those in my home the previous night.

I was on the phone with my father watching it all unfold, which was exceedingly difficult, because only a decade earlier, he worked on the 104th floor of the North Tower.

Embedded in my memory forever will be our conversation when suddenly, at 9:59 a.m., I only saw dust around one of the towers. I said to my dad, "I think the building is gone." My dad said that I could not be correct; the smoke was just blocking the view of the building he used to work in. Within minutes, the news confirmed everyone's worst nightmare, and it continued to worsen.

Along with thousands of families affected by the tragic events of 9/11, the Stenzlers lost family and friends that we loved and cared for. It could have been much worse if my dad still worked at the company he departed from years earlier. My brothers Scott and Marc and sister Haley all worked in finance, and they quite possibly would have been working with my dad at that company. While that company employed many of my dad's friends and colleagues and someone my brother Marc cared for dearly, my immediate family was spared. Unfortunately, too many other families were not so fortunate. That company alone lost at least 658 of its 960 employees.

As the day went on (before we knew names of those who perished), I began to think about some of my friends who were in my home the night before that worked on Wall Street and that I kicked out of my home the night before. Is it possible that my last interaction with some of them would have been yelling because of a stupid football game? Thankfully none of those friends were killed the next day, but they could have been. I knew right then and there that I needed to make a major change in my life.

I started to look more deeply into my life, my frustrations and my reactions and realized that they were not necessarily serving me very well. I began to acknowledge that Michael Strahan, the defensive end for the New York Giants at the time does not care how many people I adjust. That would not affect his life any more than how many times he sacks a quarterback affects my life!

I did a lot of reading, praying, meditating and professional/personal development seminars. At one of the seminars I attended, Dr. Bob Hoffman and Dr. Dennis Perman and their team at the consulting group, The Masters Circle, taught us what it means to be inner directed. This was life changing for me. Being *inner directed* in short is about not allowing outside (external) influences to control the way one reacts.

How many times have you overreacted to a situation or reacted in a manner that was not most productive? I know I have, that's for sure!

Every single day, we encounter situations and events from outside of ourselves that we had little or nothing to do with and typically cannot control. Let's refer to these as external influences. Anything outside of your own doing that can impact you physically or emotionally can be considered an external influence.

> *There are two things in this world . . . things you can control and things you cannot control. And one thing you can always control is how you respond to the things you cannot control.*

Think about your life right now. How do you react (or overreact) to external influences? When you are inner directed, you are able to create a life where you are at peace no matter what the outside circumstances may be, and your reactions are not based solely on emotion. I am not in any way suggesting that we should be robots or numb to the outside world and never have emotion, we absolutely should. However, we cannot allow those emotions to control us and affect us in ways that are not productive and in our best interests. Increased emotional reactions create anxiety, stress and discontentment. Maintaining a level of neutrality to external influences allows us to respond more effectively, thoughtfully and consciously resulting in a better outcome overall.

Much like the events of September 11, 2001, we will constantly need to deal with circumstances that we cannot control. My chiropractic brethren decided to take the pain and anguish of that attack and do something constructive with it.

For the first time in history, the chiropractic profession worked with the American Red Cross and Federal Emergency Management Agency (FEMA) to provide relief workers with support by providing chiropractic care during their rescue efforts. Organized through the New York Chiropractic Council (an organization that I was an Executive Board member of), chiropractic colleagues from around the country and I served at respite centers in Manhattan thousands of rescue and relief workers, providing them much needed chiropractic care so they could perform the best at their jobs.

Between the combination of them receiving a loving adjustment and the touch from someone who cared for them, the workers would walk into our area with their heads down feeling exhausted, sad and deflated and they would leave a different person, with more energy, comfort and exuberance. Of all the services offered at the various respite sites, chiropractic care was the one that was requested to be available to the workers 24 hours per day, 7 days per week for more than an entire year. (In 2001, I received the award of New York

Chiropractor of the Year from The Council for helping coordinate the efforts of bringing in and scheduling chiropractors from around the country to the respite sites.)

Learning to be inner directed does not take one day. It takes a lot of practice, discipline, prayer, meditation and patience. For me, one of the ways I exercised my inner-directed muscles was to learn and daily recite the Serenity Prayer by Reinhold Niebuhr.

> *"God grant me the serenity to accept the things I cannot change; the courage to change the things I can; and the wisdom to know the difference."*

Being inner directed is not just about controlling your emotions when bad things happen. It encompasses your attitude and perception toward everything, including why you do what you do the way you do it as learned in the ULT (*see Ch. 9-3*).

Some people are just wired to thrive with praise and acknowledgement for the good deeds they perform. That too is an example of an external influence, one that you have absolutely no control over. While it may be in some people's nature to desire praise (which is one of the revelations you may discover after taking the ULT as it was for me), it should not be necessary. Your goal should be to always do your best, even when no one is watching. If you are a parent of a child under the age of 16, I recommend looking into Amy McCready's work with positive parenting; she teaches parents how to avoid turning your child into a praise junkie. Children need to learn to be inner directed just as much as an adult does. Remember, kids learn by observing adults, so be a good role model.

When you can control your emotions, think and speak positively and be inner directed, you will find that it will be easier to handle all setbacks gracefully. Also, you will find much more inner joy in your life as well as self-confidence, self-assurance and self-awareness. If you do not want to practice being inner directed for yourself, at least do it for your children. They are watching!

BONUSES & RESOURCES *6 Techniques to Manage Your Emotions* Worksheet

9-5

STARTING THE DAY WITH INTENTION

♫ WE'VE GOT THE POWER

I have learned that one of the best ways to practice inner directedness is to build my armor each and every morning and prepare myself for the day that is to come.

How do you start each day? Is it reactive or proactive? Do you check your emails? Your social media? Turn on the news?

It is my intention to get you to start thinking about being proactive with everything you do. While I am sure it is important to see what you "missed" when you were sleeping, most things can wait. If not, just wake up a little bit earlier and no one will know that you could have checked your messages sooner.

When I wake up in the morning, the first thing I do is silently recite my daily affirmation. Then I visualize my day. I think about my schedule and visualize how I would like the day to go. I get into very specific detail and play the day out in my mind as if it's a movie. Once I'm done visualizing, I express my gratitude to God for all the wonderfulness that lies ahead and I also express gratitude for the past.

Once I complete this ritual, I then go into the life of most CEOs and check my messages before moving on with my morning routine.

Motivational speaker, life coach and billionaire Tony Robbins talks about starting each day with an "Hour of Power," and that has been a gamechanger for me. It does not need to be a complete hour, but it must be enough time for you to visualize and plan your day to get it started on a good footing. And it can be longer than an hour if needed and available. This may be your time for prayer, meditation, exercise, journaling, writing/reading goals and reciting affirmations. Heck, even stretching or doing a few pushups is better than doing nothing.

When I start my day off right, I find that my day flows much more smoothly. Additionally, when things occur unexpectedly (which happens a lot), I can handle the setbacks much more gracefully and skillfully.

Think about how your family starts its day. Is it chaotic or peaceful? Are people happy or grunting that they want to go back to sleep? Are you rushing to get your kids dressed, fed and off to school? Is there something you can do to inspire them to start their day with an hour of power? Consider ways you can create a harmonious start to every day at home, especially the school days.

BONUSES & RESOURCES *16 Empowering Morning Rituals* Guide

9-6

WATCH YOUR MOUTH

♫ MORE THAN WORDS

"I suck!"

That would be heard from hundreds of yards away when I was on a golf course, often followed by the sound of my club hitting a tree or snapping in half. Yes, I had anger issues, but my words did not help either. This is just another example of why an hour of power is necessary to start my day, not to mention, learning to be inner directed!

If you remember earlier in the book when you read about the power of words, you are aware that what you speak about, you bring about (*see Ch. 2-1*). When I said, "I suck," I affirmed that I suck.

If you constantly refer to the leg that hurts you as, "my bad leg," you just affirmed that you have a bad leg.

People say affirmations hundreds of times daily, whether they know it or not. The problem is, most affirmations are not positive. Worse yet, negative affirmations reinforce the exact behavior or result you do not want.

So why do we do it?

Everything you say to yourself is an affirmation, and you are affirming a belief about yourself. Every time you say that you cannot start your morning without a cup of coffee, you are affirming that you are caffeine dependent. There are an infinite number of negative self-talk examples I can demonstrate, but hopefully you get my drift. The idea of reciting purposeful positive affirmations daily is to create the habit of saying what you really want and attracting the results you desire in life.

Positive affirmations are statements that are recited to help avoid self-sabotage, degrading, and negative thoughts. The more you recite a particular affirmation, the more you will believe the statement to be true . . . and that can put you on the road to achieving the goal you have, or overcome the struggles of the past. They are generally short and specific thoughts that target a specific area, behavior or belief that you have historically struggled with. When you create a positive affirmation, make sure it is not too long. It should be easy to memorize, written in present tense and always spoken with positive words. It is not advisable to recite what you want to avoid but to only speak what you desire.

Think about how you can change your language for the better. Anytime you hear yourself say something negative, particularly about yourself, stop for a moment. Consider how you could have phrased that better and more positively. I recommend accountability partners to call you out when you do it if you really want to improve your language.

For me, I created a new habit of reciting an affirmation while playing golf. Whenever I would hit a terrible shot, I would say, "I get better and better with every swing!" I have taken so many bad shots that you would think I could beat Tiger Woods by now. While positive affirmations are helpful, they will never replace practice . . . especially when it comes to golf!

We all know that the words we say affect others, but they also affect us. Using the correct words can transform our reality. Thinking and processing a positive word in the brain can stimulate frontal lobe activity. Words can encourage and give confidence to those around us.

Through understanding the power of words, lives can be transformed. Drawing attention to the positives through words will relate a happier sense of direction and outlook for our lives. As for negative words, they connote a dangerous and anxious feeling in others; this feeling can lead to negative effects in one's mind and body. Therefore, it is important to focus on the positive, especially through words, so one's life can be optimistic and happy.

As noted earlier in this book, I'd like to re-quote the Old Testament of the Bible: *"Death and life are in the power of the tongue; and they that love it shall eat the fruit thereof"* (Prov. 18:21, 21st Century King James Version). What this means to me essentially is, "What you speak about, you bring about." You attract into your life first your thoughts, then your words (followed by your actions). Your words have the power to attract good or bad results, so watch what you say. You then "reap" what your *words* have "sown."

Unfortunately, parents are negatively affirming all too often, and this is especially dangerous when speaking with your children. "Bad boy!" "He's so shy." "You always do that!"

Negative talk, whether it is to yourself or others, is a large contributing factor to low self-esteem and the catalyst to limiting beliefs. Limiting beliefs are essentially opinions or thoughts one has about themselves that ultimately holds them back and prevents the achievement of many personal and professional aspirations.

As my little boy Zion grows up, my wife, Brooke, and I are very mindful of the words we use about him and around him. When he misbehaves, we would *never* call him a bad boy. If we do that, we are more likely to convince him that he is a bad boy, especially since young children really do not know the difference between truth and lies. Besides, why would we ever want to affirm such a thing? If we did that, based on the biblical text, we would "eat the fruit" we have spoken by potentially creating a bad boy. Instead we say, "Zion, you're a good boy but you did a bad thing." That language reinforces the behavior we desire while letting him know that he *is* good, while informing him that his action was unacceptable.

I was even reminded of this myself recently when speaking with my good friends Barrett and Tram who have a son a little younger than Zion. I was expressing to them some frustrations we were having when Zion would do things that were not in his (or our) best interest. We told them that we did not want to be yelling parents and wanted a better way to discipline him.

To be honest, it was a bit of a kick in the butt when they told me exactly what I already knew . . . tell him what we want him to do, not what we do not want him to do. They are constantly doing positive reinforcement with their son, and I came to realize I could be better at it. This is one of the many reasons why you should spend time with people who share your values in life and will keep you accountable to be the person you want to be.

Always remain mindful of the words you use every time you speak. Use words that are positive and empowering. Use words that are more likely to attract what you desire as opposed to repel what you do not.

Think of the words and phrases you may use or hear daily that are a form of self-sabotage. "That's my bad leg." "Oh, that's because of my allergies." "You know, it's because of her cancer." When we take ownership of something that is not desired in our lives, we "energetically" give it more power.

There is a field of study called Neuro-linguistic Programming (NLP) developed by Richard Bandler and John Grinder which teaches this (and so much more) in detail, and I highly recommend looking into it. The phrases above could easily be reworded using NLP: "My leg that is getting better and better every day."

Positive Psychology, a term coined by Abraham Maslow in the 1950s, is essentially the scientific study of what makes life most worth living, according to psychologist Christopher Peterson.

When people positively affirm and use positive words in their daily talk, they are typically very positive people in general. They then are able to experience many more positive emotions, such as hope, gratitude, joy, love and ultimately happiness. To me, love is the reason for life and happiness is the result.

How can you possibly love yourself when you are bombarding yourself with negative self-talk? Imagine if all the negative things you said to yourself, you actually said to someone else. Do you think that person would like you very much? Unlikely! It takes work to express the love that you have for yourself and speaking consciously positive words.

Try this right now . . . walk in front of a mirror and say out loud, "I love you."

Were you able to do it? How did it make you feel? Were you uncomfortable doing it? Would you do it if someone else were around?

I find that my relationship with God and the love I have for Him has helped me create unconditional love for myself, which in turn has helped me love others on a much deeper level.

Hope is a feeling of expectation and desire for a certain thing to happen. Hope is a promise, goal, or gift from God. While most people think that hope is wishful thinking, that is not what the Bible means by hope. The Bible understands hope as a "confident expectation." It is a firm assurance regarding circumstances that are unclear and unknown. Without hope, life loses its meaning for many. Optimistic outlooks on life generate less risks for stress, anxiety, and depression. Hope is associated with happiness, positive outcomes and even better academic achievement.

BONUSES & RESOURCES *Affirmation E-Book for Parents and Kids!*

BONUSES & RESOURCES *Promoting Positive Self Esteem in Children* E-Book

BONUSES & RESOURCES *Loving Yourself* Workbook

BONUSES & RESOURCES *NLP* Fact Sheet

BONUSES & RESOURCES *The Parent's Guide to Promoting Positive Self Esteem for their Kids*

WORKBOOK ACTIVITY *Family Affirmation* Worksheet and Action Guide

WORKBOOK ACTIVITY *Overcoming Limiting Beliefs* Worksheet

9-7

GOAL SETTING

♫ WE ARE THE CHAMPIONS

As you probably picked up on when you read about my need for the Giants to always win, or my previous golf antics, I am a rather intense person. That is not only consistent with being a loud New Yorker, but it is also shows up in my ULT results (*see Ch. 9-3*). Being an intense individual, I also lacked patience and had a short fuse. In summary, it did not take much to frustrate me and set me off. Never in a violent way, but in an unbecoming way.

Year after year, I had set a New Year's resolution to be more patient and less frustrated and to react more calmly. Nothing changed. Not until I set a goal. And by setting a goal, I do not mean just saying that I wanted to change. I took a methodological approach toward goal setting and followed the process until it was achieved.

Goal setting is the process of identifying something that you want to accomplish, as well as establishing measurable goals in timeframes. It is important to set goals that motivate you. There is an immense amount of benefits to goal setting, especially when done correctly and with the best intentions. By creating goals and sticking to them, this provides direction in one's life. It provides a clearer focus of what is important as well as clarity in decision making. It gives you control of your future and provides motivation. Lastly, it gives you a sense of personal satisfaction and purpose in life.

Your goals should be tied to your values and your purpose. Your purpose is ultimately your why.

Why were you brought into this world? Why do you exist? Why do you wake up every morning? What purpose do you serve?

I encourage you to determine your purpose statement before you set your goals. Once you understand your why, you should set your goals in accordance with it. If you have a goal that does not impact your purpose, you should think about whether that goal is really worth pursuing, or perhaps you should modify your purpose statement.

Your sense of purpose motivates and drives you toward a satisfying future; a sense of purpose helps prioritize your life. Striving to fulfill your purpose creates focus on what is most important in your life. Living a life "on and of purpose" allows you to invest your time, energy, talents, and passions. Fulfillment in your purpose allows you to live a value-based life. This means that you can really focus on your core values.

Your purpose can demonstrate your true integrity. Trust and faith are very important in understanding and believing in one's purpose. Having this trust and faith is crucial in living a positive life. Lastly, people who know their purpose in life can go with the flow and allow what is going to happen, happen.

If you consider yourself a spiritual person and open to ideas that may be different from your religious background (if any), two books that I recommend that can help you understand and find your purpose are *Your Best Life Now* by Joel Osteen and *A Purpose Driven Life* by Rick Warren. In spite of having been raised in Long Island in a Jewish family, I can tell you that both books from Christian pastors have been tremendously positive influences in my life.

My purpose is, "To serve God by assisting all people in realizing their true perfection." By having a clear purpose in life, I can look at my actions and goals and see if they are in *alignment* (*see Ch. 4-1*) with that purpose. For example, whether I am providing a chiropractic adjustment, challenging someone in a coaching session, inspiring an individual in an audience or motivating a reader . . . I am proudly serving my purpose because that person will be better than before.

Tony Robbins says that people are motivated by one of two things . . . to move away from pain or to move toward pleasure. While I very much agree with Robbins, I believe that there is a third group of people: those who are motivated by purpose. People living with purpose will find themselves moving through both pain and pleasure to ultimately serve their purpose.

I knew that my issues with frustration were not helping me serve my purpose. That became an additional driver for me to make that change. I began to think about people in my life who would never show their frustration the way I did. I thought of a mentor of mine who coached me when I was a member of The Masters Circle, Dr.

Janice Hughes. Janice was always cool, calm and collected. She had her sh*t together! I could never visualize her punching a wall because she got mad at something.

Everyone in the goal-setting world these days talks about SMART goals. They must be specific, measurable, attainable, relevant and time-bound. As part of my methodology of goal setting, I include two more extremely important elements . . . mimic the thoughts and actions that led to someone else's success (relative to your goal) and visualization.

If you want to play basketball as well as Michael Jordan played, you may want to see how he trained. If you go to the gymnasium once per week to practice, you will probably never shoot free throws like he did. What was his mentality? What was his thought process? What was his WHY? When you can get into the head of these people and take on their attributes, you have a much greater chance of achieving a goal.

Think of someone who has already achieved a particular goal you desire or already lives a certain way. I started to exercise my "I am Janice" muscle whenever a frustrating circumstance came my way. I would think, "What would Janice do and how would she react?" Each time, my reaction got less and less intense. I now believe that I have almost complete control over my reactions. It does not mean that I do not get frustrated anymore, I do! However, I no longer respond in an unproductive way or out of emotion. This goal achievement not only made me look less foolish but also helped me express more inner directedness.

Teaching kids goal-setting strategies will certainly provide them an advantage that they can benefit from throughout their lifetimes. People who set and achieve goals and live with purpose are among the healthiest, happiest and most successful on the planet, and they demonstrate incredible discipline.

WORKBOOK ACTIVITY *Defining Your Life's Purpose* Worksheet
WORKBOOK ACTIVITY *Setting Personal Goals* Workbook

9-8

VISUALIZATION

♫ I CAN SEE CLEARLY NOW

"The only thing worse than being blind is having sight but no vision"
—Hellen Keller

Earlier, I referenced the story of the archer and the "village genius" (*see Ch. 2-1*).

I like to think of visualization as yet another muscle to exercise. The more you think about something, the more likely you can bring that thought to reality (within reason of course). Visualization is a cognitive tool that accesses the imagination and is used to realize all aspects of an object, sound, place, or outcome. This can often include a mental sensory experience of sound, sight, smell, taste and touch. Visualization is often used to bring relaxation to someone and can help navigate through a seemingly uncontrollable situation. Visualization is especially helpful for people dealing with anxiety. With the aid of visualizing a vacation place, people with even severe anxiety and depression can be brought to a place of relaxation and even contentment.

Visualization is especially helpful in everyday life for people of all ages, especially children. Visualizing positive imagery before professional interactions, all types of tests, academia, performances, health issues and so much more can potentially help create the outcome you desire. Visualization can help people organize their thoughts, mentally prepare themselves and reduce stress.

As in the story with the archer, you have the opportunity to create a life that you desire to a large extent, just by choosing to see it that way.

I believe wholeheartedly that the vision board I created specific to my DREAM wife (*see Ch. 9-2*) helped me attract Brooke into my life.

BONUSES & RESOURCES *Take Back Your Family's Time* Guide
WORKBOOK ACTIVITY *The Guide to Creating Your Family's Vision Board*

9-9

"THOUGHTS BECOME THINGS"

♫ IF YOU COULD READ MY MIND

Remember the Lao Tzu quote you read earlier in this book:

> Watch your thoughts, they become words;
>
> Watch your words, they become actions;
>
> Watch your actions, they become habits;
>
> Watch your habits, they become character;
>
> Watch your character, for it becomes your destiny.

If your very thoughts ultimately lead to your destiny, wouldn't it be great if you could consciously control them? Well you can . . . it just takes practice and the understanding of where your thoughts come from.

I do not believe that most of your thoughts are random, but more so a reflection of your lifestyle. Studies have shown that the average person has around 6,200 thoughts per day and the vast majority of those thoughts were related to the previous day. To me, it sounds like a waste to constantly be living in the past!

I see prayer, meditation and even dreaming (awake or asleep) as great tools to get thoughts and inspiration from the Divine. When your mind is clear and your intention is pure, you allow a higher power to speak and enlighten you.

Your thoughts are also greatly formed from the reflection of everything you see and hear in your daily life. Think about the television and movies that you watch and books and articles that you read. Think about these external influences in your life and categorize each of them as constructive or destructive. A constructive influence is one that is building up and positive, whereas a destructive influence is negative and tears down.

If you are watching the news for example, does it make you feel good about the world, or scared and angry? Your television, movies, magazines and books . . . are they inspiring or demonstrating horror, pain, gratuitous sex and violence?

Now consider the people you spend the majority of your time with. Do they speak life and inspiration to you? Do they build you up and encourage you to be your best, or tear you down and tell you what can't be done? Do they speak highly of others or enjoy gossiping about other's woes of life?

Remember the Jim Rohn's line, "You are the average of the five people you spend the most time with." Think about the five people you spend most of your time with. Are they happy? Are they successful? If you could be like anyone in the world, what are the characteristics of that individual? How many of those characteristics live in the people you spend most of your time with?

Remember the old computer term GIGO, garbage in, garbage out (*see Ch. 4-1*). Well, if you put garbage into your mind from your eyes and ears, what do you think you will get out?

If you want to control your thoughts and keep them as positive and constructive, you must live consciously. Consider where the information you are putting into your mind is coming from and whether it is more constructive or destructive and then eliminate as many destructive influences as possible.

Studies show that watching violent movies can cause people to become more aggressive. It is even more dangerous for those who have an abrasive past to start with. Watching and experiencing violence and negative aspects in films can wrap one's mind up in gore, destruction and anger. This is a dangerous mindset to live in as it can cause anger, anxiety, and depression. Extensive research indicates that violence in film and media contributes to aggression, desensitization of violence, nightmares and the fear/anxiety of being harmed.

Lastly, violence in the media can desensitize viewers to experiencing emotional responses to acts of violence. It can also lead to a decreased or no feeling of guilt for conducting violent or negative acts. All in all, watching or playing violent video games, films or television shows can lead to an increased aggressive behavior. If this behavior eventually becomes unchecked or not helped, the brain may change to release less serotonin, leading to an increase of violence. In an article by L. Rowell Huesmann published in the *Journal of Adolescent Health*, Huesmann concluded, "Research evidence has accumulated over the past half-century that exposure to violence on television, movies, and most recently in video games increases the risk of violent behavior on the viewer's part just as growing up in an environment filled with real violence increases the risk of violent behavior."[17]

When you are mindful of what you are watching, what you are reading and the people you spend time with, you are increasing the odds that your thoughts will resonate at a much higher frequency. When you take control of your thoughts . . . you take control of your destiny!

9-10

DISCIPLINE: TURNING DEPRIVATION INTO EMPOWERMENT

♫ EYE OF THE TIGER

I think we can all agree that the people with the most discipline are the most likely to achieve their set goals and enjoy success in life. Whether the goal is achieving a certain body weight, earning a particular income or scoring 100% on an exam, one must behave and work in a strictly controlled and regular manner.

Think about yourself or child in the past where a desired outcome was not achieved. How much planning and consistency took place throughout the process? What was the level of impulse control? How would achieving that goal have impacted your life or that of your child?

People are quick to admit fault by affirming that they just are not disciplined enough. Unfortunately, they often try to make themselves feel better by shaming the achiever as being too disciplined, as if that achiever is unhappy because of his/her choices.

Happiness and discipline are not mutually exclusive. Those who do not need instant gratification feel that the accomplishment brings them more long-term joy than the temporary satisfaction had they not controlled their impulses.

Discipline often defers temporary satisfaction for long-term joy, but that's not always the case. The key is to not allow discipline to lead to deprivation, but rather to empowerment. You should feel good about the choices you make and the temporary satisfaction you may be passing on. If you regret that choice, then it is important to re-evaluate your values. Every choice you make is value clarification.

For example, if you want to slim down, you first must consider why you want to weigh less. Whether the reason(s) is related to health, looks, clothing fit, attracting a mate, performing in a sport or getting a role in a movie, it doesn't matter for this point. What is important is that the reason for the desired weight must be valued higher to you than the things that are keeping you from releasing the weight. If you prefer to regularly eat decadent desserts, skip your exercise and sit around watching television, then you are essentially putting those activities at a higher value than the reason you want to lose the weight.

The goal is not to deprive yourself in life of the things you enjoy, even if they may not all be that good for you. As mentioned in the preface of this book, everything in moderation leads to mediocrity. I believe that we should fill ourselves with excessive goodness and make an excessive amount of constructive choices—and very little of the destructive stuff—as the result will be more joy, contentment and ultimately happiness.

WORKBOOK ACTIVITY *How to Strengthen Your Self-Discipline* Action Guide

9-11

BEING GRATEFUL

♫ GRATITUDE

"Always have an attitude of gratitude; and if for some reason you can't be grateful, at least be graceful" —Dr. Bob Hoffman.

Cultivating gratitude is a positive emotion that must be practiced and learned. Gratitude is all about expressing appreciation; it is being content with one's experiences. Being aware of positive and negative effects is key in achieving gratitude. With gratitude comes a feeling of well-being and mindful awareness. Alongside the mental benefits that come from gratitude, one can also reap physical benefits.

With a healthy mind comes a happy body. Gratitude has been shown to lower blood pressure, strengthen the immune system by increasing white blood cell count, and even reduce aches and pains. As Bing Crosby's character in the movie *White Christmas* would advise, count your blessings instead of sheep. Gratitude has been proven to help people fall asleep quicker, get better sleep, and wake up more refreshed and rested. Expressing gratitude also strengthens relationships as well as encourages paying it forward. Grateful people tend to be more compassionate, generous and helpful.

Some people use what's called a gratitude rock and keep it in their pocket as a reminder to be grateful every day. It's a great reminder for kids too! All you need to do is write something inspirational on the rock or paint it a certain color. Be creative if you so choose. Any time you feel down or worried about something, take the rock out of your pocket. Think of three things to be grateful for and see how your mood changes.

Maintaining a gratitude journal is also a great tool. If you are constantly recording things that you are grateful for, the impact compounds greatly when you read it and reflect back on them.

Brooke and I are often teaching Zion different ways to express gratitude, including before every meal. It is especially heart-warming when he jumps in to say grace. And every night just before going to sleep, Zion is asked these three questions (and then he asks them back):

1) Who did you help today?
2) What did you learn today?
3) What are you grateful for?

BONUSES & RESOURCES Your very own Gratitude Journal!
WORKBOOK ACTIVITY *Gratitude Journal* Worksheet
WORKBOOK ACTIVITY *Express Your Gratitude* Activity
WORKBOOK ACTIVITY *Top 5 Ways to Feel Gratitude* Factsheet

9-12

FORGIVENESS

♫ ANGRY YOUNG MAN

"Holding onto anger is like drinking poison and expecting the other person to die," —Buddha

Letting go of anger, grudges and bitterness toward others makes way for an improved and positive peace of mind. Forgiveness leads to healthier relationships. Through trust and faith in friends, significant others and colleagues, relationships become stronger. Also, an overall improvement of mental health can occur through forgiveness.

By choosing to focus on the positives rather than the negatives, people will see a decrease in worry and anxiety, leading to less stress and hostility. From this, people will experience lower blood pressure, decreasing one's risk for heart disease. Improved heart health and a stronger immune system can manifest themselves through this as well.

Forgiveness will also lead to fewer symptoms of depression and melancholy. Focusing on the positives of life really excels one's mind to become hopeful and trusting.

Lastly, forgiveness can lead to self-confidence and an improved self-esteem. Having more positivity and self-worth will create a balanced and happy life.

REFLECTION OPPORUNITY

Is there someone or something still upsetting you that you may not even realize? Maybe something your spouse/partner/child's other parent may have done? Maybe something your child said or did?

What from your upbringing/parents or family dynamics have you still not let go of?

Are you teaching your kids about the importance of forgiveness?

WORKBOOK ACTIVITY *The Busy Parents Guide to Better Connection and Communication with Your Kids*
BONUSES & RESOURCES *Forgiveness Meditation* Video
BONUSES & RESOURCES Purchase multimedia sets on forgiveness at a discount.

9-13

CHOOSE HAPPINESS

♫ DON'T WORRY, BE HAPPY!

As discussed earlier regarding the ULT test (*see Ch. 9-3*), there are some people who have the natural talent of creating security and protection. In a healthy mental state, these people serve humanity in so many meaningful ways, including police officers, firefighters and parents of toddlers, to name a few. However, when people with this talent as a primary driver are under stress, they may demonstrate potentially dangerous behaviors, including panic.

When we choose to worry (and yes, it is a choice), we are stealing happiness from the current moment in life. Chronic worriers can face extreme troubles when trying to shake away their worries and anxiousness. This causes them great distress and disability. After all, when did the emotion of worry ever solve the issue that was concerning?

Ongoing fear and anxiety can be harmful to one's mental and physical states because of its nature to create irrational realities, causing one to not think clearly. People with high anxiety find it extremely difficult to get rid of theses worries and anxious thoughts.

Chronic worrying can take a toll on one's health. The fight or flight (*see Ch. 8-4*) response within one's sympathetic nervous system releases stress hormones such as cortisol. The release of this hormone increases the body's blood sugar, leading to an increased state of anxiety in some people. Anxiousness can lead to a decreased appetite and a lack of zest for life.

Other symptoms can lead to chronic headaches and muscle tension. The constant rate of stress that one lives in can lead to clinical depression. Letting go of worry can be very difficult but it is important to focus on the positives of life and be thankful for the good that life gives.

Clinical anxiety is a serious health condition and must be diagnosed and handled by an appropriate mental health provider.

Teaching your children to put everything in perspective is an excellent strategy to help prevent them from worrying needlessly. Instead, teach them how the issue that is concerning them is either not really a problem or that an opportunity lies in the solution of that concern. There is no doubt, we live in a dangerous world. Between natural disasters, threats of crime and terror and pathogens in the air, you can understand why some people do not want to leave their homes. That said, all of those dangers are part of this wonderful thing we call life. Rather than live in fear, we should teach our children to live in gratitude (*see Ch. 9-11*). This is a great opportunity to turn your kids from chronic worriers to capable warriors.

BONUSES & RESOURCES *Daily Routines to Tackle Unnecessary Worry* Action Guide

BONUSES & RESOURCES *How to Help Your Child Deal with Worry & Anxiety*

9-14

LOOKING FORWARD

♫ LET IT GO!

As Gusteau, the fictional chef from the 2007 Disney movie *Ratatouille* said,

> *"If you focus on what you left behind, you will never be able to see what lies ahead."*

Like worry, focusing on the past is yet another behavior that steals the happiness of today. Continuing to review the past, or constant rumination, is a common symptom of anxiety. Living in this kind of mindset can be very unhealthy and can create psychological distress. Often people create different endings to these past events. This idealization can cause a warped sense of reality. While it can be helpful and nostalgic to reflect upon a memory, many people end up demonizing the present and romanticizing the past. Also, through focusing on the past, present expectations can be set in a "backwards mentality" as many cultural norms from the past have changed.

There are some people who have an innate talent that accompanies a natural swing of emotions that would be revealed from the results of the ULT (*see Ch. 9-3*). One moment they are spontaneous and the next, manic. There is genius that lives in this talent. However, if these people do not care for themselves properly and find themselves outside an appropriate environment, they can end up suffering from a series of mental health issues.

Through focusing on the present moment, distractions are limited. Concentration and effectiveness are improved, relaxation is increased and outmoded beliefs disappear. Positive reinforcement through positive thinking can really improve one's quality of life.

Rather than focusing on the past, it would be advantageous to surround yourself with those who inspire you to move forward. Inspired people generate ideas that create future movement. In being surrounded by inspiration, people can find the ideas and beliefs that influence them to be better people. In being around a positive environment, one is generally happier and experiences less stress and anxiety. Being around those who inspire you creates a healthy sense of competition that allows people to be challenged. Also, inspired people can shed light on positive possibilities and an optimistic future. Lastly, being surrounded by inspiration can teach someone how to live a positive life with endless opportunities and possibilities.

This is obviously not typically a concern for very young children, but kids of all ages do have memories. When your children bring up a memory that saddens them, like remembering a deceased grandparent, let them have that moment. Afterward, however, be sure to help the child appreciate the time they spent with the loved one and take the opportunity to explain that everything and everyone is temporary and that we should be grateful for the time they were in their lives. Turn it into a positive experience.

BONUSES & RESOURCES *Learn to Let Go* Action Guide
BONUSES & RESOURCES Learn how the ULT can help you understand why you may have more emotional swings than others.

9-15

HEALTHY RELATIONSHIPS

♫ YOU'VE GOT A FRIEND

Healthy relationships are vital for emotional and physical well-being. They require communication from everyone involved. Communication allows people to have a good understanding and connection with one another. Mutual respect is key for a healthy relationship. Speaking up when things are bothering you, compromising and supporting one another all play huge roles in a healthy relationship. The importance of honesty and trust can also greatly improve one's relationship.

Healthy relationships lead to a less stressful life, and people in committed relationships are known to be less likely to produce the stress hormone, cortisol (*see Ch. 7-4*).

Emotional support from a significant other is crucial in the healing process. Reassurance from a trusted someone is very important in managing stress and fear, especially in situations such as surgeries or illnesses.

Healthy relationships also build the foundations for an overall healthy lifestyle. It is much easier to inhabit healthier lifestyles if one is surrounded by other people doing the same. Being in healthy relationships cause people to feel wanted, and as if they are a part of something more; in these instances, people tend to have a greater sense of their purpose in life.

Lastly, being a part of healthy relationships is likely to add years to one's life. It has been found that having healthy relationships leads to a healthier mind and body. With less stress and more encouragement and support, people can live their lives with more positive influences, helping them become the best they can be.

Not only is it important for you to personally engage in relationships that are constructive, but it is especially important that your children do as well. Take a close look at the other kids that your children spend time with. If you do not feel that they set a good example for your children and "lift" them up, then perhaps intervening appropriately may be valuable. Be mindful, however, there are effective ways to encourage your kids to engage with "better" friends. It is one thing to nudge them in a certain direction and it is an entirely different thing to forbid a certain relationship that causes them to lose trust in you. It is ultimately up to you as a parent to walk that tightrope and find the perfect balance. I believe that the best way to teach your children to foster healthy relationships is to set an example by engaging in them yourself.

WORKBOOK ACTIVITY *10 Ways to be a Better Friend* Action Guide
BONUSES & RESOURCES Use the ULT to learn more about yourself and how to better relate with those you spend time with.

9-16

AVOID GOSSIP & DRAMA

♫ DON'T BRING ME DOWN

"Ships don't sink because of the water around them; ships sink because of the water that gets in them. Don't let what's happening around you get inside you and weigh you down" —Anonymous

---

A great way to ruin healthy relationships is to engage in gossip. I mentioned that one of my dealbreakers when it comes to my diet is gossip and that is because I believe it to be as bad for our health as corn syrup.

Gossip will not help the situation in which you are gossiping about, so there really is no reason to gossip. Gossiping does not only hurt the ones who you are talking about but can also hurt you. Gossiping can stress you out and impact your mood negatively.

It is no secret that gossip draws negative attention. Walking around with this negativity shows a lot about your character as well and only brings hate and disgust into your thoughts. Thinking negatively takes a toll as it creates anxiety and, in some cases, depression.

Also, gossiping causes those around you to lose your trust. Your integrity and trustworthiness go way down by talking down about others. The people you are speaking with may think ill thoughts about you, even if they are egging you on and seemingly enjoying it. And if they genuinely enjoy hearing bad stuff about another person, are those the type of people that you really want to be around? Additionally, who knows what they are saying about you when you are not around? And they may wonder what you are saying about them when they are not around, which leads to all kinds of trust issues.

This is a great lesson to teach children at early ages. Gossiping is just another form of bullying. It may start with words from one person, then a group of people ganging up on another and then it can lead to mental or physical abuse and even violence.

If you have been "wronged" by someone talking "smack" about you, it seems appropriate to lash out and do the same to that individual. By doing that, however, the situation only worsens. You probably teach your kids that two wrongs don't make a right. The lesson for you is, it is important to not treat people the way they treat you, but rather to treat them the way you would want them to treat you.

Gossiping about others hurts your reputation and can even isolate you. It is important to focus on the positive aspects of yourself, others, and the world. Many times, gossip leads to drama, and we know how that turns out.

Drama has the power and opportunity to negatively affect your life. There is no reason to involve yourself in someone else's drama when it does not affect you, unless you can help without getting caught up in it.

Along with drama comes stress. Aside from the mental stress that comes with drama, physical stress and impairment accompany it as well. Stress has numerously been linked to cancer, lung disease, fatal accidents, drug and alcohol abuse and more. When one is exposed to stressful drama, they experience an increase in cortisol (*see Ch. 7-4*), which increases one's heart rate and blood pressure. From this, one's blood vessels are constricted, and their heart muscle can become physically damaged.

Some drama is inevitable; people will experience everyday drama. However, unnecessary drama can be avoided. It is important to distance oneself from people who bring negative drama with them. Focus on positive, uplifting people. This does not mean that you should ignore or not help people in need. It just means that you need to rise above the drama itself and work on solutions. If the person you are trying to assist is not interested in fixing the issue, then prepare to move on and not get caught up in unnecessary negative talk.

Here is the bottom line . . . some people just love drama and love to complain about it. They also love to bring others into it as misery loves company. No matter how many good things they could have in their life, they always seem to attract more drama. Whether their drama is brought on by poor decisions (and the drama is real) or the drama is created because being a "victim" gives them their sense of purpose, allowing them to bring you into their darkness puts you in a very vulnerable position.

Holocaust survivor and author of *The Choice: Embrace the Possible*, Dr. Edith Egar, said, "Just because you've been victimized doesn't mean you need to be a victim." Egar encourages all people that, no matter how bad a situation may have been for an individual, there is always a pathway out of victimhood.

There are some people we can choose to have in our lives and others we are stuck with. Either way, you can choose how much time you spend with them (at least in most cases) and you can always choose how you receive their baggage.

BONUSES & RESOURCES *How to Eliminate Drama in Your Life* Action Sheet

BONUSES & RESOURCES *Should You Say It or Remain Silent?* Action Sheet

9-17

OCCUPATIONAL FULFILLMENT

♫ (I CAN'T GET NO) SATISFACTION!

Success is having your purpose, passion and paycheck in alignment.

Everything you have already read about goal setting, visualization and discovering your purpose will hopefully land you in a job that is rewarding and enjoyable. Additionally, the ULT test (*see Ch. 9-3*) will help you focus on what occupations are most appropriate for you based on your inner nature.

When one is satisfied with their job, they tend to have a greater sense of their purpose in life. Also, employees with job satisfaction tend to have less stress and worry regarding their job. They tend to be satisfied with their pay, relationships with colleagues, and status of their career path and development.

Job satisfaction is not only crucial in improving employees' performance and productivity, but it is also crucial for their mental state of mind. If you are happy at work, you will most likely be happy at home. This in turn will make you a happier parent.

While salary is an important factor to most people, it actually falls at the bottom of the list of importance for most people. That is, of course, provided that the salary is enough for the employee to make ends meet and to feel valued. Respectful treatment of all employees is vital in one's job satisfaction. Along with this, appreciation of your work, learning, career development, and good relationships with your colleagues, among others, are all very important to your job satisfaction. Survey after survey regarding why people stay at their places of work reveals that more important than money is the culture and environment of the company; the feeling that their work is meaningful, recognized and appreciated; that they are mentored; that they enjoy their coworkers; and that they have trust in the leadership.

This perspective goes beyond job satisfaction and takes it to a level of fulfillment.

If you are employed and do not love your job, consider finding a place of employment that will check the boxes above. If you are an employer, think about your company's culture and determine if there is something you can do to keep happy, healthy employees long-term.

When your children are at the age of getting their first job, encourage them to seek a role that will lift them up rather than just seeking a minimum wage job at any place that will hire them. The younger someone enjoys being part of the workforce, the better it will be for his or her future, not just financially.

BONUSES & RESOURCES *Make Your Job More Fulfilling* Action Sheet

BONUSES & RESOURCES *Changing Careers after 40* Action Sheet

BONUSES & RESOURCES *How to Pick a Career You'll Love* Action Sheet

BONUSES & RESOURCES *My Job Adds Satisfaction & Fulfillment to My Life Affirmation* and Action Sheet

9-18

CONSTANT LEARNING

♫ SCHOOL'S OUT!

Whether it be at a fulfilling job or during play, it is essential to ensure you are learning new things every day. This provides opportunities to have fun in finding new passions. Learning new things is like a kid in a candy store: fun and excitement is around every corner. It creates a sense of accomplishment and pride; few things can make one prouder than learning something new.

These new opportunities from learning also facilitate the creation of new relationships and friendships. Meeting like-minded people is a great way to start friendships with people that share your new interests and passions. With learning new things, your self-esteem will also rise, giving you more self-confidence. Also, you can experience immense personal growth through your new experiences. Creating new routines in your life will allow your mind to grow. Lastly, you may discover a hidden talent and reveal an untapped potential through learning new things.

For kids, learning should not end in the classroom. Encourage them to engage in activities that foster creativity, culture and friendships. Whether it be an after-school activity or during summer break, be wise as to where you send your kids. And always keep your children involved in the decision-making process so you know that they will be interested and look forward to the activity.

9-19

LOVE

♫ ALL YOU NEED IS LOVE

Love is a variety of different emotional and mental states, typically strongly and positively experienced, that ranges from deepest interpersonal affection to simple pleasure. In the beginning stages of love, it has been found that patterns of hormones and brain activity show signs of stress and even addiction or obsessive disorders. While at first this can lead someone to make rash decisions, these circumstances fade to calm and joy.

Oxytocin is a hormone that is released when one is in love. It is known to lower blood pressure, decrease stress and even boost the immune system. It can reduce aches and pains, increase energy, and even enable us to live a life with optimism. Being in love generally makes for a happier life. Familial love gives fulfillment and comfort to one's life. The gratifying experience of giving and receiving love can reap not only mental benefits but also physical benefits as well.

As a parent, the most important thing you can do for your kids is make sure they know they are loved. Consider your daily interactions with your children not just what you say, but also what you do with them. They need to feel like an essential member of your household, but more importantly, they need to know they are an indispensable member of the family.

Do Your Children Feel Loved?

One of the greatest responsibilities of a parent is to ensure your children feel loved and happy.

While every parent knows that kids don't always listen (or at least they don't *choose* to listen), it's important to realize the kids are *always* watching. You can use this fact to help increase your child's happiness by remembering that what you do is often more important than what you say.

Kids are especially sensitive to noticing when a parent chooses a person or activity over the child. As they grow and learn about the world around them, children naturally assign meaning to what they see. When you're too busy for them, they can easily begin to feel that they're not worthy of being one of your priorities.

Apply these ideas in your household to help your child feel secure, loved, and happy:

1) Let them know you're genuinely excited to see them. When you see them for the first time in the morning and after school, ensure they know just how happy you are to see them. Use their name (everybody likes that) and show genuine pleasure.

- Think about how happy you would be if the person you love the most did the same for you.

2) Make sure they know that your work is less important than they are. Most kids are constantly being put off because of work or some other task. Avoid scheduling your kids around your tasks. Take care of the kids first and schedule work around them. This technique shows them how important they are.

3) Teach your kids at home. Don't assume that everything they need to learn they are learning sufficiently outside the home. While I have the greatest respect for teachers, just like every other profession, some simply aren't very good at teaching the way your child needs to learn. Help your child with their schoolwork.

  - Many of the most important things children learn have nothing to do with academics. That's your responsibility. If you don't do it, who else will?

  - Consider all the things you wish you had known when you were a young adult heading out into the world. Those things would be a great start.

4) Model good behavior. Children assume that the appropriate way to handle a situation is the same way their parents handle it. Are you behaving like a strong, patient, persistent person? How successful and happy will your children be if they handle challenges the same way that you do? Remember, they're always watching and copying.

5) Let the kids make a few of the rules around the house. People naturally resist and rebel when they feel like they

don't have any control. It can be something small. Perhaps they can choose which days to clean their room each week. Or they can choose what's for dinner (from choices that you give them). Simple things like this really help.

6) Limit the amount of media/technology exposure. It's easy to let the TV entertain the kids when you're busy or frustrated. But most parents instinctively know that their kids watch too much TV. As kids get older, cell phones, the internet, and social media become an issue. Technology is hypnotic, but it doesn't make people happy.

- Many studies have shown that people who use technology the most tend to suffer from loneliness at a greater rate than those that use it less.

Have fun with your kids. Teach them everything you think they need to know and be a good example. Ensure they feel special and loved. Simply doing your very best is a great place to start.

9-20

PRAYER

♫ LIVIN' ON A PRAYER

I truly believe that faith is an important, if not essential component of a wellness lifestyle. An active way of practicing one's faith is through prayer. This is not something I was exposed to very much as a child.

As mentioned earlier, I was raised on Long Island in a non-religious, Jewish family. We acknowledged and appreciated God and participated in many of the Jewish holidays and traditions. However, I had no relationship or understanding of God. I only knew the history and stories of the Hebrew Bible. The prayers that I recited were usually memorized and almost always in Hebrew. Honestly, they meant very little to me because I did not understand them. I was just saying them because I was supposed to. I am sure that many of you can relate.

In 2005, my "almost" stepbrother, Steve Lindner (see Ch. 1-4), introduced me to the book *Your Best Life Now* (mentioned earlier), by a pastor named Joel Osteen. I am not going to lie, at first, the book was very uncomfortable for me to read. I was not accustomed to reading books that mentioned God and especially Jesus so many times. I felt like it was sacrilegious for me to be reading it. However, as I read it more and more, I found myself getting incredibly inspired. I was always into Tony Robbins and other personal development books, and this was a combination of those and the Bible.

This book ended up being a launching pad for me to build a relationship with God and to begin a new journey in personal development, one that put God at the forefront. I began to see the world through a different lens which led to new experiences and friendships.

I began to *voluntarily* visit synagogues (as opposed to being obligated as a kid), as well as attend churches for extra spiritual "nutrition." I now have a great fondness for the sermons I hear, regardless of the specific religion or denomination. The Bible is rich with ideas and inspiration that can lead people to atonement (*see Ch. 4-1*). I now better understand the context of the Bible and the promises God made to the Jewish people and the world.

Prayer has a different meaning to different people in different contexts of life. For some, prayer is a religious tradition done with a congregation during a ceremony perhaps in a church, synagogue or mosque. Within that context, some may feel a connection with God while others just do it for ritual purposes and recite from memory or by reading.

For the context of this chapter, I will be referring to active prayer where a person engages in some form of conversation with God outside of the confines of a place of worship. This conversation may be silent or spoken and memorized/planned or off the cuff. Many people consider prayer to be their opportunity to speak with God (whereas meditation is when they listen).

I see prayer as an extremely important activity. It can be done with a particular theological or religious frame of reference, or just a spiritual one where God is the higher power that is spoken to like a friend or parent. It is important to not make it complicated and it can take place in any location at any time. Additionally, I believe that since God is omniscient (all-knowing), He understands all languages. So, if your Hebrew, Aramaic or Latin is not up to snuff, don't fret! English works just as well.

While prayer draws one closer to God and lets one feel more connected to Him, it also brings light where darkness existed. People use prayer for protection, promotion, healing and peace. When we feel connected to a higher power, we often modify our habits and lifestyle so we do not contradict our beliefs and we remain in *alignment*. Many people, including myself, have seen prayer bring incredible breakthroughs in life and even help create a sense of purpose.

Just like conversations with friends and family, be mindful of how you speak with God. The words you use along with the intention will often bring about a certain outcome. Speak life, say positive words and come from a place of gratitude. When I pray, rather than beg God for something to occur or not, I prefer to thank Him for what I would like to see come to reality and phrase it as if it already did.

For example, if I want millions of people to be inspired by this book, I could pray, "God, please help me get this book into the hands of millions of people." That would not be wrong, but I would more likely say, "God, thank you for using me as a vessel to put your words of wisdom onto paper so that these words can inspire and positively impact the lives of millions of people."

Also, rather than pray for a sickness to go away, I would thank God for the healing, and I would consciously and intentionally see the healing as 100% perfect and whole. Yes, I use NLP (*see Ch. 9-6*) even when speaking to God! Thankfully while I do believe that the words, whether spoken aloud or in my own head, are important, God knows my heart. I believe that He knows what I am thinking before I even have the thought, so I don't get too caught up in my head and I just make sure that I commit the time to have an intimate relationship with Him.

I cannot say that there is 100% evidence in the existence of God or a higher power, or even the benefits of prayer, but that is why it is called faith. I personally have 100% faith that God is real and the Creator answers prayer . . . but even if I am wrong . . . I am still affirming my exact intentions. I can say with certainty that my life is better, if for nothing else, than for the belief that prayer is effective.

I feel strongly that prayer should be a big part of every household. The sooner you introduce it to your children, the better. Be cautious to not force it on your kids but rather to find ways to make it enjoyable, inspiring and empowering. The stories of the Bible are typically very entertaining for kids and chock full of lessons for all.

REFLECTION OPPORTUNITY

How well do you *know* yourself?

Do you feel that you are inner directed? If not, what can you do to exercise that inner-directed muscle?

Think about the 5 people you spend most of your time with. Do you enjoy spending time with them? Are they positive? Do they build you up? Can you be honest with them, all of the time? Are the relationships meaningful?

Is there someone in your life that constantly brings you down? If so, what should you do about it?

Are you conscious of your purpose in life?

Do you spend time on social media? If so, how do you feel during or after?

Do you currently have anger or hatred toward someone? If so, what can you do today to put an end to that emotion?

What inspires you?

Are you where you want to be in life, or at least working on it?

What are 3 things you can do today that will make your life better tomorrow (or the upcoming days)?

If you have children, how positive is their home environment? Are you expressing gratitude as a family, even when things may be tough? What type of words are being used at home toward one another? Is your home an uplifting environment?

PART III

CONCLUSION: BRINGING IT HOME

Throughout this book, you have been exposed to new terms, concepts and rationale for taking specific action required to live your DREAM, every day.

Part I enabled you to see the world through a different lens. You were exposed to what is working and what is not working when it comes to our current healthcare system. You also learned about the impact your thoughts, words and actions will have on your health and that of your family. Hopefully you completed Part I with an understanding of what your body is capable of accomplishing without the constant need for outside interventions and gained a new appreciation for the amazingness of life and vitality. And finally, Part I concluded with introducing the five keys to a wellness lifestyle.

Part II dove deeply into the depths of the five keys through the Wellness Wikis™. You learned about food and other input through your senses and how they impact the health of your family. You learned about the importance of taking time to rest, repair, regenerate and rejuvenate. You were hopefully inspired to move more and to do it properly for your body. And to teach your kids the importance of physical activity.

You became aware of the importance of a fully functioning nervous system and how that impacts everyone's health. And finally, you learned how to see yourself and others through a different lens— one of perfection. This understanding, along with appropriate action will help you have more harmonious relationships with yourself and those in your life, leading to greater happiness and fulfillment.

Here is the best part . . . the hardest part is complete. As I wrote in the preface regarding principles of "be, do and have," the first two parts of the book are all about who you need to *be* and what you need to *do* for you and your family to *have* a lifetime of physical and mental health. When you bring all that you have learned *home* to your family and start implementing the recommendations you learned, salutogenesis will be the result.

This final part of the book will show you how the fruits of your labor will lead to salutogenesis as you and your family embark on a happy, healthy existence for a lifetime and for generations to come.

10-1

SALUTOGENESIS VS. PATHOGENESIS

As defined earlier (*see Ch. 1-3*), *salutogenesis* ultimately focuses on the factors that lead to the creation of health. This is contrary to pathogenesis.

Pathogenesis is the formation of disease. The word comes from the combination of the Greek words "pathos," meaning suffering or disease, and again "genesis," meaning origin or creation. All disease processes have a starting point and many are avoidable. (This of course is excluding diseases that are 100% genetic, congenital or traumatic in origin.)

You were all born with 100% vitality. So were your children. Some people may not be as fortunate to express their perfection 100%, but we all still have 100%, nonetheless. Conscious living is about living by choice, not chance. It is about making good choices and incorporating all five keys as discussed within this book.

When you do not get adequate sleep or relaxation, do not maintain a nutritious diet, or you choose to not have a positive attitude or exercise regularly, the likelihood of adapting to chemical, physical and emotional stressors is diminished greatly. When your body is unable to adapt to these stressors, your body loses balance, increases tension and will likely no longer be in *adjustment*. (Remember, being in adjustment is being in balance mentally, physically, spiritually and emotionally and having optimal brain-body communication.)

When you are out of *adjustment*, you are demonstrating the first phase of dis-ease, dis-harmony and dis-connect. Vertebral subluxations often occur at this point, preventing optimal nervous system performance (*see Ch. 8-5*). When this occurs, the expression of innate intelligence is reduced, regardless of how you feel.

When you are out of *adjustment*, you will likely begin to experience what I refer to as asymptomatic pathology. This is a fancy way of saying you have problems beginning to form but you are not aware just yet. If you let it go for too long, that is when you may experience a symptom or known disease process. The real problem is, you may think that the problem just started when the symptom started. However, you can see by the illustration below that the symptom was just the tip of the iceberg. You will have to make a choice once a symptom presents itself as to whether you want to treat the symptom, correct the cause, or even better, go back to the beginning and live a lifestyle of consciousness and a near perfect DREAM lifestyle.

D.R.E.A.M. Vitality Spectrum

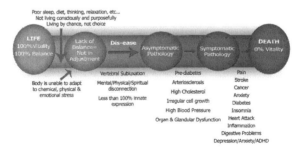

10-2

NEW BEGINNINGS

♫ STAYIN' ALIVE

Health is your natural state of being. You were born to be healthy. Your body was created with a natural ability to constantly heal and regulate; and if you choose to care for your body everyday of your existence, you will be keeping the odds in your favor that you will not only remain healthy and reduce the negative effects of aging, but you also have the opportunity to grow and expand your health and strength as you age. Same goes for your kids.

Living the DREAM will provide the opportunity not only to add years to your life but to also add life to your years!

How do you do this? It's easy . . . make a choice to live your DREAM everyday.

If you made it to this point, you may be overwhelmed with information. Depending on your current lifestyle and starting point, you will have more or less work cut out for you to begin this wellness journey. As the saying goes, "How do you eat an elephant? One bite at a time!" I will do my best to chunk it down for you into bite-size pieces. Here are three easy steps to begin your journey and become the best version of you.

Step 1: Take the DREAM Score questionnaire if you have not already done so (https://DREAMWellness.com/DREAMScore). It has just under 100 questions and should take 20 minutes to complete. Based on your score and report, begin your journey by working on your biggest weaknesses and make improvements immediately. In many areas of life, people are encouraged to work on their strengths and make them stronger. That, however, is not the case when it comes to health. Have other members of your household, if applicable, do the same.

Think of the 5 Keys as the five wheels of a car. You have two in the front (let's call them *Diet* and *Relaxation*), two in the rear (*Exercise* and *Mental Wellness*) and one that steers your vehicle (being in Adjustment/Alignment/Atonement, which is fitting for this analogy because it is the brain that tells the other body parts what to do, much like the steering wheel tells your car where to go). If any of the four tires have less air than the recommended amount, the lack of balance and alignment will cause your tires to wear unevenly and possibly even swerve off the road or into another vehicle! (If all four tires are low, you are in big trouble.)

How you score on the questionnaire will give you a good idea about whether you are on the path of salutogenesis or pathogenesis and whether your "battery" is charging or depleting. We all know what happens when we run out of "battery life." Conversely, think about how good it feels when you know that your devices are fully charged!

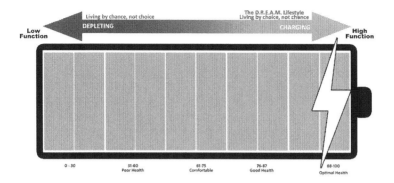

Those who score an 88–100 are likely to be experiencing optimal health, they generally feel and function great, and they experience contentment and fulfillment. They engage in exceptional relationships, enjoy living a purposeful life and their energy level has a full charge.

Those who score a 76–87 are likely to be in good health and they are rather happy individuals in good relationships. Their body feels good and seems to function well and their energy level is sufficient.

Then we get into the "Comfort Zone" with scores of 61–75. These people are typically comfortable most of the time with no significant health concerns. Their happiness is often determined by circumstances and they maintain the status quo with unpredictable energy levels.

For the individual who scores a 31–60, they are extremely likely experiencing poor health and typically have at least one ailment that requires medication. They are often in challenged relationships and have a loss of normal function. Their energy levels are draining.

And then there are the people who score a 0–30. They have disease and disability and are almost certainly aware of their many health challenges. They are likely taking multiple medications and experience a poor quality of life. Grief and disappointment is probably a common theme for them, and their energy level is near empty.

Step 2: Unless you score 100, it is important to recognize and accept the reality that your lifestyle has room for improvement when it comes to salutogenesis. Visit the bonus and resource page and download as many resources as you can and read this book while going through the workbook (https://DREAMWellnessbook.com/bonuses).

Step 3: Decide to enact lifestyle changes. It must start with your thoughts, then your words and finally your actions. If there is another parent in the picture, I recommend having a conversation to get the other on board. I have added bonuses in the resource section to provide you with strategies on how to communicate these important changes with another parent/caregiver. Calm and focused conversations with the entire family is a must for significant change to take place. Start taking action immediately. Baby steps are fine, just do something.

Once you successfully apply the first three steps to your lifestyle, the rest of my advice in this book should be a breeze.

I recommend retaking the DREAM Score at least four times per year. Hopefully your score will improve each time. And even if you scored in the 90s, taking it regularly will help keep you accountable and remind you of the important little things that you may forget about here and there. Also, it is recommended to retake the DREAM Score any time you experience a life changing event.

BONUSES & RESOURCES *DREAM Score* Questionnaire. If you haven't taken it yet, stop procrastinating and get on it! It's my biggest gift to you, so please take advantage of it.

BONUSES & RESOURCES *Calm, Focused and Safe Conversation Blueprint*. Whether you are partnered to your children's other parent or co-parenting from different households (if there is another parent in the picture), this bonus will help you communicate your desires to implement this material into your children's lifestyle.

10-3

BUILD WISELY

An elderly carpenter was ready to retire. He told his employer of his plans to leave the house-building business and live a more leisurely life with his wife enjoying his extended family. He would miss the paycheck, but he needed to retire. They could get by.

The contractor was sorry to see his good worker go and asked if he could build one more house as a personal favor. The carpenter said yes, but in time it was easy to see that his heart was not in his work. He resorted to shoddy workmanship and used inferior materials. It was an unfortunate way to end a dedicated career. When the carpenter finished with his work, the employer came to inspect the house. He handed the front door key to the carpenter.

"This is your house," he said, "My gift to you."

The carpenter was shocked! What a shame! If he had only known he was building his own house, he would have done it all so differently.

So it is with us. We build our lives, a day at a time, often putting less than our best into the building. Then, with a shock, we realize we have to live in the house we have built. If we could go back and do it over, we'd do it much differently. But we cannot go back.

You are the carpenter. Each day you hammer a nail, place a board, or erect a wall. Life is a do-it-yourself project. Your attitudes and the choices you make today, build the house you live in tomorrow.

—Anonymous

Your choices and actions of today will build your future of tomorrow. Diet, Relaxation, Exercise, Adjustment and Mental Wellness are the keys to help you and your family experience life at its fullest potential and live your DREAM every day.

Here's to wellness for you, your family and many generations to come.

ACKNOWLEDGMENTS

There are numerous acknowledgements that I would like to make for helping me make this DREAM a reality. First and foremost, I would like to thank God for giving me inspiration throughout the book and for giving me the strength to continue on and not quit as I wanted to do on many occasions.

Of all accomplishments to date, completing this book and making it what it is today is by far the most difficult undertaking of my life. Yes, even more difficult than chiropractic college and receiving my master's degree. I am not trained as a writer; I am a healthcare provider with a passion to share a message. The amount of research and editing that went into this book over the past decade seems insurmountable in retrospect. But somehow, I did it through the grace of God. And as difficult as it was, I maintained a DREAM lifestyle as much as possible. I was not perfect. I will admit that throughout the process, I got frustrated. I got sad. I got mad. I wanted to quit, many times! But in the end, I feel that humanity will be better because of it.

In fairness, however, I really could not have done it without the love and patience of my exceptionally supportive wife, Brooke. I started writing the book before I even knew her. However, through the experiences we shared as a couple first dating, then wedded and now a dynamic duo as parents, I grew an incredible amount; and the book got richer and richer as my life did. She not only provided me with the time and inspiration to complete the writing, but she gave me so much insight that is interwoven throughout the entire book. I know that this book would not be what it is if not for her, and I am incredibly grateful.

And for my son, Zion, the boy we test all this stuff on . . . thank you for being our guinea pig. God could not have blessed this family with a better example of His shining light. You literally epitomize the very example of what is possible when this lifestyle is put into action. I can only hope and pray that the readers of this book attain similar success in creating their DREAM family. We know you are still young, and challenges may come, but as we continue to put the contents of this book into action, I have faith that you will grow into the adult that Brooke and I visualized you to be before you were even conceived.

To my mom Linda . . . you have always supported me, no matter what. You would also let me know how proud you were of me, even when I didn't deserve it. You taught me right from wrong my entire childhood, and I know that the integrity my peers commend me for is because of how you raised me.

To my dad, Lenny, and stepmom, Robyn . . . thank you for always being there for me. Your undeniable commitment and love for family is incomparable. Thank you for teaching me so many of the values I live by and raising me to become the man I am today.

To my brother Scott and sister-in-law Nancy, my sister Haley and brother-in-law Jonathan, my brother Lee, my brother Marc and sister-in-law Ashley . . . thank you for still loving me in spite of moving

3,000 miles away to live my DREAM and leaving "the parental units" with you. Thank you for all the continued love, support and grace you have always given me. Thank you for the lessons you have taught me over the years on how to be a good brother to you and uncle to your amazing kids, who inspire me every day. Mostly, thank you for putting up with me and all my antics.

To my honorary brother, Dr. Steve Lindner . . . thank you for introducing me to the chiropractic profession and taking me under your wing. I don't know what I would be doing today if not for you and your dad. The impact you have had on my life is immeasurable. You continue to inspire and teach me, and I am so incredibly grateful to have you in my life.

To my friend, fraternity brother and DREAM "partner in crime" Dr. Gregg Baron . . . thank you for helping develop the concepts of DREAM with me since the early 1990s. Your knowledge and insight are unrivaled, and this book would not exist without you. I continue to seek guidance and wisdom from you, and you always come through big time. I am forever grateful to have you by my side as we continue to create and bring DREAM to reality.

To my friend, mentor and coach Dr. Bob Hoffman . . . thank you for teaching me everything you know. In actuality, it would take me 20 lifetimes to gain the knowledge that you have, but I am incredibly grateful that you have shared so much with me over the past several decades. As I wrote this book, I heard your voice on almost every page. So much of this could be your book . . . heck, so much of it *is* your book. Thank you for never holding back and for helping me become the healthcare leader I am today. I owe so much of my success to you, and I only hope that I am making you proud.

To one of the greatest sages in my life to whom I owe so much, Dr. Zannah Hackett . . . thank you for releasing information about Y.O.U. to the world and for sharing it with Brooke and me. Your guidance and mentorship have without a doubt helped shape me into the husband, father, doctor and coach I am today.

To the other coaches, mentors and friends whose wisdom is intwined throughout this book . . . thank you! There are too many names to mention, but I must give extra thank you mentions to Dr. Dennis Perman, Dr. Janice Hughes, Rick Itzkowich, Dr. Guy Riekeman, Dr. Patrick Gentempo, Dr. Christopher Kent, Dr. Eric Plasker, Dr. Fabrizio Mancini, Dr. Ron Oberstein, Dr. Gilles LaMarche, Dr. David Jackson, Dr. Billy DeMoss, Dr. David Fletcher, Dr. Jason Deitch, Dr. Armand Rossi, Dr. Stuart Warner, Dr. Theresa Warner, Dr. Tony Ebel, Dr. Claudia Anrig, Dr. Daniel Matzner, Dr. Adam Glassman, Dr. Heidi Haavik, Dr. Chuck Plante, Dr. Peter Seguinot, Dr. DD Humber, Dr. Matt Hubbard, Dr. Sandra Castro and Dr. Danny Gambino; and those who have passed on from this plane of existence and continue to inspire me from a great distance . . . Dr. Pasquale Cerasoli, Dr. Sid E. Williams, Dr. James Sigafoose, Dr. Reggie Gold, Dr. Fred Barge, Dr. Tom Klapp, Dr. Frank Sovinsky, Dr. Larry Webster and Dr. Jeanne Ohm.

To the board members and staff of the New York Chiropractic Council, California Chiropractic Association, San Diego Senior Games Association, OneChiropractic and Congress of Chiropractic State Associations . . . thank you for constantly demonstrating your never-ending commitment to helping people live a better life. Your sacrifices for others should be an inspiration to all and should never go unnoticed. You have all helped shape me into the leader I am today, and I am grateful for having the opportunity to serve alongside you.

To my unofficial editors, copywriters and beta readers . . . Kari Johnson, Shelley Hickox, Barrett Zoltai, Genia Enders, Dr. Zannah Hackett, Dr. Gregg Baron, Dr. John Travis and the dozens of "advanced readers" . . . thank you for turning this "manifesto" into a book! Without you, I have no idea if I would have had a product that anyone would have purchased or benefited from. Kari, I will never forget your first comment (as you were the first person after Brooke to read the manuscript) when you said, "I know there is a book in here, somewhere." With your guidance and that of so many others, we now have a book that we can all be proud of. Thank you ALL so much for making this possible.

To Emily Petty, my unofficial researcher . . . thank you! Years ago, when I was stuck on what to write next, you stepped in and provided me with information and research that was much needed to take the next steps. Thank you so much for your tireless work. Though it is finally paying off years later, I am incredibly grateful for the great work you put into this project. I hope you can take pride in seeing some of your words be put into print for (hopefully) millions to read.

To Jeremy Jones and the entire team at Jones Media Publishing. I don't know what to say. Had Rafael not reached out to me when he did, I don't know if the book ever would have gotten finished. You have provided me with all the tools and resources anyone would need to create a best-selling book. Your insight and caring through this entire process will never be forgotten, and I will be eternally grateful.

To JJ Virgin, Karl Krummenacher and fellow Mindshare Mastermind and Vistage members . . . thank you for helping me take this project through the finish line. Your guidance and inspiration helped make the success of this book what it is.

To my current and former DREAM Wellness practice members (patients) and DREAM Team members (employees and providers) . . . I just can't thank you enough for letting me "practice" on you over the past several decades. Though it was Life University that gave me the education, skills and knowledge I have, you all have made me the doctor I am today. I am beyond grateful that you have trusted your health and your babies' well-being with my team and me. There is no bigger compliment a doctor can receive.

And finally, to whom I dedicate this book, Nat Lindner . . . Thank you Nat for loving my mom until your last breath. More importantly, thank you for taking the time to introduce me to Steve, which ultimately launched my interest into the chiropractic profession. I always say that you were the angel who changed the trajectory of my life. Your impact has unequivocally been the most pivotal. Thank you!

NOTES

1. Klodian Dhana et al., "Association between maternal adherence to healthy lifestyle practices and risk of obesity in offspring: results from two prospective cohort studies of mother-child pairs in the United States," British Medical Journal, no. 4 (July 2018): 362, https://doi.org/10.1136/bmj.k2486.

2. Kaare Christensen, Thomas E. Johnson, and James W. Vapel, "The quest for genetic determinants of human longevity: challenges and insights," *Nature Reviews: Genetics 7* (June 2006): 436–48, https://doi.org/10.1038/nrg1871.

3. Sean C.L. Deoni et al., "Breastfeeding and early white matter development: A cross-sectional study," *NeuroImage* 82 (November 2013):77–86, https://doi.org/10.1016/j.neuroimage.2013.05.090.

4. Karl G. Hill et al., "Family influences on the risk of daily smoking initiation," *Journal of Adolescent Health* 37, no.3 (September 2005): 202–210, https://doi.org/10.1016/j.jadohealth.2004.08.014.

5. Jason Lazarou, Bruce H. Pomeranz, Paul N. Corey, "Incidence of Adverse Drug Reactions in Hospitalized Patients: A

Meta-Analysis of Prospective Studies," *Journal of the American Medical Association* 279, no. 15 (April 1998): 1200–5, https://doi.org/10.1001/jama.279.15.1200.

6. "Leading Causes of Death," National Center for Health Statistics, Centers for Disease Control and Prevention, https://www.cdc.gov/nchs/fastats/leading-causes-of-death.htm.

7. Kimber L. Stanhope, Jean-Marc Schwarz, and Peter J. Havel, "Adverse metabolic effects of dietary fructose results from the recent epidemiological, clinical, and mechanistic studies," *Current Opinion in Lipidology* 24, no. 3 (June 2013): 198–206, https://doi.org/10.1097/MOL.0b013e3283613bca.

8. João Ricardo Araújo, Fátima Martel, and Elisa Keating, "Exposure to non-nutritive sweeteners during pregnancy and lactation: Impact in programming of metabolic diseases in the progeny later in life," *Reproductive Toxicology* 49 (November 2014): 196–201, https://doi.org/10.1016/j.reprotox.2014.09.007.

9. Wayne H.F. Sutherland et al., "Effect of meals rich in heated olive and safflower oils on oxidation of postprandial serum in healthy men," *Atherosclerosis* 160, no. 1 (January 2002): 195–203, https://doi.org/10.1016/S0021-9150(01)00561-5.

10. Hui Gao et al., "Bisphenol A and Hormone-Associated Cancers: Current Progress and Perspectives," *Medicine* 94, no. 1 (January 2015): e211, https://doi.org/10.1097/MD.0000000000000211.

11. Kent C (2018) Chiropractic and Mental Health: History and Review of Putative Neurobiological Mechanisms. Jou Neuro Psy An Brain Res: JNPB-103.

12. P.C. Brennan et al., "Enhanced phagocytic cell respiratory bursts induced by spinal manipulation: Potential Role of Substance P," *Journal of Manipulative and Physiological Therapeutics* 14, no. 7 (September 1991): 399–408; D.R. Murray et al., "Sympathetic and immune interactions during dynamic exercise. Mediation via a beta 2 – adrenergic-dependent mechanism," *Circulation* 86, no 1 (July 1992): 203–213, https://doi.org/10.1161/01.CIR.86.1.203; R. Pero, "Medical Researcher Excited By CBSRF Project Results." *The Chiropractic Journal* 32 (August 1989); David L. Felten et al., "Noradrenergic sympathetic neural interactions with the immune system: structure and function," *Immunological Reviews* 100 (December 1987): 225–60, https://doi.org/10.1111/j.1600-065X.1987.tb00534.x.

13. J.M. Fallon, *Textbook on Chiropractic & Pregnancy* (Arlington, VA: International Chiropractic Association, 1994), 52, 109.

14. Jeanne Ohm and Joel Alcantara, "Webster Technique: Definition, Application and Implications," *Journal of Pediatric, Maternal & Family Health* (May 10, 2012), https://icpa4kids.com/media/1160/webster_technique.pdf.

15. E Kapreli et al, "Respiratory dysfunction in chronic neck pain patients. A pilot study," *Cephalalgia* 29, no. 7 (July 2009): 701–710, https://doi.org/10.1111%2Fj.1468-2982.2008.01787.x.

16. I.A. Kapandji, *Physiology of the Joints*, Vol. 3, 6th ed. (London: Churchill Livingstone, 2008)

17. L. Rowell Huesmann, "The Impact of Electronic Media Violence: Scientific Theory and Research," *Journal of Adolescent Health* 41, no. 6, supplement (December 2007): S6–S13, https://doi.org/10.1016/j.jadohealth.2007.09.005.

INDEX

ABOUT THE AUTHOR

Dr. Brian Stenzler received his Doctor of Chiropractic degree in 1998 from Life University. In 1999, he earned a master's degree in Sports Health Science, also from Life University. Additionally, he is a Certified ULT Facilitator & Corporate Consultant and provides wellness and lifestyle coaching and consulting for individuals, families and businesses around the globe.

Dr. Stenzler is the co-founder of D.R.E.A.M. Wellness and has owned and operated numerous wellness centers in New York and California where he has helped thousands of families achieve their health and wellness goals. He also has a passion for working with athletes and has spent many years volunteering and providing chiropractic services at the U.S. Open Golf Championship Wellness Team by adjusting the players, caddies and other volunteers.

Early in his career, Dr. Stenzler was an adjunct neurology instructor at the New York College of Health Professions and continues to use his vast knowledge of the nervous system in everything he does.

Dr. Stenzler has served on numerous boards and was president of the California Chiropractic Association from 2014–2016 and has received dozens of awards and accolades over the years for his leadership and service to the chiropractic profession.

Dr. Stenzler travels the world as a guest speaker at conferences and colleges, and lectures at numerous businesses, schools and civic organizations as a health and wellness expert. He has also been featured on television and radio shows around the world.

More than anything else, he enjoys spending quality time with his wife Brooke, and their son, Zion.

Made in the USA
Middletown, DE
29 March 2022